RECONSTRUCTING THE UNIVERSITY

Reconstructing the University

*Worldwide Shifts in Academia in
the 20th Century*

DAVID JOHN FRANK
JAY GABLER

STANFORD UNIVERSITY PRESS

STANFORD, CALIFORNIA 2006

Stanford University Press
Stanford, California

Printed in the United States of America
on acid-free, archival-quality paper

Library of Congress Cataloging-in-Publication Data

Frank, David John.
  Reconstructing the university : worldwide shifts in academia in the
20th century / David John Frank and Jay Gabler.
      p. cm.
  Includes bibliographical references and index.
  ISBN-10: 0-8047-5375-x (cloth : alk. paper)
  ISBN-10: 0-8047-5376-8 (pbk. : alk. paper)
  ISBN-13: 978-0-8047-5375-3 (cloth : alk. paper)
  ISBN-13: 978-0-8047-5376-0 (pbk. : alk. paper)
    1. Universities and colleges–Curricula–History–20th century.
2. Curriculum change–History–20th century.   I. Gabler, Jay.   II. Title.
LB2361.F73 2006
378.1'99–dc22   2006006596

Typeset by TechBooks, New Delhi, in 10/14 Janson.

Contents

Acknowledgments

We owe thanks to many people and institutions for assistance with this project. For help thinking through the substance of the book, we are grateful to (among others) Karl Alexander, Aaron Benavot, John Boli, Steve Brint, Gili Drori, Georg Krücken, Michèle Lamont, Stan Lieberson, Betsy McEneaney, John Meyer, Colin Milburn, Francisco Ramirez, Barbara Reskin, Evan Schofer, Marc Ventresca, Regina Werum, and Suk-Ying Wong. Anonymous reviewers at *Comparative Education Review* and *Sociology of Education* also made helpful comments and suggestions.

Throughout the process of researching and writing, we were fortunate to be part of the extraordinary intellectual communities at Harvard University and the University of California, Irvine. The faculty, students, and staff in the departments of sociology at these institutions deserve credit and thanks for their support, advice, and good company. Additionally, the NAE/Spencer Postdoctoral Fellowship Program and the UC-Irvine Council on Research, Computing, and Library Resources provided funding at crucial junctures in the project.

We presented earlier versions of parts of this book at meetings of the Future of the City of Intellect Conference, Riverside, February 2000; Comparative and International Education Society, San Antonio, March 2000; Pacific Sociological Association, Pasadena, April 2003; American Educational Research Association, Chicago, April 2003; American Sociological Association, San Francisco, August 2004; Workshop on Entering the Knowledge Society, Bielefeld, Germany, November 2004; and, on several occasions, the Comparative Workshop at Stanford University. The project was improved at each turn, thanks to the thoughtful comments and suggestions from our colleagues at these forums.

The editorial and production staff members at the Stanford University Press have seen this project through many stages and revisions, and the finished book bears the mark of their patient guidance. We are particularly indebted to our editors, Kate Wahl, Kirsten Oster, and Pat Katayama, for their good advice and unfailing support.

Finally, on a personal note, we would like to acknowledge our families – particularly our parents, Ken and Joan Frank and Jim and Jean Gabler. We dedicate this book to them.

Foreword

Remaking the University

David John Frank and Jay Gabler, in *Reconstructing the University*, make an impressive contribution to the study of modern (or postmodern) culture and the analysis of the university that is central to the culture. They do this by tracing the rise and relative fall of academic fields and topics in universities around the whole world through most of the twentieth century. Creating the unique data sets involved is a major achievement. Analyzing them systematically is even more creative. And building an interpretive scheme that enables us to comprehend the real nature of the modern university is an extraordinary theoretical contribution.

An uninformed commentator might assume that all this knowledge is old hat – of course, everybody knows what universities teach and how it has changed over the modern period. It seems obvious that this is important information and is thus likely to be found in all central sources. This is dramatically not so, and in this Foreword I offer an explanation of why it is not so.

The reason, simply, is that we all tend to assume – and our postmodern or "knowledge" society is built on this assumption – that the university basically provides information and training relevant to the skills needed in the modern economy (or more broadly, workforce). The knowledge society needs the university, and the university services (according to some critics, at the loss of its own soul) this society. With all this assumed, the actual empirical exploration of the cultural contents of the university becomes a matter of secondary importance.

David Frank and Jay Gabler show in detail how wrong this conceptualization is. They see the university as a central location of the cultural constitution – not the technical skills – of the postmodern society. And they show that the rise and fall of academic fields in the twentieth-century university is best comprehended in precisely this way. The university builds the cosmos and structure of society. It tames and "scientizes" and universalizes nature; it rationalizes models of society; and it celebrates the extraordinary capabilities for agentic action of the supreme modern individual. It thus creates the cultural conditions enabling the contemporary society, rather than providing a sort of storehouse for technical activity within this society.

In this Foreword, I review the story of the expansion of the modern university and the conventional interpretations of this expansion. Against this background, it becomes clear what an extraordinarily creative achievement *Reconstructing the University* is. And why it is such a unique study, with almost no parallels – whether competitors or supporters or alternatives. This book, in short, commands the attention of anyone interested in the modern university and its cultural role in society.

Background

University-level education has expanded enormously in the modern period. Most of the expansion has occurred in the last half-century. So almost 20 percent of a cohort of young people in the world is now found in an institution of higher education – fifty years ago, it might have been 2 percent, and fifty years before that it might have been a fraction of 1 percent.

Of course, in developed countries, it is common for more than half a cohort to be participating in higher education at any time. But the more striking phenomenon is the very rapid expansion of higher education in the developing world, where it is routine for countries to have higher rates of enrollment than Britain or Germany or France had a few decades ago. A country like Kazakhstan, for instance, might have as many higher education students as the whole world had in 1900.

For better or worse, this huge social change has come to seem obvious, even to those social scientists whose job it should be to provide analysis and explanation. It now seems to make sense that young people should normally aspire to higher education and that societies should normally provide it: Education is now seen as "human capital" and as benefiting both individuals and societies in the great races to achieve success and progress. The ideas that

there could be too much higher education, that there would be great ineffi
ciencies from "overeducation," and that anomic social disorder would result
from unemployed youth with unrealistic expectations have receded into the
woodwork of conservative muttering. A recent report from the World Bank –
by no means a center of radical thought and action – simply celebrates the
virtues of higher education for the developing world's progress and worries
only that the quality and character of it might not be adequate to meet all
the social needs.

Our limited understanding of the great expansionary change in higher
education is concealed in descriptive words that do not really analyze what
is going on. It is said that we now live in a knowledge society or information
society. Globalization is thought to demand a highly schooled labor force, as
if the Honduran banana worker must go to college if the banana is to go all
the way to Canada.

The underlying aim of the descriptive words that try to routinize or nor-
malize the great educational expansion is quite clear. The very traditional idea
is that schooling in general – and higher education in particular – is about
giving people skills to do "jobs" and that as the jobs change with economic
growth, technical professionalization, and globalization, the schooling has
to change too. Thus, the knowledge society requires expanded higher education.

This idea is not entirely unreasonable. But it leaves unexplained why
higher education should expand so rapidly in economically very peripheral
Third World countries. And it leaves unexplained why higher education
should expand in the developed world so much more rapidly than economic
or occupational change.

And importantly, a more subtle matter is left unexplained by notions that
so much higher education is necessary for substantial proportions of required
job performance in the modern system. It is generally understood that training people for jobs goes on most successfully if the training is linked closely to
the job. It can be on the same site, involve working with the same experienced
people, employ the same tools and models, and so on.

Expansive higher education around the world systematically violates these
obvious requirements of job training efficiency. It occurs in socially (and
physically) bounded and separated places. It involves working with teachers
who are rarely real practitioners and who are instructing under very artificial

conditions. And it generally involves all sorts of abstract models and tools, far removed from the tasks of daily practice. We live in a world, for instance, in which people being trained to be physicians are required to spend long years – far removed from the human ills they are to deal with later – learning things like organic chemistry and calculus. And maybe sociology.

Reformers confronting this situation historically propose small correctives. (The large corrective, getting rid of the schooling complex, was proposed some years ago by Ivan Illich in *Deschooling Society*, but his proposal was not really taken seriously.) For instance, one can partially correct the insulation of training from work with the field trip, or the internship, or the laboratory experience, or with temporary workshops and in these fashions have the segregated trainee glimpse normal reality from a kind of catwalk. But the more fundamental problems are to understand why the institutional segregation occurs in the first place, why it replicates itself so regularly, and why it has expanded to become a worldwide norm.

One solution to this whole nest of explanatory problems is to imagine that higher education and, in good part, modern education in general are not mainly about training people for extant jobs. They are about training people for a progressive and expansionist future – for activities that may not exist, or may be transformed in great new ways, or could and should be so changed. Education, unlike the apprenticeship, is about progress.

This line of thought helps explain the otherwise odd phenomena noted above – the extreme expansion of education in the Third World, its apparently over-rapid expansion in the First World, and its peculiar separation from the life it is nominally to enhance. But this argument also raises new questions and ones that are much more interesting and fruitful than all the traditional ones in this field that are based on the utterly unconvincing assumption that higher education is tightly interdependent with society as it exists.

If we are training people to live in a world that does not exist – a world that will be created by progress as carried along by the people we are training – how do we know what to teach them? Obviously, we *do* have confidence that we know, because the university expands apace on a worldwide scale. An analysis of this confidence seems core to understanding higher education in the modern world.

David Frank and Jay Gabler's extraordinary research in *Reconstructing the University* analyzes changes in the world's knowledge system through the greatest part of the twentieth century. But their core insight characterizes the university – a unique Western institution now gone global – throughout most or all of its history of almost one thousand years. It is that the university is more about establishing the cultural or religious map of the cosmos and of human action and structure in this cosmos than about facilitating particular activities within this system. The university is more about creating and installing the frame for the demonic powers of "man" than about technically enabling the powers themselves.

This was true in the expansionist medieval world that created the model of a university, which understood the cosmos in a way that would give power and authority (not really job training) to the emerging state and church and economic actors of the world. The cultural scheme worked out a distinct religious version of theology and law (two of the four core agenda items of the period) and a sanctified secular version from ancient philosophy (for medicine and philosophy, the other agenda topics). It is a customary conceit of interpreters to imagine that some real skills were transmitted in this process (e.g., the reinforcement of Latin as the language of civilization), but the whole argument is not strong.

Frank and Gabler do not provide data on the early modern period, but their argument is strong there too. The great battles over university secularization and over religious versus statist ties were not principally about any occupational or functional skills at all. They were about fundamental cultural assumptions, carried in different ways by different versions of the university and empowering different models of emerging modern society. (The most famous of these battles, actually carried out outside the domain of the university, has everything to do with cosmology and nothing to do with the immediate functioning of any social role. Galileo got into trouble, not by advocating usury, but by observing some moons around Jupiter. It should go without saying that this issue was not at the forefront of the concerns of the capitalists of the period. Nor was it a policy concern of the murderously mobilizing nation-state elites.)

The nineteenth century, too, can provide much fodder for the argument of *Reconstructing the University*. It is striking how much the actual cultural expanding university of the period is irrelevant to the direct social functioning of society and its roles, and how close the connections are with the cultural base of the system in its specification of a changed cosmos and a grossly altered place of humans and social organization in that cosmos. Modern analysts try to ignore this close connection and try to fit the university into the functioning technical role they envision for it – this effort involves the absurd celebration of the creation of an occasional engineering school or the successes of a few German chemistry professors, but is at gross odds with the actual cultural content of the universities in question. (The German university, on its secular side, was excavating philology more than the periodic table.)

Decoding the Knowledge Society

The extraordinary data and analyses that David Frank and Jay Gabler provide in this book achieve their full force not in abstract theory about the nature of the university or in analyses of its past, but in an aggressive and historically situated analysis of our own knowledge system. They see this university-based knowledge system as carrying a whole modern cosmology and framework for human action and structure, not a job training scheme for an elaborate and technical modern social machine. They see it, in other words, as culturally supporting the assumptions and mythology of the machine, not principally the particular skills of the human components involved. And their arguments make it quite clear why the great expansion of education in the modern period occurs in a rather unified university (serving as a kind of church for postmodernity), rather than in differentiated technical training institutions linked closely to workplaces and job sites.

The knowledge society is based on extreme cultural assumptions. It takes an enormous amount of university research and teaching to make them make sense. Thus, the twentieth century experienced an extraordinary expansion of public (often state) authority in social life, with the spread of the nation-state system around the world and its penetration down into the details of social life. The huge expansion of the rationalistic social sciences, emphasized by Frank and Gabler, provides the needed supports for this explosion of what Foucault called governmentality. And the relative decline in the humanities helps weaken the alternatives – the senses of the power of tradition, of local particularities, of the gods and spirits, or of natural human desires and needs. And the dominance of the sciences continuously expands the frame in which empowered humans can walk the earth as rational actors – small gods, empowered with legitimate purpose and comprehension.

The fact that all this cultural formation goes on, not in specialized re- search institutions and oracles, but in educational institutions, is crucial to understanding the contemporary world. This world is filled not only with a knowledge system authorizing enormous control over humans, society, and nature but also with persons authorized to undertake this control. Agentic humans, full of degrees and esteem, can take rational action and assemble rationalized social structures across an incredible array of social domains.

Beyond the rough classification of fields into natural sciences, humanities, and social sciences, Frank and Gabler are able to go into great detail. Field by academic field, they spell out the qualities that make a subject especially relevant for the postmodern knowledge society. So fields that celebrate tra- dition (classics), that leave human action in the distance (astronomy), or that limit the centrality of natural and social structures and agents (religion) do not do so well. And within the special academic field of history, Frank and Gabler show the rise of universalized versions (world history) and the relative decline of particularistic traditions (nation-state history, ancient history).

In all this extraordinary work, Frank and Gabler almost never find any reason to stress the technical utility (or lack of it) in any field for particular job activities. In the same way that the great religious traditions do not provide much instruction on how to make bricks, the modern university rarely places emphasis on teaching people how to make the widgets of the information highway.

Dialectics

The medieval and early modern university was a cultural-constitution locale, like the modern one. It was probably even worse at training people for actual job performances than the modern one is. But in a perverse way, it did link up to the limited professional job "markets" of the period – in the church, in the central mysteries of the state, in medicine, and in the schools. In each case, the university did this not by serving some sort of needs of society, but by *defining those needs in the first place*. Thus, the university pulled down out of ancient culture some knowledge, which we now know to be useless and counterproductive of human health, called medicine and gave it authority. And much law. And theology. And very odd sorts of cultural material we might loosely call philosophy (learning an ancient language, useless unless the university said so).

In the modern world that Frank and Gabler analyze, the same phenomenon has gone wild. Enormous numbers of "professional" jobs in the modern world exist and gain authority principally because they carry university-based "knowledge." Consider all the consultants and professionals and therapists and teachers that make up our modern labor force. For many of these positions, there would be no market were it not for the special knowledge certified by the university and carried by degrees.

An enormous number of other jobs might exist, without educational certification, under a variety of cultural conditions. But in the contemporary world, schooled knowledge can be made a requirement by legal or social definition. Thus, in developed countries, primary-school teachers are required to have university training; increasingly, so are day care workers; it goes without saying that all sorts of counselors must have certificates.

Even when certificates may not be required, gratuitous tasks can be attached to any job, making it practically necessary that a good deal of formal education be attained. Thus, a small plumbing contractor must not only have some skill at working with pipes but must also have the knowledge to deal with laws and agents of multiple regulatory agencies, suppliers, technical manuals, and the arcane worlds regulating financial transactions and legal liabilities. In job after job, the modern world has a preference, rooted in a faith in educational knowledge, for the gratuitous schooling of work tasks.

So it turns out that education is the most important component of essentially every modern stratification system. Sociologists write as if jobs are the important thing. But jobs gain status inasmuch as they require educational training – empirically, this is by far the most important component (transcending, for instance, income). And people gain jobs and other dimensions of social standing inasmuch as they have education.

Of course, the central point of this book remains intact. The schooled plumber, primary-school teacher, or clerk does not really acquire the relevant skills in typical schooling programs. What the education does is prepare the person, and the whole modern society, for life and activity under general principles, subject to abstract analysis, and amenable to disciplined linguistic performances.

Thus, postmodern society is indeed a knowledge society. But the point stressed over and over in the analyses of Frank and Gabler is that this is centrally a cultural matter, not a technical or functional one. That is, the knowledge generated and transmitted in the university is mainly cultural framing, not technical skill. It is knowledge taming the cosmos and rendering it suitable for and comprehensible by the extraordinary numbers of young people receiving its blessings. Understanding the power of this core point is central to our comprehension of the nature of the modern university and of the reasons this formerly narrow institution has broadened to cover virtually every substantive domain in practically every country in the world, with huge populations of participants.

John W. Meyer
Professor of Sociology, Emeritus
Stanford University

Introduction

The Ongoing Reconstruction of the University

In deep and resounding ways, the teaching and research emphases of universities shifted over the twentieth century, altering their academic core. During this period, for example, the relative prominence of university activities in such fields as philosophy, the classics, and botany all declined precipitously. The social sciences, meanwhile, came unbridled, and various types of engineering were born. In the distribution of its main academic endeavors, the university changed extensively.

The shifts occurred at all levels of the university organization: among the main branches of learning (the humanities, the natural sciences, and the social sciences – both basic and applied), among the various disciplinary fields (e.g., art, chemistry, psychology), and also within the subject matters of particular fields. The transformations – in the heart of what the university is and does – appeared in countries around the world.

Indeed from places near and far and from universities new and old, stories of reconstruction abound. For instance at 800-year-old Oxford, the post-World War II period witnessed rapid expansion beyond the university's traditional strongholds in the humanities, with the founding of a business school (an endeavor once considered too philistine for a great university), the winning of six Nobel prizes in the natural sciences (endeavors once too technical and applied), and a sharp increase in the percentage of undergraduates reading the social sciences (endeavors once essentially unknown). In the composition of its basic activities, the new Oxford looked rather different from the old, ivied one.[1] During the same postwar period at the University of Chicago, an institution seven centuries younger than Oxford, the humanities themselves were transformed. According to the dean, the humanities moved away from (without abdicating) "the notion of transcendent geniuses" and "the concept of a canon" organized around "fixed, prescribed ideas of artistic worth." Accordingly the classics faculty, once devoted to the likes of Plato and Cicero, embarked on "studies of magic, religion, popular belief, and gender studies." English professors, previously faithful to Shakespeare and company, engaged "popular genres and mass culture." And the music department, a former bastion of European classical composers, embraced ethnomusicology, including "Middle Eastern popular romantic crooner songs."[2] At Chicago as at Oxford – and as at virtually all their peer institutions – teaching and research portfolios changed sharply over the twentieth century.

Similar reformations transpired far beyond the elite universities and core countries. Academic emphases at Nigeria's University of Ibadan, for instance, altered greatly even during the short span of 1963 to 1980. In 1963, Ibadan's humanities faculty was virtually the same size as its natural sciences faculty and 3.8 times larger than its social sciences faculty. By 1980, just seventeen years later, the humanities faculty had shrunk to 0.8 times the size of the natural sciences faculty and 1.8 times the size of the social sciences faculty. In relative terms, Ibadan's humanities lost substantial ground in a very short frame of time. It seems that outside the global elite, as well as within it, academic rosters underwent substantial revision.

Beyond particular universities and regions, there were twentieth-century expansions and contractions of entire knowledge domains, even on a global basis. For instance, of universities worldwide in 1959, fewer than half had economics faculties, whereas twelve years later, almost two-thirds did. The proliferation of economics programs happened broadly and swiftly. Likewise at a lower level of analysis, there were striking developments within the field of history. In history departments worldwide, for example, the average share of courses on Greece and Rome fell by more than half between 1895 and 1995, even as the share devoted to world history quadrupled. What counted as meaningful "history" shifted acutely.[3]

In fact, over the twentieth century, one finds extensive alterations in the composition of the university's most essential activities throughout the world, at every level of the university organization, as well as across indicators of change – be they curriculum reforms, departmental closings, degrees granted, or whatever. The whole body of university knowledge seems to have morphed during this era, reconstituting the academic core. This is the starting point of our endeavor.

Change in the Academic Core

To some extent, of course, change is built into the modern university's foundations. The institution's animating quest for discovery requires the evolution of teaching and research priorities; its commitment to progress demands them. Thus in the year 1904 in a parting speech to the Board of Trustees, Jane Stanford extolled, "Let us not be afraid to outgrow old thoughts and ways, and dare to think on new lines as to the future of the work under our care." Let us embrace, in other words, constant renewal.[4] Similarly in the year 2000, the mission statement of the University of Botswana declared, "Naturally a modern university must recreate itself on a regular basis to ensure its purpose is always relevant."[5] By contemporary definition, universities are programmed for continual revision to remain abreast of the knowledge frontiers.[6] Change is in the nature of the beast.

Despite such reform-oriented foundations, however, the reshuffling of university priorities elicited repeated storms of protest during the twentieth century. In recent decades from within the academy, Bloom warned of a "closing of the American mind," as the university catered academic menus to the whims of ill-informed student bodies. Around the same time, Readings deplored "the university in ruins," as higher education lost its mission-guiding attachment to the nation-state. For Kirp, the critical problem was consumerism unbound, as the university reorganized around market models to produce a dissonant mix of "Shakespeare, Einstein, and the bottom line." In Bryson's analysis, the result was nothing less than a culture "war" being fought over the university's composition.[7] The chorus of outcries from the professoriate – only briefly sampled here – conveyed an unequivocal sense of crisis.

At the same time in the popular press, imageries of basket-weaving students and comic-book-analyzing professors were conjured to illustrate the university's alleged ongoing degradation. Typical among dozens of screeds was a *Wall Street Journal* article decrying the loss of historical knowledge among U.S. students:

> No more than 22 percent [of surveyed students] had any idea that "government of the people, by the people, for the people" came from the Gettysburg Address. More than half could not identify the Constitution as the source of the separation of powers....Only 34 percent knew George Washington was the general commanding the Americas at Yorktown, the ultimate battle of the Revolutionary War....[U]niversity administrators, long cowed by the multiculturalists and pressure groups hostile to anything that might smack of Western culture, ought to consider getting up off their knees to provide young Americans with a serious education in their history and civilization.[8]

Declamations such as these leave little room for wonder: Not all academic innovations over the twentieth century were embraced across the board.

And yet for all such smoke, social scientists know surprisingly little of the fire. Many anecdotes and illustrations imply that the university's academic emphases shifted acutely and globally over the last century among the branches of learning, between the basic and applied divisions, among the disciplinary fields, and within the subject matters of particular fields. Still the contours of change remain almost totally undocumented in systematic empirical terms. Furthermore as illustrated above, many of the purported developments generated deep consternation. And yet sober analyses of the university's evolving priorities are few and far between.[9]

Thus we arrive at the inquiries that motivate our study. First empirically, exactly what changed in the university's academic core over the twentieth century? And then theoretically, what causal forces stood behind the observed changes? These fundamental descriptive and explanatory questions guide us through this book.

The Existing Literature

Large-scale studies of change in the university's teaching and research priorities are virtually nonexistent in the current literature. Given the intense scrutiny of so many other aspects of higher education, this omission is striking. At issue is the makeup of the university's most basic activities after all.

As suggested above, the literature's oversight may derive in part from the university's contemporary definition. Change in an institution built to change – "let knowledge grow from more to more," proclaims the University of Chicago's motto – can appear to be natural and therefore unproblematic, and thus researchers may disregard it. Complicating matters, summary indicators of academic priority changes are difficult to assemble in aggregate. The obvious candidates for measure – disciplinary enrollments, say, or funding allocations – are unavailable on both or either longitudinal and/or comparative bases.

What do exist in the literature are (often despairing) anecdotes of change, as digested above. Although these stories can provoke intrigue, they cannot stand in for systematic analyses of university reconstruction. What exist as well in the literature are many excellent and detailed case studies, charting developments in the teaching and research priorities of particular departments, fields, universities, and countries. These works are useful for the detail they offer and commendable for their fidelity to the gamut of available evidence. But essentially by definition, case studies present movements in academic emphases narrowly, often tracing just single threads of change through time.[10]

Altogether, the existing store of anecdotes and case studies provides a rich foundation for our investigations below. But we depart from them in three decisive ways.

First, the existing literature typically confines its gaze to single branches or fields of learning – the decline of the humanities, say, or the rise of biochemistry.[11] Characteristic pieces in this vein carefully consider the complex pressures promoting expansions and contractions in particular university domains. And yet in tightly delineating their objects of study, most such studies all but preclude the possibility of observing domain-straddling patterns of transformation.

In part, this is a problem because raising the standing of any one domain in the university necessarily lowers others: By definition, relative academic emphases are interdependent. More important, there seem to be forces of change that span across the knowledge domains, carrying implications throughout the academic core. To illustrate, we show in Table 1 the faculties and departments of the University of Tokyo in 1900 and in 2000. Considering the differences for a moment, one sector-spanning force of change seems likely to have been globalization, providing impetus not only to the new Department of Earth and Planetary Physics but also to the new out-reaching departments of Indian Philosophy & Buddhist Studies, Islamic Studies, Occidental History, and Slavic Languages & Literatures. Another broad force of change seems likely to have been the rationalization and scientization of society. The social sciences at the University of Tokyo exploded over the century – in new faculties of economics and education, for instance, and in new departments of psychology and sociology. Far from exhibiting the qualities of Kerr's "Tower of Babel" or "city of infinite variety," these data in Table 1 – although culled from one university only – show distinctly patterned rearrangements in academic emphases cutting across levels and sectors.[12] Studying knowledge domains in isolation necessarily underplays such features of university reconstruction.

In our first departure from the literature then, we regard the various knowledge domains as components of a dynamically integrated system – a unified "body of university knowledge" that metamorphoses together over time. In this, we do not mean to minimize the benefits of studying the particular stimuli of change vis-à-vis specific knowledge domains. We only mean to point out the additional benefits of studying the parts in terms of the whole. As some knowledge domains contract and others emerge and expand, they do so in interaction with one another and in the context of overarching environmental changes. The body of university knowledge transmogrifies in total. From this purview for example, the fates of physics and literature (not to mention physics and astronomy) cannot be disentangled.

As a second matter, the orthodox literature nearly always limits analytical attention to academic emphases within a single country or even university.[13] Such studies often provide full-bodied and detailed accounts of academic recomposition. Nevertheless, investigations thus confined are by design insensitive to transnational and global influences on the university's academic priorities.

Again, a quick perusal of empirical materials suggests the problems with such purview restrictions. The faculty and department listings for the University of Tokyo in 1900 (Table 1), for instance, look remarkably similar to those that would be found at a typical American land-grant university of the same era (e.g., the University of Minnesota). According to the U.S. Morrill Act of 1862, the land-grant universities were founded to teach classical studies, agriculture, and the mechanic arts, as well as military tactics – precisely what one finds at Tokyo in 1900. In particular, Tokyo's twin departments of Arms Technology and Explosives Technology suggest Morrill-Act parallels, especially given the fact that both they and their U.S. analogues were by 2000 long gone.

Even this bit of evidence suggests that analyses limited to particular country or university contexts are likely to miss encompassing forces behind university reconstruction. Accordingly in our second departure from the literature, we pursue the notion that at least some changes in the academic core have transnational and global wellsprings. We do not thus disregard university- and national-level factors; we only embed them in broader contexts. In academic-priority reforms, we argue, universities in Peru and Sweden may follow common models.

Taken together, these first two departures from the literature suggest the benefits of a research design centered on an empirical problem that at present is almost wholly absent from the social science agenda.[14] How did the body of university knowledge, as a whole and worldwide, change during the twentieth century? Where did the global academic frontiers retreat, and where did they advance? The literature's dominant case studies are ill equipped to recognize, much less address, such macro-comparative issues.

Third, beyond limitations in research design – and partly because of them – the bulk of the current literature is constrained theoretically. Most analysts adopt a loosely functionalist point of view, treating changes in the composition of teaching and research (more business, less botany, etc.) as adaptive responses to the shifting needs and interests of either society at large or of its dominant elites. In premise, one must note, such arguments are questionable. Most needs and interests could be satisfied more efficiently outside the university's encumbering walls in specialized laboratories of power and profit.[15] Nevertheless functionalist perspectives remain prevalent in the literature, taking organizational, economic, and political forms.

Table 1 Faculties & Departments at the University of Tokyo, 1900 & 2000[1]

Law	Politics	Political Science
	Law	Private Law
		Public Law
Medicine	Medicine	Medicine
	Pharmacy	Health Sciences & Nursing
Pharmaceutical Sciences		Molecular Pharmaceutics
		Functional Pharmaceutics
		Life Pharmaceutics
Engineering	Civil Engineering	Civil Engineering
	Mechanical Engineering	Mechanical Engineering
	Electrical Engineering	Electrical Engineering
	Architecture	Architecture
	Applied Chemistry	Applied Chemistry
	Naval Architecture	Naval Architecture & Ocean Engineering
	Metallurgy & Mining	Metallurgy
	Arms Technology	Urban Engineering
	Explosives Technology	Engineering Synthesis
		Mechano-Informatics
		Precision Machinery Engineering
		Aeronautics & Astronautics
		Information & Communication Engineering
		Electronic Engineering
		Applied Physics
		Mathematical Engineering & Information Physics
		Quantum Engineering & Systems Science
		Geosystem Engineering
		Materials Engineering
		Chemical System Engineering
		Chemistry & Biotechnology
Literature	Philosophy	Philosophy
	Japanese Literature	Japanese Literature
	Japanese History	Japanese History
	History	History
	Chinese Literature	Chinese Language & Literature
	English Literature	English Language & Literature
	German Literature	German Language & Literature
	French Literature	French Language & Literature
	Comparative Philology	Linguistics
		Chinese Philosophy
		Indian Philosophy & Buddhist Studies
		Ethics
		Religious Studies

Table 1   Continued

		Aesthetics
		Islamic Studies
		Oriental History
		Occidental History
		Archaeology
		Art History
		Japanese Language
		Indian Languages & Literature
		Slavic Languages & Literatures
		South European Languages & Literatures
		Modern European & American Languages & Literatures
		Greek and Latin Classics
		Psychology
		Social Psychology
		Sociology
Science	Mathematics	Mathematics
	Astronomy	Astronomy
	Physics	Physics
	Chemistry	Chemistry
	Geology	Geology
	Zoology	Zoological Sciences
	Botany	Plant Sciences
		Information Science
		Earth and Planetary Physics
		Biophysics and Biochemistry
		Anthropology
		Mineralogy
		Geography
Agriculture	Veterinary Medicine	Veterinary Medicine
	Agriculture	Applied Life Sciences
	Agricultural Chemistry	Bioenvironmental Sciences
	Forestry	Biological Production Studies
		Regional Economics and Resource Studies
Economics		Economics
		Business Administration
Education		History and Philosophy of Education
		Social Sciences in Education
		Educational Psychology
		Teaching, Curriculum, and Learning Environments
		Educational Administration
		Physical and Health Education

[1] *Sources:* 1899–1900 Tokyo Imperial University *Calendar* and 2000–01 University of Tokyo *Catalogue.*

In their organizational variant, functionalist explanations view altered teaching and research emphases as responses to the evolving needs and interests of university actors per se. Professors, for instance, who are protected by professional autonomy and motivated by career pressures (e.g., to publish or perish), may flock to some fields more than others – perhaps those perceived to be pioneering.[16] Similarly, an enlarging and increasingly diverse student population may demand new or different (for example, more "pertinent") courses of study.[17] Along the same lines, wealthy alumni and well-placed administrators may push study rosters in particular directions – for example, toward higher status or higher revenue-generating disciplines.[18] In perhaps the most common incarnation of the organizational argument, universities themselves are the salient actors, differentiating from one another in order to enhance their survival prospects in an increasingly competitive environment.[19] This process presumably precludes the appearance of population-level trends, as universities seek out unique organizational niches. Common to all these organizational arguments is the imagery that the university and its internal constituents are autonomous and effective actors, implementing academic-core changes over time to fulfill their needs and advance their interests.

In the economic version of the functionalist story, actors outside the university come into focus. Their financial needs and pecuniary interests are allotted the catalyzing roles in academic reconstruction. Corporations typically headline such analyses, encouraging the expansion of potentially profitable knowledge domains.[20] To illustrate, the Boeing professorships (e.g., of Aerospace Engineering at Penn State and of Global Learning at Wichita State) seem rather obviously oriented toward developing technical and marketing expertise favorable to Boeing's bottom line. Sometimes, economic functionalists also assign centrality to nation-states, which may selectively invest in particular "higher education units that aid in managing or enhancing economic innovation and thereby competitiveness."[21] The rise of the so-called knowledge economy, for instance, spurs many countries to fund university-based computer engineering programs. All arguments along these lines share the basic notion that actors external to the university – in pursuit of profits, economic development, or other monetary benefits – shape and reshape academic portfolios over time.

Political functionalisms also invoke outside actors, but they focus on those – especially states and state officials – with agendas of power and governance.[22] In the Manhattan Project, for example, the U.S. government funded university science and engineering units in pursuit of military objectives.[23] Similarly with the proliferation of benefits programs, the welfare states of Europe spurred the growth of economics. More broadly, England, France, and the other colonial powers are seen to have profoundly shaped university priorities in the colonies, conveying Western worldviews that then enabled postcolonial domination.[24] In addition to such state-level influences on university priorities, political functionalists sometimes also highlight efforts by social movements to implement their agendas with academic-core revisions.[25] Across all these strands of thought recurs the idea that actors outside the higher education orbit enhance their powers and further their political agendas by promoting alterations in the university's academic composition.

Altogether, these functionalist explanations have been helpful in moving the literature beyond the once-accepted notion that shifts in the body of university knowledge represent pure enlightenment – progress toward unfettered truths.[26] The same functionalist arguments, however, share empirical and theoretical deficiencies.

A first problem is that many university activities are difficult to fathom in needs-and-interests terms. Let us consider again the changes observed at the University of Tokyo between 1900 and 2000: It is straightforward enough to imagine the economic needs satisfied by establishing a Faculty of Pharmaceutical Sciences or the political interests served by creating and then disbanding the Department of Explosives Technology. But what needs and whose interests can be said to have prevailed in founding Tokyo's Department of Aesthetics or in dismantling its Department of Forestry? Such additions to and departures from the academic menu defy easy functionalist logic.

The same case can be made from the standpoint of individual courses. Some components of nearly every degree program flout needs-and-interests categorizations – as proponents of credentialism theory well know.[27] It is the rare doctor who employs organic chemistry in the diagnosis of whooping cough or advanced calculus in the treatment of bone cancer. And yet both subjects stand central to medical schooling. It is likewise the exceptional lawyer who uses Constitutional law in a contract dispute or felony case – let alone the garden-variety divorce – despite which the course is a cornerstone of legal education. At Rhodes University in South Africa, the Department of Ichthyology and Fisheries Science – "promoting the study of fish and the sustainable utilization of aquatic resources" – requires its undergraduate majors to complete an array of natural science courses, but notes as well, "Undergraduate students in Ichthyology are encouraged to study Management and Introduction to Philosophy as credits towards the degree."[28] Functionalist imageries seem too limited to explain such features of the academic landscape, especially given their everyday appearance.

A second problem with functionalist arguments arises from the fact that dominant needs and interests are highly variable by country, given overwhelming dissimilarities in such basics as socioeconomic development. Were the makeup of university teaching and research to follow from these factors, one would anticipate much greater cross-national variation than appears in fact. To illustrate, take Jordan and the United States around the year 2000. The two countries differed economically: The gross domestic product per capita in Jordan was one-tenth that of the United States and centered on natural resources. The two countries differed politically: Jordan was a constitutional monarchy with about 4 million people, whereas the United States was a democracy with about 280 million people. And the two countries differed culturally: One was Muslim based (mainly Sunni,) and one was Christian based (mainly Protestant). Although the needs and interests prevailing in the two countries – both at large and in terms of their elites – undoubtedly overlapped to some degree, they had every reason to diverge much more. And yet contrary to any functionalist imagery, academic emphases at the University of Jordan looked remarkably similar to those found at a typical American state university of the same period, with Faculties of Arts, Business Administration, Science, Medicine, Nursing, Agriculture, Educational Sciences, Engineering and Technology, Law, Physical Education, Pharmacy, Dentistry, Humanities and Social Sciences, Graduate Studies, Rehabilitation Sciences, Information and Technology, and Arts and Design.[29] Only Jordan's Faculty of Islamic Studies seems at all distinctive from the Western purview, although its Western analogues are perfectly obvious (departments of theology, religion, Biblical studies, etc.). Around the world, country-to-country differences in university priorities seem a good deal smaller than those implied by functionalist arguments.

By the same token, universities themselves are characterized by diverging congeries of needs and interests – different types of student organizations, variously esteemed faculty groups, and so on. Were such organizational stakeholders wielding significant influence over the composition of teaching and research, one would expect to find substantial university-to-university differentiation as above.[30] On the contrary, however, the academic rosters of places as different as Harvard and the College of the Ozarks overlap remarkably in form and distribution. The more one observes isomorphism – an issue we explore further below – the less that functionalist explanations seem adequate to explain changing university emphases.

A third problem with functionalist arguments is that most needs and interests – aside from those explicitly linked to the common good – are denied legitimate standing vis-à-vis university agendas. Thus, although there can be little doubt that throughout the modern period, rich and powerful actors have sought to reshape academic emphases in hopes of winning private advantage, it is equally clear that the university's "claim[s] to objectivity and universality" have limited the success of those attempts.[31] Indeed it is precisely because they represent boundary transgressions –threats to academic integrity – that needs and interests based influences on teaching and research gain public notoriety, mobilizing the policy arsenals of expert panels, professional review boards, administrative bodies, and so on.

Take, for example, a corporately funded university biochemist.[32] The extent to which market forces can shape the scientist's findings – as the functionalist vision implies – is severely limited by prevailing scientific standards of objectivity. These standards are enforced by peer review and given rigorous attention when mandatory conflict-of-interest disclosures mark potential interpretative bias. Such rules and procedures exist to ward off sectarian advances on the academic core, and they are built into the university's standard operating procedures (and are often required for accreditation).[33] Researchers in even the most extremely "applied" disciplines, with potentially immediate impacts on wealth and influence (petroleum engineering, applied genomics, information technology), must adhere to precisely detailed work protocols to clear the hurdles of objectivity. Indeed in the late 1800s, Germany's *Technische Hochschulen* spent decades meeting the exacting standards of basic research before building sufficient credibility to branch into studies of "concrete industrial development."[34] Examples along these lines highlight the barriers protecting university studies from needy and interested actors, at least as much as they illustrate the incursions thereof.

In summary on three grounds we critique functionalist explanations of change in the body of university knowledge: (1) We observe many features of the academic landscape that are difficult to characterize as needs fulfillment or interests appeasement, (2) we see more homogeneity in university portfolios than needs- and interests-based arguments imply or predict, and (3) we find carefully policed boundaries around the academic core, warding off needy and interested trespassers. At best it seems, functionalist analyses offer only partial explanations of academic recomposition over time.

In what follows, we therefore develop an alternative approach to the university's ongoing reconstruction, taking account of the issues just delineated. In developing this alternative, we draw heavily from the global-institutional or world-society school of sociology, which starts at the point of questioning the assumed naturalness of actors, needs, and interests and then directs attention to the evolving world-cultural models from which such entities and characteristics derive.

Thus in our third departure from the orthodox literature – further articulated below – we treat the evolving global-institutional frame as embodying basic assumptions about reality that condition the contents of the academic core. This does not mean that we take no notice of the actors, needs, and interests highlighted by functionalists, only that we see them as socially constructed within wider institutional environments.

Mapping Reality

Our main arguments can be stated simply. We propose (1) that the university is definitionally committed to mapping reality and (2) that changes in the assumed features of reality thus reconstitute the academic core. To develop this argument, we begin here by exploring the relationship between university knowledge and reality.[35]

In Shils's terms, the distinctive task of the university is "the discovery and transmission of truth." In Bourdieu's postmodern language, the university is "an institution which has been socially licensed as entitled to operate an objectification which lays claim to objectivity and universality."[36] The appellation "university" emphatically conveys the institution's primary obligation: By cultural fiat and organizational rule, the university presents reality in objective and universal terms. The field of economics, for example, "presents itself as a universalistic paradigm. Its main rhetorical tool – model-building – is often taken-for-granted as a 'natural' product of the cumulative development of scientific knowledge." Violations of the standards of objectivity and universalism disqualify an organization from *being* a university.[37]

These basic parameters establish what a university is and does, and they are deeply institutionalized in the culture and organization of world society. They appear in encapsulated forms in university charters, mottoes, mission statements, and so on. For instance in a report from 1853, Yale made clear that its purpose was not to impart particular job skills but to convey broad understandings of reality:

> In laying the foundation of a thorough education, it is necessary that all the important faculties be brought into exercise. When certain mental endowments receive a much higher culture than others, there is a distortion in the intellectual character. The powers of the mind are not developed in their fairest proportions by studying languages alone, or mathematics alone, or natural or political science alone. The object, in the proper collegiate department, is not to teach that which is peculiar to any one of the professions; but to lay the foundation which is common to them all.

More than 100 years later, South Dakota State University echoed many of the same themes, setting its sights not only on "professional," "vocational," and "citizenship training" but also on "general education essential for the understanding and appreciation of the American way of life." Threaded throughout such statements, one sees the institution's commitment to *veritas*. In the university, exalts the anthem of the Universidad del Valle de Colombia, "truth shines triumphant."[38]

Of course few would claim that such grand ambitions are always fulfilled. But clear misrepresentations of reality, in subjective and particularistic terms, can catalyze unforgiving reprisals. For example in 2003, after a yearlong investigation, the Danish Committee on Scientific Dishonesty found

Bjørn Lomborg guilty of having "clearly acted at variance with good scientific practice" by presenting "systematically biased" data and thus perverting the depiction of reality in his book *The Skeptical Environmentalist.* The journal *Nature*, around the same time, published a harsh review of Lomborg's book, and *Scientific American* printed a point-by-point rebuttal. The World Resources Institute, meanwhile, stated that Lomborg had "no professional training...in ecology, climate science, resource economics, [or] environmental policy," whereas the Union of Concerned Scientists concluded that Lomborg's book was "seriously flawed," failing "to meet basic standards of credible scientific analysis."[39]

Although the Lomborg case is extreme, it vividly demonstrates the rigorous and sometimes punishing process of peer review, which is dedicated to defending the standards of truth. Thus we begin to see that the university's defining feature lies not in its capacity to serve the needs and/or interests of society or its elites but rather in its devotion to enlighten the objective and universal truths of reality. Where the primacy is reversed, placing needs and interests first, something other than a university – for example, a pharmaceuticals laboratory or policy think tank – is at hand.

As regards the body of university knowledge, all of this suggests that the university's very definition excludes from the academic core some forms of understanding – i.e., those that fail to conform to the fullness of reality. For example when the government of India called on universities to "rejuvenate the science of Vedic astrology," it "stirred a hornets' nest" of resistance from "widely disparate groups of scientists." Given the "overwhelming scientific evidence that the positions of planets and the time of birth do not dictate the course of human affairs," the scientists united behind the position that astrology's inclusion in the university sciences would only "erode the credibility" of India's universities.[40] The university's academic composition, thus, is set by the terms of reality.

Seeing the university through this lens helps clarify and resolve the main difficulties that vex functionalist arguments. First, there is no reason to see the decoupling of teaching and research activities from needs and interests as anachronistic, given that the university's first obligation is to map reality. Second there is every reason to expect isomorphism in academic emphases, given the institution's commitments to overriding truths. And third there is every reason to expect the university to demand the highest standards of academic integrity – keeping the rich and powerful at bay – given that its identity and purpose are antithetical to particularism and subjectivity.

Although the university's academic core undoubtedly bears the marks of societal needs and actor interests – as recent work on the multiversity reiterates – we expect that the broader contours of the body of university knowledge are established by its defining task of mapping the ultimate facts and transcendent principles of reality. In the end, even Kerr himself conceded that the university's members must "pay their devotions to truth."[41]

Changing Reality

Thus, we make the first assertion of our argument. University knowledge maps reality, and before catering to particular needs or interests, items on the academic menu must first jump the hurdles of objectivity and universalism. Our argument's second assertion – again simply stated – is that changes in the assumed nature of reality alter the raw materials of university studies. In a nutshell, this is the argument of our book. Modifications to the body of university knowledge (less zoology, more chemistry, etc.) arise not only to satisfy needs and interests but, more important, follow from revisions in globally institutionalized models of reality.[42]

Global institutions are built into the cultural scripts and organizational rules of world society. They take form in empirical "facts" (often of a scientific variety), natural "laws" (e.g., those underlying human rights), and general principles (often purveyed by professionals as "best practices").[43] Democracy, mass schooling, and environmental protection are all examples of global institutions; their rule-like-ness is implicit in the unlikelihood of any public leader speaking, even *sotto voce*, against them. The most egregious polluters, for example, vigorously claim to support environmental protection.[44]

One subset of global institutions is key to our arguments. We care less about particular institutions (such as democracy) than we do about the overall global-institutional frame, which is constructed from the most fundamental assumptions about reality's origins (the cosmology) and being (the ontology). The cosmology, specifically, supplies the master tale of manifestation, whereas the ontology establishes the nature of "action" and "structure" in the manifest world. Together, these sets of assumptions provide the root elements in the world culture's periodic table – designating the baseline features of global reality and the premises according to which objective and universal truths can be established. They thereby lay the foundations on which university knowledge arises.[45] Shifts in the global-institutional frame foment shifts in the academic core.

This argument about university reconstruction draws broadly on sociological neo-institutionalism, and it involves four main assertions. The first is that theories of origins and being establish frameworks of reality that determine the supply of foundational building blocks to university studies. If the distinctive task of the university "is the methodical discovery and the teaching of truths about serious and important things," and if what is "true" and "serious" and "important" are not spontaneous facts but rather cultural and organizational accomplishments, then changes in the institutional frame – altering the taken-for-granted aspects of reality – should reconstitute university activities.[46] One is less likely to find a theology department, for example, if the cosmology assumes no god. There must be a *there* there for university studies to occur.

The second assertion of the argument is that it is not just *any* institutional frame but rather the *global* one that delivers the main constituent materials to university teaching and research. Given the rule of universalism, global institutions take priority over local and national ones.[47] Even at its genesis in medieval times, the university adopted the most general posture – using a universal language (Latin) to educate a pan-European student body in universalistic forms of knowledge (i.e., reason and then later science).[48] Accordingly today, an education from the University of Liberia should "not only enable [graduates] to assure the future growth and development of Liberia but make it possible for them to contribute to the world at large."[49] The priority given to the global-institutional frame also derives from the universalism inherent in contemporary models of national state and society: To be a nation-state is to have and sponsor a "world-class university," meaning one that conforms to academic-priority standards (currently, for example, promoting information technology for the knowledge society).[50] Finally, the preponderance of the global-institutional frame is caused by recent increases in globalization itself, meaning both the sense and the fact that the world is one, whole interconnected entity. On economic, political, and cultural grounds, the "globality" of the world is rapidly intensifying, widening the global streams feeding university pools.[51] For all three of these reasons, we expect the body of university knowledge to be founded predominantly on assumptions embedded in the global-institutional frame.

Our argument's third main assertion is that the global-institutional frame provides, in Foucault's terms, a "basis or archaeological system" that is common to all the university's knowledge domains across organizational levels.[52] In constituting the heart of imagined reality, the frame's foundational blueprints of origin and being provide a platform of premises for everyday life and thus simultaneously establish foundations on which rest the humanities *and* the natural sciences *and* the social sciences, including all of their respective disciplinary fields (both basic and applied), as well as all of the subject matters within them. The retreat of God from the cosmology, for instance, affects biology as much as sociology.

Finally our fourth assertion lays out a causal pathway – from altered theories of origin and being (the latter along both its key action and structure dimensions) to altered university priorities. Although by no means a one-way street, the reality-to-university causal flow predominates, given the obvious precedence of reality in both historical and logical terms. Nevertheless in incremental ways, university professors rearticulate reality, feeding materials back into the global institutional frame. We further elaborate our causal imagery below.

Although empirical research on global-institutional explanations of academic-priority shifts is limited, what does exist is encouraging. In particular, several studies have documented world-level trends in disciplinary fields and subject matters that transcend the usual local/national and needs/interests accounts. The analyses that follow test the global-institutional perspective on the university's academic contents more generally than previously.[53]

Thus we make our central case, summarized in Figure 1. Shifts in the global-institutional frame reestablish reality's baseline assumptions and thus alter the plausibility, authority, and legitimacy of various academic activities, reconstituting university priorities. As a first step in fleshing out this argument, we turn now to the task of describing the major global-institutional reframings that characterized the twentieth century.

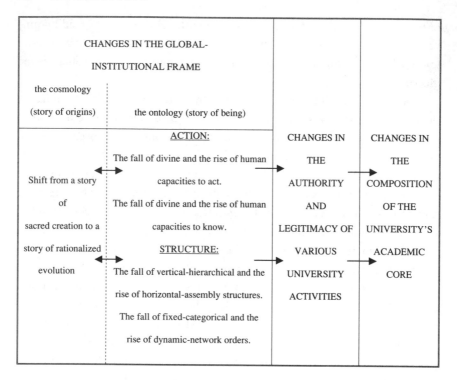

Figure 1   Causal model of university reconstruction.

Cosmology and Ontology during the Twentieth Century

If, as we claim, university knowledge must be objective and universal in order to count as truth, and if the conditions for establishing objective and universal truth are embedded in a dynamic global-institutional framework of reality, then the immediate question is, How did the global-institutional frame – in its basic stories of origins and being – change over the twentieth century? According to our argument, after all, it is these changes that reset reality's baseline assumptions, thus catalyzing reforms in the body of university knowledge.

In describing the changing framework of reality, we attend only to the broadest cosmological and ontological developments documented in the historical and social scientific literatures. Our descriptions here are necessarily in summary form, given that our primary energies are devoted to taking the step beyond global-institutional reframing – to its ramifications for the academic core.

One other qualification warrants mention before proceeding. Many of the changes described below not only originated in Western thought and science but also permeated Western societies earlier and more thoroughly than societies elsewhere. Their Western genesis and early success contributed importantly to the processes eventuating in their global institutionalization. With global institutionalization, however, the fact of their Western origins lost much of its salience, becoming a detail largely whitewashed by the universalism of world culture. The transformations became embedded in the understanding and production of knowledge in the world culture writ large.[54] From the perspective of Sri Lanka or Botswana, to take a concrete example, mass schooling is not a Western innovation but rather a feature of global modernity, and this is all the more so from the perspective of UNESCO (and its Global Coordinating Drive: Education for All by 2015).

RATIONALIZATION AND SECULARIZATION IN THE GLOBALLY
INSTITUTIONALIZED COSMOLOGY

As Weber and many others have observed, the modern theory of origins differs sharply from the traditional one. Over several centuries in a process set in motion by the Enlightenment, the picture of the genesis as a sacred creation – a picture dominant for many centuries, with variants around the world – slowly gave way to a picture of the genesis as a mundane evolution. In this way, a reality that once was seen to have emanated fully formed from the hand of God came instead to be seen as having been distilled over billions of years from a natural-physical primordial soup; An origin that was once shrouded in divine mystery acquired the transparency of a logical and predictable law-like system.

The roots of rationalization and secularization in the global cosmology date back at least to seventeenth-century Europe, with the onset of the Scientific Revolution. An important and representative figure from this age was Frances Bacon, whose denunciations of deduction (reasoning from first, typically religious, principles) and endorsements of induction (reasoning from empirical observations) laid some of the essential groundwork for the broad disenchantment of reality that attracted Weber's notice 300 years later. Already by the late eighteenth century, the contributors to Diderot's twenty-eight-volume *Encyclopédie* almost unanimously advocated skepticism (demanding that all assumptions be questioned) and rationalism (asserting that unaided human reason could attain truth): Having examined and rejected religion's foundations, they proclaimed reason's independence from faith. By that time throughout Europe, long-held assumptions about God and the creation were being steadily surrendered to conceptions of natural law. "[S]oon the possibility of miracles and revelation was denied, while mysteries were regarded as absurd."[55]

Nevertheless even with these forerunners, the publication of Darwin's *Origin of Species* in 1859 provided a new and powerful catalyst to the reformulation of the origins story that was taken for granted in world society. Darwin's theory of evolution – first suggested by Lamarck in 1801, who incorporated even earlier ideas – "fundamentally changed our view of the universe and our place in it. By providing a radically new vision of the origins of human beings, it challenged long held assumptions about our own significance, and undermined the major arguments for the existence of God."

These interrelated cultural changes – long underway – congealed over the twentieth century, producing a fundamental revision in the global-institutional frame.[56] In world society, the origins of reality were decreasingly assumed to lay in a sacred creation and increasingly assumed to lay in a mundane evolution.

The evidence for rationalization and secularization in the globally institutionalized cosmology is at once slippery, refusing easy measurement, and also pervasive, being written into much of the constitutional matter of contemporary world society. One gauge of the change is the substantial relative decline in religion-based international associations during the twentieth century. Whether the issue was AIDS or terrorism, assertions of divine will or sacred design lost virtually all legitimacy in global discourse.[57] From the flipside, one sees a shift toward the evolutionist cosmology in the extraordinary authority gained by science in international forums during the period in question, when science became the ultimate measure of truth in almost every realm. Today as a result, most governments in the world have cabinet-level science ministries (including the likes of Sudan, Iran, and Kazakhstan), and both sides in many global-issue conflicts never depart from scientific terrain, pitting scientist against scientist (as in the current climate change debates).[58] Also more specifically, testimony to the changing cosmology appears in the recalibrated benchmark story of human origins, no longer assumed in almost any international setting to be a unique episode of sacred creation – the birth of the children of God – but rather now conceptualized as a mere step in a mundane evolution from protoplasm to the animal *Homo sapiens*.[59] The key point here is not that people traded faith for reason during the twentieth century; it is rather that the taken-for-granted cultural scripts and organizational rules of world society decreasingly assumed that reality originated in a sacred creation and increasingly assumed that it arose in a mundane evolution.

Of course, no single piece of evidence has sufficient weight to prove the transformation at hand. The motivating processes, after all, proceeded slowly and unevenly, and they met with considerable resistance in particular world sectors and locales (and still do). Nevertheless, when observed from a bird's-eye view over the whole era, global-institutional reframing appears pronounced. According to many indicators, the authorized and legitimated world theory of origins seems to have changed profoundly. Now in world society, one may embrace a creationist cosmology as part of one's private, expressive cultural apparatus, but one may not, with few exceptions, use creation-based imageries to guide instrumental action in the public arena (e.g., to reduce environmental degradation or to address the grievances of indigenous peoples).[60]

For the university, of course, this global-institutional reframing carried deep ramifications, bringing forth a reality with critically different premises from those of its predecessor. The altered cosmology replaced divine and diabolical forces, which randomized reality so as to flout analysis, with systematic and law-like forces, which rendered reality as predictable and amenable to inquiry. Thus steadily over time, rationalization and secularization in the globally institutionalized cosmology opened more and more territories of nature and society to reasoned scientific examination, boosting the relevance and stature of universities tremendously. Indeed during the twentieth century, universities sprang up with great rapidity around the world – laying claim to vastly expanded areas of study, attracting sharply higher student enrollments, and generating substantially heightened demand for their certified degree holders. The new premises of the globally institutionalized cosmology helped fuel massive university expansion.[61]

The same altered premises also carried implications for the theorized nature and relations of being (the ontology). Indeed in terms of academic-core priorities – our primary object of analysis in the book – we expect the main effects of rationalization and secularization to be mediated through revisions to the globally institutionalized ontology in both its action and structure facets.

REDEFINITION OF ACTION IN THE GLOBALLY INSTITUTIONALIZED ONTOLOGY

In tandem with cosmological renewal over the twentieth century there came a double redefinition of action in the cultural scripts and organizational rules of world society. Along a pathway paved by the Renaissance, the conventional assumption that the gods (or spirits or divinities) controlled the ultimate capacities to author and comprehend reality was questioned more and more vigorously, at the same time as the notion that humans possessed inherent capacities to act and understand became increasingly routine. Thus, over several hundred years, a world that had long been assumed to be motivated largely or even exclusively by God came increasingly to display what appeared to be markings of self-conscious human intervention. And an ontology that enduringly had granted God the principal means to effect first-order changes in reality came instead to locate master capacities both to act and to know in the hands of individual humans.

The first and more general of these interrelated changes – concerning the reallocation of all-purpose action capacities – had multiple origins. These include Thomas Aquinas's thirteenth-century meditations on free will, according to which humans were conceived to be rational agents, possessing abilities to choose courses of action among alternatives, independently from God. Here were the early stirrings of an autonomous human actor. The redistribution of actorhood was furthermore spurred by the fifteenth- and sixteenth-century Renaissance in Italy – the so-called birthplace of the modern individual. Against the orthodox notion that all creative powers were ultimately vested in the Deity, Renaissance thinkers asserted the power and potency of the human individual – celebrating the virtues of individual freedoms and the possibilities for individual accomplishments (the Renaissance Man was thus one of diverse endeavors).[62] Increasingly over the centuries,

God was deactivated and humans were activated in the prevailing global-institutional frame.

The rationalization and secularization of the master origins story, discussed above, added heft to these early developments. To the extent that creation-based imageries continued to reign in world society, the presumption that God ultimately designed, built, and operated all the pieces of the universe maintained rule-like status. But as the cosmology shifted in the global-institutional frame, the plausibility of divine action capacities gradually decreased, and the plausibility of human action capacities steadily increased. Assertions of the existence and operation of human reason and foresight gained credibility on the evolutionist scaffolding, which installed predictability in the natural and social worlds and exceptionality in the human brain. Thus, with the institutionalization of evolution-based origins, the world-level accounting system increasingly reoriented itself around a human center, such that now, for instance, it can be said that deadly landslides represent human misjudgments, rather than acts of God.[63]

In short by the onset of the twentieth century, a syndrome of forces had come together to propel a profound shift in the globally institutionalized ontology. The taken-for-grantedness of divine actorhood was in rapid decline, and to humans were increasingly attributed broad-spectrum capacities to pursue specified ends.

Evidence of this process is at once plentiful and difficult to pin down, as was the case vis-à-vis the origins story. At life's entry and exit points, the effects of altered action premises appeared rather strikingly. Early in the twentieth century, the scripts of human birth and death assumed the operational priority of God's will.[64] By the end of our study period, in contrast, the assumptions inscribed in world culture and organization endowed individuals with extensive action capacities in both realms. The rise of contraception, for instance, dramatically demonstrated the widening latitude of the human actor over birth. To cite just one relevant statistic: the share of couples in the developing world using contraceptives quadrupled from 15 to 60 percent between 1960 and 1997. Meanwhile to an increasing extent, humans also assumed the reins of death. This is vividly apparent in the spectacular advances of medical science made during the century. But the same move also materialized in the fact that between 1980 and 2004, the World Federation of Right to Die Societies gained 23 country chapters, each one working to secure the individual's right to die under conditions of his or her own choosing.[65] Vis-à-vis both birth and death – over which God was assumed to wield chief influence at century's dawn – human action capacities came to be extensive and *de rigueur*. These are just two measures of a singular change in the global-institutional frame. As the story of being underwent revision during our period of study, divine actorhood gradually dissolved and human actorhood increasingly solidified.

Hand in hand with this first change in the globally institutionalized ontology came a tightly linked second one. Over the twentieth century, cultural scripts and organizational rules were rewritten such that humans acquired from the gods not only all-purpose action capacities but also authorized and legitimized access to and control over knowledge (i.e., over universal and transcendent truths).[66]

In some ways, this redistribution of knowledge capacities began with the sixteenth-century Reformation, a religious revolution in Europe that attacked the closed authority of the church and the passive faith of its members. Before the Reformation, free thought was the province of philosophers, and only those divinely constituted were presumed capable of understanding divine mysteries. In this context and in opposition to centuries of tradition, Martin Luther insisted that every believer could read and interpret the Bible and establish direct communication with God. He thus bestowed upon individuals the keys to their own salvations while commandeering for laypersons the capacities to understand sacred texts. With the onset of the Scientific Revolution in the seventeenth century, nascent human knowledge capacities were elaborated rapidly. More and more broadly, traditional philosophies privileging faith over reason fell under attack. For example, Francis Bacon argued that all important knowledge was empirically rooted in nature and that only scientific inquiry could give humans access to it.[67] As such ideas took hold, passive meditations on the sacred texts, guided by faith and moral conviction, were increasingly displaced by active investigations of empirical evidence, guided by science and principles of reason.

This divine-to-human shift in knowledge capacities was further sparked by the cosmological shift discussed earlier. Under creationist assumptions, knowledge was largely inaccessible and incomprehensible to humans. By design, the secrets of the universe were hidden and shrouded by mystery, and humans could do little but contemplate God's handiwork and await revelation.[68] The rationalization and secularization of the origins story gave new opportunities to the human knower. Proscriptions on knowledge fell away as religion's public authority waned, and the emergent evolution story increasingly rendered the world as a lawful and orderly – and thus knowable – place.[69]

As these several historical forces intertwined with others over the twentieth century, they promoted a second shift in the globally institutionalized ontology. Over the territories of knowledge, divine actorhood decreased and individual actorhood increased. Transcendent knowledge – once a gift from God – came to appear as the output of self-directed human endeavor, providing a means to advance human ends.[70] To an ever greater extent, human capacities to know were built into the cultural scripts and organizational rules of world society.

Once again, proof of this shift in the global-institutional frame is both elusive and easy to come by. The handover is somewhat ironically represented in the main outcome of Vatican II (1962–65), after which the Catholic Church began to permit the use of vernacular languages in the liturgy – finally conceding to the laypeople the same access to and abilities over knowledge that Luther had demanded centuries earlier. More concretely and pervasively, the deepening presumption of human knowledge capacities in world reality was embodied in the global proliferation of primary schools – along with international treaties guaranteeing the rights of all boys and girls to have access to them – which sprouted up from the Ethiopian high plains to the Amazon river valley and Siberian steppe. As the ontological shift proceeded, knowledge that once was restricted to the blessed few and later limited to the disciplined and gifted became universally available to the schooled masses. Under the new ontological scheme, even young children were assumed to enjoy extensive capacities to know.[71]

As regards this book's main focus – twentieth-century transformations in university teaching and research emphases worldwide – the significance of action's two-fold redefinition seems likely to have been both wide and deep. For instance, all of the experimental sciences – which took form around the assumption of effective human capacities to act and know – most likely benefited from action's relocation in the global-institutional frame, with their university profiles following suit. Once we have substantive questions and empirical data in hand in subsequent chapters we discuss such implications in detail.

Thus, in widening arenas during the twentieth century, humans were imbued with great authority and legitimacy both to act and to know in the globally institutionalized ontology. What is more, as these premises of reality evolved, action's ontological counterpart – namely, structure – also exhibited substantial flux in the global-institutional frame.

REDEFINITION OF STRUCTURE IN THE GLOBALLY INSTITUTIONALIZED ONTOLOGY

Just as there were twin shifts in action over the twentieth century, so also were there twin shifts in structure – altering basic assumptions about the fit and order of reality in the global-institutional frame. Especially via its incarnations in the French and U.S. revolutions, Enlightenment liberalism catalyzed a process that steadily stripped authority and legitimacy from long-entrenched structural templates – of vertical hierarchies and fixed categories – and heaped them instead upon horizontal assemblies and dynamic networks. Thus along dual dimensions, the structural premises of world society underwent long-term and widely recognized transformations. Increasingly on the international stage, the natural *fit* of reality was seen to consist of team-like interconnections rather than top-down subordinations, and the natural *order* of reality was seen to consist of elastic co-minglings rather than rigid separations.[72]

The first of these sibling transformations in the ontology – concerning fit – sprang out of many historical wells. From Aristotle's *Scala Natura* to the Renaissance's Great Chain of Being, reality long was depicted as a vertical hierarchy, the major premise of which "was that every existing thing in the universe had its 'place' in a divinely planned hierarchical order.... At the bottom, for example, stood various types of inanimate objects... At the very top was God." This was a conception of structure that "most educated men were to accept without question."[73] The inception of Enlightenment liberalism, however, stirred change in the supplies of structural templates. Both Hobbes in the seventeenth century and Rousseau in the eighteenth century asserted a state of nature in which all humans stood equal and free. Their ideas joined with others in challenging traditional notions of supremacy and hierarchy. For example in the Declaration of the Rights of Man and Citizen, written in the wakes of the U.S. and French revolutions in 1789, the principles of equality and sovereignty were set as foundation stones of democratic polities. With such developments, structures of horizontal assembly gained ascendancy over structures of vertical hierarchy in the global-institutional frame.

This template shift was additionally fueled by the reconstituted origins story summarized earlier. Creation's fit was explicitly hierarchical. Out from the hand of God issued forth reality's elements, ranked in a downward cascade from the Supreme Creator. Each rank was superordinate over those beneath it: archangels over angels, nobles over peasants, and lions over leopards, down to the lowliest fleas and mites. With the installation of evolution as the default origins story, however, basic assumptions about structure began to change in world society. The fit of reality leveled. Lions and fleas were placed on equal footing, the form of each paying respect to the other (fleas carry diseases, resistance to which enhances the reproductive chances of particular lions, etc.). With the institutionalization of the evolution story over the twentieth century, in other words, structural templates increasingly depicted a flattened reality, with linked and interdependent parts. Under the new assumptions, reality's pieces fit together in recursive loops of horizontal assembly.

Testimony to this redefinition of structure in the global-institutional frame is again prolific and again, on any single count, inconclusive. Certainly over the twentieth century, vertically structured political empires lost authority and legitimacy and indeed almost disappeared entirely. Following in spades, scores of former colonies won recognition as sovereign and juridically equal nation-states, most of which immediately joined the United Nations, which itself embodied the horizontal-assembly structure from its 1945 founding – granting one vote per member nation-state, from Guatemala to Guinea-Bissau. Although it would be naive to conclude that such changes spelled the demise of international domination, it might be just as naive to conclude that the international landscape remained fundamentally unaltered. Of course, structural remodeling took place quite broadly during these decades and pervasively not only in political realms. Even the IQ test, which once fit students into neatly delineated ranks, grew suspect in the final years of the time interval, as researchers laid the groundwork for intelligence mosaics, in which every student could excel.[74] Thus, although the twentieth century hardly saw the vanquishing of vertical hierarchies, much evidence suggests that horizontal assemblies grew increasingly dominant in the global-institutional frame.

Along a second dimension, too, structural templates shifted during this period. Not only were the rule-like principles of *fit* fundamentally recast in the premises of world society but so also were the rule-like principles of *order* – moving steadily from fixed categories to dynamic networks.

In part, the delegitimization and deauthorization of fixed categories derived from the same political movements discussed above. The *ancien régime* in France was not only hierarchical but also locked in place as such, with the nobility and clergy claiming irrevocable positions of privilege. To oust the *ancien régime* meant both to overthrow hierarchy and to depose fixity. Many complementary forces lent aid to the reestablishment of order. One of these was the triumph of progress over tradition in eighteenth-century Europe. Under the latter, continuity was the natural and desirable state of affairs, whereas in the former, change was paramount. The notion of dynamic order was fundamental to the work of Marx and appeared even earlier in the writings of Condorcet. His *Outline of a Historical Picture of the Progress of the Human Mind* (1795) traced human development through nine historical epochs, predicting in the tenth the ultimate perfection of humanity, replete with freedom, equality, justice, and humanitarianism. Thus as progress trumped tradition in the baseline order of reality, dynamism trumped fixity in world society. Also representing and promoting the new order was the invention of society – an entity that emerged from the shadows of the state and church as the likes of Hobbes, Locke, and Rousseau developed the idea of the social contract, whereby society formed around an implicit pact made by its members to give up certain freedoms in exchange for certain rights. The imagery at the heart of this new entity – the contractual agreement – prioritized active interrelationships, incorporating dynamically network orders into the global-institutional frame.

Naturally, many other cultural and historical forces reinforced this course of change in the globally institutionalized ontology. One additional prop came from the transforming theory of origins. Under once-prevalent creationist assumptions, reality was ordered into fixed categories; that which was ever would remain so: the bees as bees and the birds as birds, according to God's own divine plan. Thus the original act of sacred invention was imagined as demarcating the fundamental and everlasting classes of creation, embodying the fixed categorical order.[75] The transition to an evolutionist cosmology reset the premises of the global-institutional frame in ways that favored new dynamic-network structural templates. Given that evolution's trademark feature was deemed to be change itself, it came to be assumed that that which was would not long be so; the bees would become birds and the apes would become humans in a process of natural modification over successive generations. With evolution as a matter of course, reality came to be understood as being continually reshaped by forces of reciprocal influence, rendering as temporary whatever distinctions might at one point demarcate the entities in a class. Thus with the rise of evolution over the twentieth century, dynamic network orders grew increasingly entrenched in the baseline assumptions about reality.

Altogether, these and other historical forces combined to promote a second redefinition of structure in the global-institutional frame. The assumed naturalness once attributed to fixed distinctions began to falter, and new structural templates emphasizing contingency and relationality won increasing cultural priority in world society.

As before, the evidentiary basis for a fundamental shift in the templates of order in the culture and organization of world society is diffuse but pervasive. Rather prominently, the transition is substantiated in the fall of categorically fixed states and the rise of dynamically networked markets worldwide during the twentieth century.[76] Across many domains, states' umbrellas shrank and markets' umbrellas grew during the era. To take the obvious example, international trade decreasingly followed logics of the state (protectionism, tariffs, etc.) and increasingly followed logics of the market (liberalization, free trade areas, etc.). Market assumptions, celebrated for their flexible and ever-changing circuitry, were thus increasingly incorporated into global institutions – a clear move toward dynamic-network orders. The same reconstruction of order in the theory of being also appeared in the delegitimization and deauthorization of immalleable human groupings based on citizenship, race, class, sex, sexual orientation, and so on (fixed categories of ascription) and in the rising centrality assigned to fluid human systems, formed by so-called intersectionality among old groupings and by the multimodal dimensions of individual experience (dynamic networks of expression).[77] Indeed with the modification of structural templates during the study period, even the tradition-bound occupational and marital orders traded premises of enduring constraint for those of transient interconnection. Of course, many fixed categories persisted. But across domains and levels of social life, an unambiguous change occurred in the structural templates of reality over the twentieth century, moving toward dynamic network orders.

Turning briefly to the book's main question – concerning worldwide changes in the body of university knowledge during this period – it seems almost certain that structure's dual-faceted redefinition in the global-institutional frame had ramifications for every corner of the academic core. For instance, the Great Books tradition in classics, philosophy, and literature almost certainly lost authority and legitimacy as hierarchical structures were dismantled, dimming the prospects of these fields in the university over time. We discuss such implications in detail as appropriate in the empirical investigations below.

In sum, to an increasing extent during our period of study, there were shifts in the global- institutional frame, as the taken-for-grantedness once tied to vertical hierarchies was retied to horizontal assemblies, and as the naturalness once assigned to fixed categories was reassigned to dynamic networks. These changes in reality's structural templates, together with those relocating action and those rerooting origins, fundamentally reshaped the platform of assumptions on which rise university teaching and research activities. Throughout the rest of this book, our main agenda involves articulating and exploring the implications of global-institutional reframing – both theoretically and empirically – for the university's academic core.

Mechanisms

Before proceeding with that agenda, however, we wish to address the question of mechanisms. Our argument, after all, sometimes has a metaphysical edge: Over the twentieth century, changes in socially constructed reality altered the assumptions embedded in the global-institutional frame and thus changed the supply of building blocks available to authorize and legitimize various activities in the university's academic core. In the conventional sense, mechanisms may seem peripheral to our scheme.

But of course every time a new department was founded or an existing faculty line was withdrawn– no matter what the country – there were individual and collective human actors immediately involved, expressing needs and pursuing interests.[78] Two points are central.

The first is that from our theoretical perspective the actors – along with their needs and interests – that provide the proximate mechanisms of academic-core change (making demands, issuing reports, etc.) are themselves outcomes of global-institutional processes. They are not the autonomous, free-standing actors essentialized in functionalist accounts, in other words; they are rather socially constructed actors (or enactors) constituted in the cultural scripts and organizational rules of world society. Given these shared origins, the actors on the scene at the moment of change – the students, the grant-making agencies, the professional associations, etc. – tend overwhelmingly to operate in tandem, pursuing common goals to a much greater extent than most functionalist accounts would predict. New professional guidelines may coincide with new student demands; new publication outlets may open at the same time as new funding initiatives. This is one factor contributing to the remarkable homogeneity in academic emphases found among universities around the world (documented in Chapter 1). Although sociologists delight in locating conflict – where professors want to read Shakespeare and students want to watch *The Godfather* – the most remarkable fact about such conflicts is how rarely they occur. The mechanisms of change are formed of global clay.

Given that this is the case, one's attention is deflected up a level of analysis – from the actors on the scene to the global-institutional environment within which they are constituted. According to Meyer and colleagues, this environment – a.k.a. world society – consists primarily of what, following Mead, might be called "rationalized others." Rationalized others are

> social elements such as the sciences and professions (for which the term "actor" hardly seems appropriate) that give advice to nation-states and other actors about their true and responsible natures, purposes, technologies, and so on. Rationalized others are now everywhere, in massive arrays of international associations and epistemic communities, generating veritable rivers of universalistic scientific and professional discourse.[79]

More than acting per se, rationalized others construct environments within which action is legitimized and authorized. A concrete example helps demonstrate the process. As scientists have increasingly united around the position that humans play some role in speeding up the natural rate of climate change, they have, in the guise of rationalized others, stored the armory on which actors rely in calling for academic-core change. With new journals (such as *Climatic Change*), new funding opportunities (such as the National Science Foundation's Earth System History program), and new action templates (e.g., "Strategies for Developing the College Course on Global Climate Change"), rationalized others did not so much knock on the doors of university administrators and demand the founding of climate-change programs as they did create opportunities for actors to do so.[80] And indeed the actors act, providing the proximate mechanisms of change in founding, for example, the Earth Institute at Columbia, the Environmental Change Institute at Oxford, and the Climatology Research Group at the University of the Witwatersrand. From our perspective, it is this higher level of analysis that is crucial, for from it emerge the actors, the needs, and the interests that appear on the scene at the moment of academic-core change.

Data and Methods

Thus, we have laid out our orienting questions: How do university teaching and research emphases change worldwide over the twentieth century, and why are the changes patterned so distinctly? And we have also sketched out our basic argument: Changes in the academic core follow from changes in the global-institutional frame. Now we turn to empirical matters. With which research design and what data can we document and enlighten long-term, worldwide shifts in overall teaching and research emphases?[81]

To test the notion that global-institutional reframings alter the university's building blocks both globally and across knowledge domains, we begin with twentieth-century data on three levels of the university organization drawn from a worldwide sample of universities. First and most broadly, we present evidence of priority shifts in the university's major divisions (the three main branches of learning and the basic and applied fields). Second and more specifically, we show data on the changing composition of each branch of learning's disciplinary fields (sociology, economics, etc.). Third and most particularly, we introduce information on the shifting subject matters within a single discipline – history. As we telescope downward, addressing each level of the university in turn, we review the major global-institutional frame changes discussed above and then draw out their implications for the particular aspects of the academic core under review. We finish by presenting relevant world-level trends in the university's academic emphases. Although imperfect, the data we present are unprecedented in scope – both longitudinally and cross-nationally – and allow us to shed new light on a much-discussed but little researched topic: the composition of the academic core.

Like any, our approach has drawbacks. For one, it trades depth for breadth in order to capture effects that transcend particular nation-states and specific domains of university knowledge. Given the rich supply of case studies in the literature, we believe this sacrifice is warranted. For another, our research design foregoes attempts at quantitative analyses, given the difficulty of measuring dependent and independent variables as diffuse as changes in globally institutionalized reality. We hope future work may make progress toward this end.

The strengths of our approach, in counterweight, lie in its capacity to examine the effects of changes in the global-institutional frame on the whole body of university knowledge on a worldwide basis – across the branches of learning, basic and applied divisions, disciplinary fields, and subject matters within them. With reference to very basic alterations in prevailing theories of origin and being in world society, we illuminate a great many changes in the university's academic priorities worldwide.[82]

To document the transformations empirically, we work with two types of data: faculty composition and course composition over the twentieth century. We use the faculty data in Chapters 1–4 to characterize redistributions of emphases at the higher levels of university organization: among the three main branches of learning, between the applied and basic divisions, and among each branch of learning's disciplinary fields. We then use the course-level data in Chapter 5 to characterize shifting priorities within the subject matters of history. For our purposes, history's advantage over other disciplines is that its subject roster has been shown by many to be quite flexible, such that the same historical event may be interpreted very differently over time and across place.[83] Thus, although we expect global-institutional reframing to spur the reconstitution of subject matters in all of the university's fields, history seems likely to be a rapid responder, with especially sharp and transparent transformations.

Data availability limits our focus to the twentieth century. By this time, as is clear from our cosmology and ontology discussions above, the global-institutional frame shifts we deem central were already well underway. Longer term data would clearly be preferable. Nevertheless, the twentieth century was pivotal in the process of university reconstruction, as accelerating cosmological and ontological changes coincided with the extraordinary profusion of universities worldwide.

FACULTY DATA

Our data on faculty composition come from three university directories: the *Commonwealth Universities Yearbook*, published from 1914 onward; the *Index Generalis*, published between 1919 and 1955; and the *World Guide to Universities*, published only in the 1970s.[84] The first two directories originated around World War I, embodying the notion that knowledge shared across international boundaries might foment peace. All three directories list faculty by disciplinary field (for example, Physics: Binotti, King, Lo), and all three have broad coverage of universities around the world, although the *Yearbook* includes only those located in British Commonwealth countries.

From all of the available directory listings, we sampled one university per nation-state, preferring the most central, where centrality is assessed by official association with the state and/or prestige (in many cases, this meant choosing the national university). This sampling method – in effect, of the population of nation-states – follows from our argument: We sought a world-level sample of universities on which to test our world-level ideas. The main alternative – i.e., sampling the population of universities directly – results in a data set too dominated by U.S. universities to serve our purposes (see Appendix A for a list of sampled nation-states by time period).[85]

The lists of faculty by disciplinary field provided the raw materials for our main variables of interest. To construct these, we first created a series of domain-specific ratios for each university in our sample (e.g., the number of basic social scientists relative to total university faculty, the number of political scientists relative to total university faculty, etc. We then averaged these ratios across university cases to come up with the mean percentages shown in the chapters below.

We performed this operation at ten-year intervals from 1915 to 1995, later aggregating the data into twenty-year intervals to maximize our case base. This left us with four time intervals: 1915–35, 1936–55, 1956–75, and 1976–95. In the first two periods, we have data from the *Index* and the *Yearbook*. In the third interval we have data from the *World Guide* and the *Yearbook*. In the final time interval, we have only *Yearbook* data (although its case base is considerably broadened relative to earlier time intervals because of decolonization).

Indeed we face considerable shift in the case base across the four time periods, owing in part to the disappearance and appearance of the source directories but also because of the growing number of independent countries. Our strategy for dealing with this shift in the case base is three-fold. In the main presentations of the trends below, we show only data from the *Commonwealth Universities Yearbook*, as they alone are available for all four time periods. But then in supplementary studies, we compare (a) the main *Yearbook* data with all available data for the earlier three time periods, (b) the main *Yearbook* data with constant-case *Yearbook* data for all four time periods, and (c) the main *Yearbook* data with UNESCO data on student enrollments by disciplinary field for the later two periods. This three-pronged approach allows us at once to avoid misleading jags in observed trends resulting from extreme case-base shifts and also to ensure that *Yearbook*-based trends are neither peculiar to the sample nor the indicator. We return to these points and show several direct comparisons toward the end of Chapter 1.

In creating the faculty-composition variables, we relied on the disciplinary codes used by the editors of our data sources: For example, a sociology professor to them is a sociology professor to us. Fortunately with three overlapping data sources, we were able to check for any biases in the application of these labels. We found none that affect our results. Reporting procedures and coding practices were broadly similar in the *Index*, the *Yearbook*, and the *World Guide*.

As an indicator of academic priorities, faculty composition has the benefit of capturing both teaching and research activities. Of course, relative faculty size does not perfectly measure a university's undertakings in any given area: Faculty members differentially contribute to and make demands on the university as a whole. Nevertheless, relative faculty size has considerable strengths as an indicator, most notably its availability for a large number of country cases and its commensurability across different types of university organizations. Indeed we know of no other indicator of teaching and research emphases (e.g., student enrollments, degrees granted, and funding streams) with comparable scope. Even for the university's most basic features – in this case, changes in the academic core – global-historical data sources are notably scarce.

COURSE DATA

The course data come from 335 course catalogues representing 89 countries between 1895 and 1994 (see Appendix B). Such catalogues are housed in archives at Stanford University and at the headquarters of the International Association of Universities in Paris. Together, the archives have wide international scope and include catalogues dating to the middle 1800s.

We sought one course catalogue for each independent nation-state per ten-year period from 1895 to 1994, preferably from a single university and always from the most central university obtainable. We selected the available catalogue that fell closest to the midpoint of the ten-year period. And when a complete set of catalogues for a single university was unavailable for a country, we cobbled together catalogues from different universities, always again preferring the most central.

Even with these flexibilities, the data set has relatively few complete cases (i.e., countries with data in every ten-year period from either 1895 or from independence). This is true because World Wars I and II slowed the international flow of materials, because catalogues became expensive to circulate (though some are now available on microfiche and the Web), and because catalogue collections grew burdensome to warehouse. Some countries enter the data set only once, often around independence. To compensate for missing data, we shifted to twenty-five-year time periods in the analysis, averaging the available data for each country per period.

The cases missing from our data set may be more idiosyncratic than those collected: Countries that fail to participate in the circulation of course catalogues may also fail to join in the circulation of constitutive cultural materials. Compared to others, European countries are better represented in the early decades, as universities in much of the world only arose in the post-World War II period. Nevertheless, the breadth of our data on course contents far exceeds any other collected to date. When we began our study, we doubted even that the course catalogue itself existed worldwide. We did not expect to find extensive collections of such catalogues dating even to the 1860s, and we were surprised at their comparability, in terms of content and organization. We had been misled to expect variability, in other words, by prevailing local-functional perspectives on higher education. What we found in fact was that course catalogues are global forms, just like university curricula and universities themselves.[86]

With the catalogues in hand, we located the history courses. Universities following English or American models typically designated distinct history departments. Universities following the French model were sometimes less direct, embedding the courses in less precisely differentiated organizational units, such as a Faculty of Philosophy and Letters. Still even in these cases, the history courses were easy to locate. They were nearly always grouped together, taught by discipline-identified professors.

In coding these materials, we used information contained in course titles and, whenever available, accompanying descriptions (present in about half the catalogues). We coded in particular five dimensions of each history course: self-representation, area, time period, subnational groups, and special subjects.[87] We explain and describe these dimensions further in Chapter 5.

Together, the faculty- and course-composition data allow us to characterize century long shifts in the academic emphases of universities for many countries worldwide. Whenever possible, we supplement these data with supporting materials from case studies and/or information on trends in primary or secondary school curricula. Altogether, our data allow us to establish world-level transformations in the academic core and to assess our argument's strength in explaining them.

Conclusion

Little analyzed but extensive change in the university's academic composition took place over the twentieth century worldwide. Teaching and research emphases underwent deep and widespread revision. Although some such changes elicited storms of protest, they nevertheless spurred little in the way of systematic research. Accordingly, we here pursue simultaneous descriptive and analytical agendas vis-à-vis university reconstruction – documenting the changes that have occurred and seeking to explain them within a global-institutional theoretical framework.

Certainly our theory cannot enlighten each and every development in every university in every field in every country. This is not our goal. The case-study literature is prolific already. Rather our goal is to explore determinants of change that are not only country- and sector-specific but also world- and university-wide – at intradisciplinary, interdisciplinary, and meta-disciplinary levels – connecting dots from the universities of Austria to Zaire over the entire twentieth century.

We set off on this course by first taking up the broadest empirical story, which concerns alterations in the emphases accorded the university's three main branches of learning and its applied and basic divisions. We begin by considering the implications of global-institutional reframing for each of the relevant domains.

Notes

1. See Ramirez (2002) for a discussion and comparison of Oxford and Stanford universities.
2. See http://magazine.uchicago.edu/0012/campus-news/journal-humanities. html.
3. Fourcade-Gourinchas (2001) discusses the expansion and internationalization of economics. Frank et al. (2000) present world-level data on the subject matters of history.
4. Cited in the Message from the President in the 2001 Annual Report of Stanford University. Of course it was only in the modern period that the university's raison d'être even shifted from knowledge conservation to knowledge production (Ramirez 2002).
5. From the university's website at http://www.ub.bw/about/index.html.
6. We use the word "core" here in its organizational sense (Scott 1992). Teaching and research (as opposed, say, to student health services or intramural athletics) comprise the university's core endeavors.
7. See Bloom (1987), Readings (1996), Kirp (2003), and Bryson (2005).
8. November 23, 2001. Sirens of concern over youthful ignorance, including the *Wall Street Journal's*, are of long standing in the United States. In 1699, Cotton Mather intoned, "Outrageous wickedness will make the rising generation loathsome, if it have not schools to preserve it." The university's uselessness is also a common refrain. In the late twentieth century, university research projects often won Senator

William Proxmire's Golden Fleece Awards for "outrageous" waste in governmental spending. See Wong (1991) for a broader view on the shift from historical and geographical knowledge toward social studies after World War II.

9. Gumport and Snydman (2002) call for longitudinal and comparative research much along these lines, and Frickel and Gross (2005:205) note that, although case studies have proliferated, "general theories of intellectual dynamism . . . have been slow to emerge."

10. For an exception to the narrow-band approach, see Drori and Moon's (2005) exploration of UNESCO data on higher education enrollment patterns by field, further discussed below. Even within the United States, systematic data on academic-priority shifts are rare. One exception is Adelman (1995), on course taking in U.S. colleges 1972–93.

11. For example, see Fourcade-Gourinchas (2001) on economics, Small (1999) on African-American studies, and Schweber (2004) on statistics. Studies in the history of science (e.g., Bender and Schorske [1997]) almost always fall into this group.

12. See Kerr (2001:31, 98).

13. Country-specific works include Babb (2001) on economics in Mexico, Lamont (1987) on the reception of Derrida in France and the United States, and our own early work on the subjects of history in the United States (Frank, Schofer, and Torres 1994). University-specific works include Soares (1999) on Oxford, Abbott (1999) on sociology at Chicago, and Camic (1995) on sociology at Chicago, Columbia, and Harvard.

14. According to Jepperson (2002), one of theory's main purposes and payoffs is to raise new questions. In opening this terrain to empirical inquiry, we offer a first contribution to the literature.

15. Napoleon's assault on universities derived directly from this premise – i.e., that the complexities of modern society required more specialized and differentiated centers of inquiry (Riddle 1993). Note that we use the term "functionalist" broadly here to include all those theories that treat the university's priorities as means of fulfillment, whether for collective or sectarian benefit. The origins of the needs and interests arguments can be found, respectively, in Merton (1973) and Mannheim (1936).

16. Jencks and Riesman (1968) provide the classic statement on scholarly autonomy. In Collins's version of the organizational argument (1985, 1998), the university rewards novelty, which in turn promotes differentiation. Abbott (2001) introduces the specific notion of fractal differentiation, whereby academic emphases change cyclically as professors discard and rediscover old ideas.

17. See, for example, Altbach (1998) and Bloom (1987).

18. Chait (2002) and Slaughter and Rhoades (2004) make organizational arguments along these lines. Sociologists of science (e.g., Latour 1987; Knorr-Cetina 1999) offer a different approach. They see particular aspects of social organization (e.g., laboratory layout) as switch-points in knowledge production, altering local academic priorities often unintentionally.

19. On worldwide university expansion, see Schofer and Meyer (2005) and Frank and Meyer (forthcoming).

20. Powell and Snellman (2004) and Geiger (2004) provide different takes on this argument.

21. Slaughter and Leslie (1997:14). See also Bocock et al. (2003) and the World Bank's report on higher education in developing countries (2000). For general needs-of-society arguments, see Clark (1995).

22. See, for example, Jenniskens (2000), Musgrave (1994), and the papers in van Vught (1989).

23. Geiger (1986) and Bertrams (2004) document similar processes during World War I.

24. Thaman (2003), for example, presents this view vis-à-vis higher-education contents in Oceania.

25. Binder (2002) takes this view in the context of U.S. secondary schools. Kimball (1990) makes a related argument, although in his version, the social movement radicals have infiltrated the professoriate.

26. See Bloor (1991).

27. For an excellent review of credentialism theory, see Brown (2001).

28. From the department's website at http://www.ru.ac.za/academic/departments/difs/.

29. See the university's website at http://www.ju.edu.jo/faculties/index.htm.

30. Camic (1995) and Small (1999) offer evidence of such university-level effects.

31. From Bourdieu (1988: xii). See also Chait (2002), Clark (2002), and Slaughter (2002) for various warnings concerning the mostly adverse impacts of states and markets on university activities.

32. Powell and Owen-Smith (2002) discuss market forces and knowledge production in the life sciences. Bok (2003) cautions more generally against the commercialization of higher education.

33. Accreditation standards are now global phenomena. For instance, the Universiti Malaysia Sarawak announces on its website (http://www.unimas.my/aboutus.htm) that it "was awarded ISO 9001: 2000 quality certificate by SIRIM as a recognition of the high quality in the management of academic activities from the intake of new students to the award of degrees to graduates."

34. From Shinn (2003:136).

35. Meyer, Boli, and Thomas (1987) and Meyer et al. (1997) provide the theoretical foundations here. See Berger and Luckmann (1966) on the social construction of reality.

36. See Shils (1997:3) and Bourdieu (1988:xii). See also UNESCO's policy guidelines and university accreditation rules at http://www.collegedegreeguide.com/articles-fr/accredit.htm.

37. The economics quotation comes from Fourcade-Gourinchas (2001). Merton (1973) discusses the universalism of science, and Lenhardt (2002) discusses the universalism of the university.

38. The quotations come respectively from the 1853–54 Yale College Catalogue of the Officers and Students, the 1956–57 South Dakota State College Catalog, and the anthem of the Universidad del Valle, at http://www.univalle.edu.co/ simbolos/himno.html. The courses required of agriculture students at South Dakota display the importance accorded to general knowledge. They include Introduction to Literature, Advanced Exposition, National Government, and Principles of Sociology.

39. The quotations and relevant information can be found at http://www. spacedaily.com/news/earth-03b.html and at http://en.wikipedia.org/wiki/The_ Skeptical_Environmentalist.

40. See Balaram (2001). Fish (2002:33) claims that even postmodernists use standards of objectivity "all the time without any metaphysical anxiety."

41. From Kerr (2001:34). In 1963, Kerr popularized the term "multiversity," which attracts continued attention today (e.g., Brint 2002a; Krücken forthcoming).

42. From similar bases, Drori et al. (2003) investigate the institutionalization of science in the world polity and its impacts on national societies.

43. See Loya and Boli (1999) for a general discussion of world standards. See Wallerstein (1991) and Drori et al. (2003) on science; Boyle and Meyer (1998) and Tsutsui and Wotipka (2004) on natural laws and humans rights; and Meyer et al. (1997) on professionals.

44. See Ramirez, Soysal, and Shanahan (1997) on democracy; Boli and Ramirez (1987) and Ramirez and Ventresca (1992) on mass schooling; and Frank (1997) on environmental protection. Clearly, the university also ranks among global institutions. It is regarded as an essential ingredient of modern societies, feeding wellsprings of progress and justice (e.g., Riddle 1993; Schofer and Meyer 2005).

45. On cosmology and ontology as cultural frame, see Evans-Pritchard (1940), Colson and Gluckman (1959), and Turner (1967). On the action and structure facets of ontology, see Giddens (1979). For related arguments, see Foucault (1994) and Ramirez (2003).

46. The quotation comes from the opening of Shils's classic essay on the academic ethic (1997).

47. We are cued by Meyer, Kamens, and Benavot (1992) and Kamens, Meyer, and Benavot (1996), who document cross-national similarities in primary and secondary school curricula. See also McEneaney's comparative analysis of primary school texts (1998, 2003). Even if the global frame were not prioritized in our argument, it would be reasonable to expect global-institutional effects, which have now been widely demonstrated. See, for example, Barrett and Frank (1999), Bergesen and Lizardo (2004), and Hironaka (2002).

48. See Altbach (1998) and Lenhardt (2002:275), who writes that "from its very beginning the university is an institution with supranational character."

49. From the 1967-68 University of Liberia Catalog and Announcements.

50. See Riddle (1993) and Meyer et al. (1997).

51. See Chase-Dunn (1998) on economic globalization, Rosenau and Czempiel (1992) on political globalization, Boli and Thomas (1999) on cultural globalization,

and Robertson (1992) on globalization generally. Of course, globalization is also seen in the rise of international scientific collaborations (e.g., Basu and Kumar [2000] and Narváez-Berthelemot et al. [2002]).

52. See Foucault (1994:xi).

53. On history, see Frank et al. (2000). Meyer, Kamens, and Benavot (1992) and Kamens, Benavot, and Meyer (1996) demonstrate surprising similarities in primary and secondary curricular outlines across disparate countries. McEneaney (1998) finds evidence of global culture in primary-school math and science texts.

54. Boli and Thomas (1997) rank universalism among the defining features of world culture.

55. The quotation on the Encyclopedists is from the online Catholic Encyclopedia, where more information may be found at http://www.newadvent.org/cathen/05418a.htm.

56. See Dupre (2003) on Darwin's legacy. According to Kerr (2002:1), the West began "abandoning the Bible as the main source of knowledge" after 1800, inaugurating the deinstitutionalization of creationism. Inasmuch as Europe dominated world society into the twentieth century, the preferred creation story was Christian in content. Its contours were sufficiently broad, however, to accommodate the imageries of other world religions. See Weber (1978); Meyer, Boli, and Thomas (1987); Meyer (1994); and Drori et al. (2003).

57. To the extent that religion continues even now to be acknowledged as a global force, it is typically so in the guise of identity-based social movements, not as a cultural frame offering an authoritative origins story.

58. On religion-based international associations, see Boli and Thomas (1999) and Thomas (2001). On science in world society, see Drori et al. (2003). On the use of science in international disputes, see Yearley (1996). On the global diffusion of science and technology ministries, see Jang (2000).

59. It is increasingly taken for granted in world environmental discourse that humans are embedded in and features of the Earth's natural systems (Frank 1997).

60. Evidence of the rise of science's public authority is nicely captured in the appearance of religion-science hybrids, such as Islamic science and creationist science.

61. On expansion in university numbers, see Riddle (1993); in enrollments, Schofer and Meyer (2005); and in knowledge sectors, Frank and Meyer (forthcoming). For a general discussion, see Lenhardt (2002).

62. According to Mansfield (2004:78), "Modernity might be quickly defined as the notion of rational control by humans of human life rather than piously or philosophically accepting the rule of God or nature."

63. The current debate over human cloning makes sense in terms of this historical shift: Cloning represents a controversial extension of human actorhood into territory even now partially controlled by God/nature. Note that the debaters tend to be MDs and PhDs more so than DDs. The terms of debate are set by science.

64. Haynes (1994) offers a thorough account of the scientist who intervenes in nature to be punished by God.

65. For contraceptives data, see United Nations Population Fund (1997). For information on the World Federation of Right to Die Societies, see http://www. worldrtd.net/about/.

66. In contrast to knowledge, which is formulated in universalistic terms, more local perceptions occupy such categories as wisdom. See Frank and Meyer (forthcoming).

67. For more on Bacon, see http://www.blupete.com/Literature/Biographies/ Philosophy/Bacon.htm.

68. See White (1967) and Kerr (2002). Weber (1946 [1919]:136) captures the arbitrary nature of this form of knowledge: "Ideas occur to us when they please, not when it pleases us. The best ideas do indeed occur to one's mind . . . when smoking a cigar on the sofa."

69. See Drori et al. (2003) and McEneaney (2003).

70. See Brint (2002b) and Brint et al. (2005) on the "practical arts." Alchemy, according to Jung, was never so much for turning lead into gold as it was for pure enlightenment. Its object was to reveal the ultimate design of nature, and thus the mind of God.

71. Ramirez and Ventresca (1992) analyze the rise of compulsory mass schooling worldwide. McEneaney (2003) and Gabler (2002) present data on children as knowers.

72. See Haraway (1989) and McEneaney (2003) for related discussions. Sociologists such as Bourdieu (1984) and Lamont (2000) emphasize the ongoing centrality of distinctions within human societies, and we take no issue with their arguments. Our point here concerns world-level trends over a century's time; we do not mean to suggest utter transformation.

73. From http://academic.brooklyn.cuny.edu/english/melani/cs6/ren.html. See Lovejoy (1936) on the Great Chain of Being. In the 1700s, Linnaeus grouped human mammals with "primates," meaning first in rank.

74. On decolonization, see Strang (1990). On multiple intelligences, see Gibbons et al. (1994). Davis (2000) offers a fascinating discussion of vertical-to-horizontal restructuring in China. In the rise of the horizontal-assembly model, one sees the groundwork for recent celebrations of the diversity ideal.

75. See the classic discussion by Douglas (2002).

76. See Fourcade-Gourinchas and Babb (2002).

77. On transnational citizenship, see Soysal (1992). On intersectionality, see Collins (2000). On the profusion of individual identities, see Frank and Meyer (2002).

78. Frickel and Gross (2005) offer an actor-centric theory of what they call "scientific/intellectual movements." Harvard Professor Harvey Mansfield provides a concrete example when he writes, "[T]here need to be more professors in religion and in the military. We should not be taking the present composition of the faculty for granted" (2004:78).

79. From Meyer et al. (1997:162). Meyer and Jepperson (2000) provide further discussion. See Mead (1934) on rationalized others, Boli and Thomas (1999) on international associations, and Haas (1992) on epistemic communities.

80. The strategies can be found at http://egj.lib.uidaho.edu/egj21/klock1.html.

81. Of course, the reconstitution of academic emphases occurs at all levels of schooling. For instance, Goodson (1995) discusses the decline of Rural Studies and the rise of Environmental Sciences in secondary schools in England and Wales – a shift easily understood within our framework. See also Benavot (2004).

82. Our strategy also allows us to consider the primacy of organizational selection (according to which contextual changes should have an impact on fields as a whole) versus organizational adaptation (according to which fields should change internally). Based on the extensive organizational-ecology literature (Hannan and Freeman 1989), we expect selection to be the stronger force.

83. See, e.g., Dierkes (2001), Schissler and Soysal (2004), Binder (2002), Wong (2004), and Hymans (2005).

84. See Montessus de Ballore (1919–55), Association of Commonwealth Universities (1914–95), and Zils (1971, 1976).

85. Even in 1995, the average number of universities per nation-state (excluding the outlier United States) was only thirty-one in the West and eleven in the rest of the world. In 1965, the comparable numbers were twenty and six (Ramirez 2003).

86. By and large, the catalogues use the major European colonial languages – French, English, and Spanish. Our research team included native speakers of English, Spanish, Chinese, and Japanese. When necessary, we hired translators to assist with other languages. On the university's global roots, see Altbach (1998), Lenhardt (2002), and Riddle (1993).

87. cf. Frank et al. (2000); Mao (1995); Meyer, Kamens, and Benavot (1992); and Wong (1991).

CHAPTER I

The Branches of Learning and the Basic and Applied Divisions

By many indicators, the university's teaching and research priorities changed profoundly over the twentieth century, fundamentally altering the makeup of university knowledge. We contend that this process occurred as modifications in the global-institutional frame reestablished reality's premises and thus shifted the academic core's most elementary foundations – for universities around the world and across the knowledge domains.

In this chapter, we develop these arguments and start to assess them empirically, focusing on the broadest demarcations of knowledge in the university organization. We begin by suggesting how twentieth-century redefinitions of action and structure might have affected (1) the relative emphases accorded the university's three main branches of learning – the humanities, the natural sciences, and the social sciences and (2) the comparative priority of the university's basic and applied divisions worldwide.[1] We then present data germane to our ideas, primarily on trends in faculty composition from 1915 to 1995. We finish by testing the robustness of our empirical findings as regards both our main sample of universities and our central indicator of academic priorities. Before moving on to test our findings, however, we list the disciplinary fields that fall within each of the university's three main branches of learning and within its basic and applied units (see Table 1).

Background

Even absent systematic data, many observers have vigorously maintained that at the highest levels of organization – among the three main branches of learning and between the basic and applied divisions – the university's academic priorities shifted dramatically over the twentieth century. Once prominent knowledge domains ostensibly lost the university limelight, whereas once peripheral others came to appear center stage.

Universities of every description, it seems, experienced this wax and wane. To take a specific case for example, Table 2 presents the degree rosters at Belgium's Université Catholique de Louvain in 1930 and in 2005 by branch of learning and applied/basic division.[2] In comparing the two, one first observes that as the number of degree offerings expanded over the seventy-five-year period the profiles of the three main branches of learning shifted subtly. Specifically in 1930, 31 percent of Louvain's degree options were in humanities fields (17 of 54 degrees, folding together basic and applied), whereas only 27 percent remained so by 2005 (17 of 62). The natural sciences, more surprisingly, also lost standing among the branches, falling from 50 to 40 percent of total degree offerings (from 27 of 54 to 25 of 62). More surprisingly still, even the applied natural science fields taken alone exhibited relative retreat over the time interval, starting with 37 percent of Louvain's degrees (20 of 54) and ending with 32 percent (20 of 62 degrees).

Where degrees did proliferate at Louvain was in the youngest branch of learning – the social sciences.[3] The social sciences gained considerable standing over the seventy-five-year period, doubling degree options from ten to twenty, and in turn increasing their share of all university degree offerings from 19 to 32 percent. Among other new social science programs, the university added psychology, economic and social policy, sociology, and family and sexuality.

Table 1 Disciplinary Fields Included in the Three Main Branches of
Learning and the Basic and Applied Divisions

	Basic Division	*Applied Division*
Humanities	archaeology/paleography art/art history/music classics history all languages and literatures linguistics/philology philosophy/logic theology[1]	law

Social sciences	anthropology
	economics
	geography
	political science/political
	    economy/government
	psychology
	sociology
		business
		area studies
		household sciences/home
		    economics
		military sciences
		social work
		education
		communication
		advertising
		journalism

Natural sciences	astronomy/astrophysics
	biology/biochemistry/
	    biophysics
	botany
	chemistry
	geology/hydrology/
	    geophysics
	mathematics
	physics
	zoology
		medicine/public health
		agriculture
		applied sciences
		architecture
		computer science
		engineering
		forestry
		mining/mineralogy/
		    metallurgy
		statistics
		veterinary science

[1] As a hybrid case, we could include theology in either the basic or applied humanities. Our rationale for placing it among the basic fields is that we believe it increasingly became so over the twentieth century. Newer fields such as women's studies appear too rarely in our sources to warrant separate coding.

Table 2   Degree Offerings: Université Catholique de Louvain, Belgium, 1930 and 2005

Humanities – Basic	
Philosophy	Philosophy
History	History
Theology	Theology
Classical Philology	Classical Languages and Literatures
Archaeology and Art History	Archaeology and Art History
Oriental Philology	Oriental Philology and History
German Philology	German Languages and Literatures
Roman Philology	Ancient & Modern Languages and Literatures
Roman Literature	Romance Languages and Literatures
Semitic Languages	Arab Language and Islamology
Dutch Literature	Musicology
English Literature	Religious Sciences
German Literature	Biblical Philology
Canon Law	

Applied	
Law	Law
Notary Public	Notary Public
	Theater

Natural Sciences – Basic	
Chemistry	Chemistry
Biology	Biology
Geography	Geography
Mathematics and Physics	Mathematics
Geology	Physics
Zoology	
Botany	

Applied	
Architecture	Architecture
Veterinary Medicine	Veterinary Medicine
Civil Engineering	Civil Engineering
Medicine	Medicine
Dentistry	Dentistry
Pharmacy	Pharmacy

Table 2   Continued

Applied

Agronomical Science	Agronomical Science
Brewery Engineering	Informatics
Mining Engineering	Biological Engineering
Construction Engineering	Clinical Biomedicine
Metallurgical Engineering	Experimental Biomedicine
Chemical Engineering	Clinical and Biomedical Technology
Electrical Engineering	Human Nutrition
Mechanical Engineering	Toxicology
Geological Engineering	Public Health
Mineralogy	Motricity
Applied Chemistry	Kinesitherapy and Rehabilitation
Agronomical Engineering	Physical Education
Agricultural Chemistry	Statistics
Agricultural Engineering	

Social Sciences – Basic

Social Science	Social Science
Political Science	Political Science
Economics	Economics
	Sociology
	Anthropology
	Demography
	Psychology

Applied

Criminology	Criminology
Pedagogy and Educational Psychology	Educational Psychology
Fiscal and Financial Science	Logopedics
Commercial Sciences	Education
Financial Sciences	Family and Sexuality
Consular Sciences	Management
Colonial Sciences	Communications
	Demography
	Development, Population, Environment
	Data Processing
	Actuarial Science
	Work Sciences
	Economic and Social Policy

Although the changes generally were modest in magnitude – demonstrating a fair degree of continuity in Louvain's central priorities over time – they nevertheless suggest real movements in the body of university knowledge. It is especially noteworthy that in the context of overall degree propagation (from 54 to 62 total options), the number of offerings in two of the three main branches of learning failed to rise by even one. The growth that occurred was monopolized by the social sciences.

Simultaneous with these reallocations of emphases among the branches of learning were reallocations of emphases between the basic and applied divisions at the Université Catholique de Louvain. Between 1930 and 2005, the overall percentage of total university degree offerings associated with the basic division declined from 46 to 42, whereas the overall percentage associated with the applied division advanced from 54 to 58. Moving down a level of analysis to the three branches, one observes that the applied humanities and natural sciences both outpaced their basic counterparts at Louvain, with the former rising from 12 to 18 percent of total humanities degree choices and the latter rising analogously from 74 to 80 percent. The social sciences, meanwhile, were an exception: The percentage of all social science degrees affiliated with the applied division receded from 70 to 65. We speculate that the social sciences' relatively recent vintage in the university accounts for its peculiarity in this regard. Taken altogether, the basic-to-applied shifts here suggest a fairly subtle redistribution of Louvain's teaching and research emphases from the basic to applied fields over time.

Overall, the comparison of degree rosters portrays a university whose academic core underwent visible but small-scale reconstruction during the twentieth century. Of course, the findings are particular to a single institution and may reveal little about world-level academic-core reforms. This is all the more so to the extent that Louvain's ancient and illustrious heritage – the university was founded by Pope Martin V in 1425 – means that the forces of inertia and imprinting exerted heavy hands on the institution, limiting Louvain's flexibility to an exceptional extent.[4] If this is true, however – meaning that priority shifts were detectable even in this highly inelastic setting – it seems likely that more imposing academic reshufflings appeared among universities at large over the twentieth century.

Indeed many observers have asserted that during this period the body of university knowledge showed sizeable reconfigurations, which altered strikingly the relative importance of the three main branches of learning and the basic and applied units. Two such changes have garnered the bulk of attention and the lion's share of lament.[5]

First with only anecdotal evidence in hand, the guardians of the humanities have deplored the sense that the university's twentieth-century reconstruction effectively marginalized that branch of learning, branding it as esoteric and less utilitarian than the two scientific branches.[6] Witness the consternation in this 1994 newspaper account:

> Sorrowed by what they view as the ravages of revisionism, political correctness and budget-slashing administrators, a group of Stanford University poets and professors say the declining role of the humanities must be mourned. More than 70 . . . were drawn Wednesday to a mock "memorial." . . . Appropriately funereal in ambience, the service included a floral display, the invocation of a clergyman and a pianist-and-tenor duo performing soulful classics. Although no one wept . . . the eulogies of the organizers made clear their dismay at what one speaker bemoaned as the "loss of a whole way of life" that once flourished when the works of Homer, Plato, Dante and other greats of Western civilization held sway on the nation's campuses.[7]

The siege mentality is pronounced in such discourses, and the evisceration of the humanities is assumed to be at or near crisis. The grim outlook is manifest in the titles of recent analyses: *The Humanities in Ruins*, *What's Happened to the Humanities?*, and *What Are the Humanities For?*[8]

Meanwhile, armed with nearly as little evidence and as much or more outcry, a second high-level organizational change – between the university's basic and applied divisions – has attracted notice and alarm. Higher education's overseers have roundly condemned a perceived onslaught from the university's applied quarters, which is thought to threaten the university's primary mission – the uncompromised pursuit of truth: "[P]ure research, motivated exclusively by the search for knowledge for its own sake, has suffered from the rise in technological or applied research. As industry increasingly invests in and collaborates with the academic world, some people assume that scientists have strayed from the goal of 'advancing knowledge.'"[9]

The applied division's expansion is thus faulted with increasing the vulnerability of the university to market interference in its hallmark endeavors.

Indeed to many, the evidence of ramped-up interference is already plentiful, found in rapidly increasing rates of academic patenting, rising revenues from intellectual property licensing, forays into venture capital financing, and so on.[10] Although the market is the trespasser *de jour*, it is important to remember that it was not so long ago (prominently during the 1970s) that it was interference from the state – not the market – that raised the paramount concerns. Of course, either way, the putative expansion of applied studies is asserted to have reduced the university's autonomy and compromised its primary commitment to universalistic forms of knowledge.

Both of these allegations – concerning the weakening of the humanities and the strengthening of the applied fields – have been made repeatedly in recent decades, often in strident and politicized terms. Despite the heat in the discursive arena, however, the prosaic task of empirically demonstrating exactly how the university's academic composition actually changed over the twentieth century – systematically charting the standings of the three main branches of learning and the applied and basic divisions over time – has been left at the wayside, limiting in turn efforts to analyze the causal forces driving change.

Indeed as previously discussed, the literature addressing the university's rearrangement of priorities has generally relied on data – mostly from the Anglo West – drawn from case studies, which naturally privilege specifics over generalities. For instance, although it is arresting to note that in the United States the percentage of bachelor's degrees in the humanities fell from 21 to 13 between 1966 and 1993, alone such findings divulge little about the humanities' global standing.[11] Indeed outside the Anglo West, the humanities seldom anchored universities during the twentieth century. For instance, in Continental Europe, the typical university had faculties of law, medicine, theology, and philosophy, assigning the humanities – at least the basic humanities – no more than supporting roles in the university's academic core. In Asia, the humanities were less central still. For example in 1900, China's Imperial Tientsin University offered just five degrees: in law, civil engineering, mining, mechanical engineering, and railways. In 1910, Pei-yang University granted only three degrees: in law, civil engineering, and mining and metallurgy. In university settings such as these, the humanities at best were ensemble players. Similar arguments apply to the putative rise of the applied fields. Again outside the Anglo West, most universities were strongly "applied" throughout the twentieth century. On occasion, this emphasis yielded a surprising course or program, such as Yenching University's Department of Leather Tanning. More typically, it simply meant a distribution of university activities more obviously weighted in the applied direction. The Université de Toulouse in France was fairly standard. In 1904, it had five faculties – of theology, law, medicine and pharmacy, sciences, and letters.[12]

Returning briefly to the case of the Université Catholique de Louvain: even without serious study, one sees here the perils of drawing general conclusions from case-specific evidence. In almost certain contradiction to the global trend, Louvain shuttered eight engineering departments between 1930 and 2005 – including those in chemical, electrical, mechanical, and also, delightfully, brewery engineering. Although it would be interesting to know more about these closures, the details – however captivating – would tell us little about academic reprioritizations worldwide.

The important point here is simply that the empirical literature has been too narrow to sustain general conclusions about changes in the body of university knowledge, even at the higher levels of analysis that concern us here – the branches of learning and the basic and applied divisions. In turn, the literature's empirical shortcomings, as earlier suggested, lead to theoretical deficiencies – namely, an overreliance on often implicit functionalist orientations, which depict academic reforms as responses to the needs/interests stimuli of economic/political powers. We find some validity in these approaches, but we also see their shortcomings, as previously detailed. Thus we offer an alternative approach to explaining reconfigurations in the body of university knowledge, assigning a foremost role to the evolving models of reality that are embedded in the culture and organization of world society and embodied in the global-institutional frame.

Thus we aspire to advance beyond the existing literature with two questions as guides. First, among the three main branches of learning and between the basic and applied divisions, exactly how did the university's priorities change globally over the twentieth century? And second, what causal factors contributed to the observed shifts?

Implications of Global-Institutional Reframing for the Branches and Divisions

Our core assertion, to reiterate, is that the teaching and research emphases of the world's universities are rooted in the global-institutional framework of reality. The frame consists of a taken-for-granted story of origins – a master accounting of reality's beginnings – and a taken-for-granted story of being – modeling action and structure in the everyday life world. Over the twentieth century, changes in the global-institutional frame reestablished the universal premises of known reality, thus reconstituting the university's grounding assumptions on a global basis and across the domains of knowledge.

Here we consider the ramifications of this argument for the broadest demarcations of knowledge in the university: the three main branches of learning – the humanities, the natural sciences, and the social sciences – and for the university's basic and applied divisions. To begin, we briefly review the global-institutional reframings described in the Introduction and draw out the sharpest of their implications for twentieth-century shifts in academic-core composition.

Redefinition of Action in the Globally Institutionalized Ontology

Enabled by the ongoing rationalization and secularization of the origins story – which increasingly replaced divine whims with natural laws in the built-in assumptions of world society – the meaning of "action" changed during the twentieth century. To an ever greater extent, primary capacities both *to act* and *to know* were relocated from divine to human entities.

Speaking more generally first, to act is to bring about intended consequences, rallying the forces of reality toward premeditated ends. At the beginning of the twentieth century, as had long been held true, the global-institutional frame posited action as emanating primarily from the gods, such that reality's animating sparks were seen ultimately to be sacred. At the end of the century, by contrast, humans were taken to be the dominant source-points of cause-and-effect behaviors, even to the point that "human" and "actor" had become synonymous. Increasingly over the period, human actorhood – with ever more elaborate facilities to do, to make, to affect, and to change – was secured in the cultural scripts and organizational rules of world society.

For the university's branches of learning, the redefinition of action in the global-institutional frame carried two clear implications. First, it involved the rise of a baseline reality that was hostile to the humanities. In the late nineteenth century, the German philosopher Dilthey called the humanities "the spiritual sciences," and Tolstoy remarked that "what we look for in a work of art is the revelation of the artist's soul, a glimpse of God." Both such statements echo that of Michelangelo before them: "The true work of art is but a shadow of the divine perfection."[13] In all such declarations, the humanities were taken to represent something beyond standard human endeavor. They embodied inspiration and genius, and the artists who were gifted with such inspiration and genius were more akin to celestial ambassadors than to self-governing doers. Inasmuch as the humanities thus maintained commitments to nonrationalized and enchanted notions of action over the twentieth century, the branch's assumptions about reality increasingly diverged from those borne by the global-institutional frame. The humanities' prospects in the university, we expect, grew clouded in measure.

While denoting a harshening climate for the humanities, the relocation of action capacities in the global-institutional frame simultaneously marked the emergence of a taken-for-granted reality favorable to the social sciences. Activated human individuals provided the essential building blocks of the modern entity "society" – conceived around the social contract – and conversely society provided the collective embodiment of human actorhood – mobilized around goals of progress and justice.[14] Thus as the portfolio of individual capacities and responsibilities grew over the century, society's portfolio grew in kind, and various direct objects of social scientific inquiry were rendered into being: the consumer, the rebel, the activist, and so on. Already in 1957, for instance, Korea University's Introduction to Political Science focused on "interest groups, propaganda, political parties, sectional influences, [and] class identifications."[15] In short as reality's baseline assumptions gradually redistributed action capacities from divinities to humans, the constitution of society extended and deepened, broadening the domain and raising the importance of the social sciences in the university.

Beyond the branches of learning, the shifting locus of action in the global-institutional frame strengthened the undergirdings of the university's applied fields, given their focus on concrete real-world problems, rather than abstract fundamental principles. In deactivating (the) God(s) and in activating humans, the ontological shift at issue here augmented the possibilities for everyday human impacts on everyday human affairs (which themselves became increasingly important as humans acquired status as reality's master actors). In more domains and to greater extents over the era, it became taken for granted and rule-like that humans could and should shape their immediate environs. From the most mundane to the most complex matters – global warming, the AIDS pandemic, etc. – human action came to be implicated. Thus the relocation of action capacities in the premises of global reality provided strengthened foundations for the university's applied disciplines, in which newly minted human actors could have their greatest impacts.

Along a second vector also, the redefinition of action changed in the globally institutionalized ontology. Humans gained from the gods not only broad capacities to act but also specific capacities to know (i.e., to act in the realms of knowledge). To know is to recognize, perceive, and identify that which is universal; to exert mastery over a body of facts or principles. With action's redefinition over the twentieth century, divine injunctions against human understandings fell by the wayside. Over matters formerly controlled by the fates, humans grew entitled to seek discernment and became responsible for using their understandings for individual and collective benefits.

This shift in the premises of reality bore implications for the university's main branches of learning, first by subverting assumptions at the heart of the humanities. In 1967, the gifts of the muse still inspired awe at the University of Liberia: Its course on World Literature celebrated "the great masters . . . with the view of knowing [their] message to mankind."[16] As celestial influences progressively withdrew from the realms of knowledge, however, the authority and legitimacy of nonrationalized forms of knowledge weakened acutely. The jewels of the humanities lost luster, and Flaubert and Beethoven were reduced to mere mortals. Forms of knowledge incorrigible to strict human control – including inspiration, revelation, and genius (which once directly referred to one's tutelary spirit) – disappeared from the cultural scripts and organizational rules of world society, undercutting key assumptions upholding the humanities. We speculate that the branch suffered in the university accordingly.

The very same change in the accepted story of being ushered forth an institutional environment friendly to both the natural and social sciences.[17] In taking possession of the keys to knowledge, humans acquired authority and legitimacy to conduct themselves as explorers, investigators, and discoverers – in natural and social worlds made comprehensible by rationalization. As the century progressed, few realms stood impervious to inquisition. For instance in 1982, Beirut University's Introduction to Sociology promised to lay bare matters once the strict province of God (i.e., "the basic principles that govern social relationships as well as the scientific points of view that deal with and explain social phenomena"). The enlarging hand of the Human Knower not only promised growth to the scientific fields but also wrought changes within them. For example, consider the following: "Biology once was regarded as a languid, largely descriptive discipline, a passive science that was content... merely to observe the natural world rather than change it. No longer. Today biology, armed with the power of genetics... stands poised to assume godlike powers of creation, calling forth artificial forms of life."[18]

Because the sciences took form around the premise of human sovereignty in the realms of knowledge (to run the experiment, to conduct the interview, etc.), we propose that the transition of knowledge capacities from gods to humans in the global-institutional frame solidified both the natural and social science fields' foundations, enhancing their presences in the academic core.

Finally as humans came to possess overarching permissions to know in world society, we suppose that the altering platform of assumptions increasingly funneled emphasis onto the university's applied division over the twentieth century. Much more so than its basic counterpart, the applied division presupposed that human mastery could be sufficiently extended to allow not only the rationalized acquisition but also the rationalized *use* of knowledge. In applied fields, human sovereignty stood supreme. Such notions of human command – bordering on blasphemy in realities run by gods – became increasingly tenable in the course of global-institutional reframing, and we conjecture that the applied disciplines as a result gained stature in the world's universities.

REDEFINITION OF STRUCTURE IN THE GLOBALLY INSTITUTIONALIZED ONTOLOGY

Side by side with reconceptions of action – and similarly spurred by the reconstitution of origins – came attendant reconceptions of structure in the global-institutional frame. Horizontal-assembly models displaced vertical-hierarchy models of structure, and dynamic-network templates dislodged fixed-categorical templates of order.

In the first dimension of this shift, vertical hierarchies, such as those found in the creation story, lost their status as the default model of structure in the culture and organization of world society. Horizontal assemblies, such as those found in the evolution story, increasingly took their place. Thus throughout reality (e.g., in classrooms, in marriages, and in ethnic relations), graded rankings came to be regarded as archaic and immoral at the same time as inclusive gatherings became normatively and cognitively standard. The baseline structural blueprints of reality were thus transformed.

For the branches of learning, this global-institutional-frame shift implied the withdrawal of aid from the humanities. The humanities emerged to study that which is most exalted in human thought and expression. For example in 1963, the Seminar in Classical Philosophy at the Universidad Central de Venezuela still commended "the praise of philosophy" and "the ideal life of the contemplative man." As vertical hierarchies collapsed over the century, however, the structure assumed by such studies – allowing the easy distinction of moral from immoral, coarse from fine, sublime from vulgar, subtle from crude, and so on – fell subject to confusion. Without structural blueprints to authorize or legitimize the separation of Great Artists from incompetents and imposters, the canon fell under fire, and the humanities lost their guiding lights. As a result, we expect that this branch of learning increasingly struggled to maintain its direction and identity in the university.[19]

This shift in reality's structural premises carried additional ramifications for the university's basic and applied divisions. As the "natural" models of reality were recast in the global-institutional frame, the affairs of everyday people gained public relevance. Activities aimed at grooming gentlemen to take positions atop vertical hierarchies grew marginalized, and activities aimed at educating ordinary persons to participate in horizontal assemblies grew central. At the same time, universities organized exclusively for elites lost their monopolies over higher education, and universities organized inclusively for the masses proliferated. Under the emerging structural assumptions, knowledge for knowledge's sake, blind to common-place concerns, came to be seen as a luxury, whereas knowledge connected to everyday life came to be seen as sheer necessity. Thus as the restructuring of reality validated popular affairs and promoted the "massification" of higher education, we anticipate a heightening of attention to the university's applied units.[20]

Hand in hand with this first dimension of structural redefinition over the twentieth century came a second one. Throughout globally institutionalized reality, the fixed categories of creation were progressively retooled into the dynamic networks of evolution (e.g., from melting pots to mosaics, from inherited to achieved status, etc.). Structural models portraying unchanging orders and enduring boundaries lost authority and legitimacy in world society, whereas those depicting active relationships and tangled interdependencies gained in kind.

Vis-à-vis the university's three main branches of learning, we first suggest that such changes in the substructure of reality undermined global-institutional backing for the humanities worldwide. Throughout the twentieth century, the humanities honored unique arrows in the human quiver – literature, art, music, and morality. For example when the linguistics department at the University of California at Irvine was threatened with closure, one professor protested, "Linguistics is the study of the faculty of language that distinguishes us from anything else in the animal world."[21] Here we see a definitional tie to old fixed-categorical structural models that burdened the humanities – which, after all, celebrate and study cultural phenomena imagined to be peculiar to *humanity*. As global-institutional reframing uprooted such boundary-laden models and replaced them with dynamic networks, the premises sustaining the humanities diminished in strength accordingly. In consequence, we anticipate a reduction in academic-core emphases in the humanities in universities worldwide.

We furthermore suggest that during the twentieth century, this same aspect of structural redefinition distributed authority and legitimacy to the sciences, but most especially to the social sciences. Clearly during the time period both branches assumed a dynamically networked reality, evolving over time and elaborately interconnected. Nevertheless, much evidence suggests that the distribution of societies into fixed categories (commonly known as nation-states) outlasted the analogous distribution of nature. In 1900 (and even still in 2000), for example, it was much more meaningful to speak of, say, "American society" or an "American citizen" than it was to speak of "American nature" or an "American squirrel." The universalization of nature – the breakdown of the fixed-categorical order – began in earnest during the nineteenth century, which is beyond the scope of our data.[22] By contrast, the universalization of society – the imagination of a common and interdependent humanity – came much later, notably in the wake of World War II. The new structural scheme was evident in 1986 in Geography I at the University of Adelaide, in which the elements in an environment were "perceived as integrated, interacting systems," such that a change in one part would "automatically affect all other parts."[23] In short, although the natural sciences surely benefited from the conversion of fixed categories into dynamic networks in the cultural scripts and organizational rules of world society, it seems likely that during the period for which we have data – the twentieth century – the social sciences benefited a good deal more.

This same transition in reality's structural templates furthermore implied a redistribution of emphases between the university's basic and applied divisions. As categorical orders fell into disuse in world society and as boundary demarcations failed, the static separation of the ivory tower from society at large grew suspect, and the special virtues of basic or pure university knowledge lost salience. Conversely as the dynamic network progressively acquired the status of reality's default order (assumed until proven otherwise), the benefits of university-society intercourse and the possibilities of society's rationalization – both expressed in applied knowledge – grew to seem substantial.[24] As embodiments of the dynamic-network order, university-society ties won rising approval under the emerging global-institutional frame, and we expect accordingly that the university's applied division ascended among academic priorities, forcing the basic division into retreat.

Altogether then, we claim that the shift from sacred creation to mundane evolution in the globally institutionalized cosmology (the story of origins) helped in catalyzing a pair of two-fold shifts in the globally institutionalized ontology (the story of being). With the redefinition of action in world society, we see (a) a contraction of divine and an amplification of human capacities to act and (b) a contraction of divine and an amplification of human capacities to know. With the redefinition of structure over the twentieth century, we observe (a) the descent of vertical-hierarchical and the ascent of horizontal-assembly models of structure and order and (b) the descent of fixed-categorical and the ascent of dynamic-network models of structure and order. These evolving blueprints of reality coalesced in a process of global-institutional reframing, which altered the premises of world society in ways that dimmed the prospects of the humanities, brightened the outlook for the natural sciences, and considerably brightened the horizon of the social sciences among the university's branches of learning on a global basis. The same process, we expect, changed baseline reality so as to lower the priority of the university's basic disciplines and to raise the priority of its applied disciplines during the time period. We summarize these orienting ideas in Figure 1.

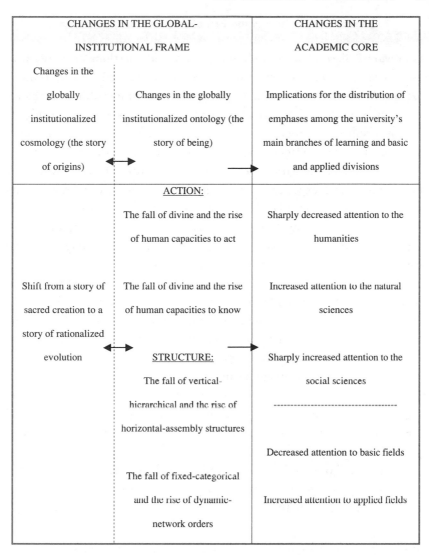

CHANGES IN THE GLOBAL-INSTITUTIONAL FRAME		CHANGES IN THE ACADEMIC CORE
Changes in the globally institutionalized cosmology (the story of origins)	Changes in the globally institutionalized ontology (the story of being)	Implications for the distribution of emphases among the university's main branches of learning and basic and applied divisions
Shift from a story of sacred creation to a story of rationalized evolution	**ACTION:** The fall of divine and the rise of human capacities to act	Sharply decreased attention to the humanities
	The fall of divine and the rise of human capacities to know	Increased attention to the natural sciences
	STRUCTURE: The fall of vertical-hierarchical and the rise of horizontal-assembly structures	Sharply increased attention to the social sciences
		-------------------------------------
		Decreased attention to basic fields
	The fall of fixed-categorical and the rise of dynamic-network orders	Increased attention to applied fields

Figure 1   Summary of argument and implications for the main branches of learning and for the basic and applied divisions.

Having thus laid out the implications of our argument for the university's upper-level organizational layers, the challenge before us is empirical. To what extent do longitudinal and cross-national data on the distribution of emphases in the academic core bear out our predictions? We consider data on the branches of learning first.

Faculty Composition in the Branches of Learning over Time

As previously described, we address our empirical questions primarily with data on faculty composition from the *Commonwealth Universities Yearbook* 1915-95.[25] The dependent variable here – faculty composition – is a gauge of priorities in the body of university knowledge as a whole and worldwide over the twentieth century. Recall that our focus is on *relative* academic-core emphases. Given huge faculty expansions over the twentieth century – driven in part by rationalization processes discussed in the Introduction – knowledge domains may have experienced declining relative emphases without losing (and even while gaining) faculty. For example, in a university that had ten humanists out of twenty faculty members in 1915 and twenty humanists out of two hundred in 1950, the humanities plummeted among university priorities even as the faculty doubled in gross size.

Bearing this in mind, we present a first look at the changing profiles of the university's three main branches of learning in Table 3. For the British Commonwealth countries in our main sample of universities, the table shows the average percentage of the total faculty in each branch of learning in our earliest time interval (1915–35) and in our latest time interval (1976–95), as well as the percentage change from the former to the latter. This final column indicates each branch of learning's standing in recent decades relative to its standing earlier (i.e., how much it expanded or contracted relative to its starting academic-core presence over the entire time period in question[26]).

In regard to both the humanities and the social sciences, the evidence in Table 3 strongly confirms our expectations. The relative emphasis allotted to teaching and research in the humanities sharply declined during the century,

Table 3 Percentage of Total Faculty in Each of the Three Main Branches of Learning for Universities in British Commonwealth Countries

	Faculty Percentage in 1915–35	*Faculty Percentage in 1975–95*	*Percentage Change Over Time*
Humanities	33.2	19.5	−41
Natural Sciences	57.5	50.6	−12
Social Sciences	9.3	29.9	222

from about one-third of total university faculty to less than one-fifth. By 1976–95, the relative representation of the humanities in the university had shrunk by 41 percent – a substantial falloff by any standard.[27] This decline, we speculate, followed at least in part from redefinitions of action and structure in the global-institutional frame, which withdrew essential lifeblood from the humanities – divine inspiration, celestial revelation, artistic greatness, and human uniqueness.

Meanwhile during the same time period, the relative precedence of the social sciences in the academic core sharply increased, from less than one-tenth of overall faculty to almost one-third. Between 1915–35 and 1976–95, the presence of the social sciences in the university increased by more than 200 percent – a spectacular climb that has attracted little notice from social scientists. The rapid ascent of this branch of learning was likely spurred, as per our argument, from reconstitutions of reality over the twentieth century, which offered the social sciences an increasingly favorable apparatus of assumptions: activated humans, with qualities of understanding and reason, joined as equal members in society, inhabiting newly universalized social spaces.

These findings unequivocally match our expectations, and they lend an initial brace of support to our argument: that master shifts in the global-institutional frame – by redesignating that which is taken for granted in reality – motivated alterations in the body of university knowledge worldwide.

Concerning the natural sciences, the results in Table 3 are slightly less supportive of our argument. During the time period for which we have data, the natural sciences as a whole registered a 12 percent decline in relative faculty share, moving from approximately 58 to 51 percent of all university faculty. Our expectations were otherwise – we thought enhanced human access to and control over knowledge in an increasingly dynamic and interconnected world would drive up attention to the natural sciences. One possible explanation for the unexpected outcome is that our data do not extend into the nineteenth century, during which time the natural sciences made strong initial inroads into universities. For example, "In the nineteenth century, geometry . . . went through a period of growth that was near cataclysmic in proportion." During that time, the University of Tübingen established its faculty of natural sciences, which led to the erection of new university buildings: the anatomical building (1832–35)... the botanical and chemical institute (1842–45); the clinical hospital for surgical cases (1846); the physiological institute (1867); the institute for pathological anatomy (1873); ophthalmic hospital (1875); medical hospital (1878–79); the physico-chemical institute (1883–85); the institute for physics (1888); the new hospital for women (1888–91), in place of the old one built in 1803; the hospital for mental diseases (1892–94); the mineralogico-geological and zoological institute (1902); the institute for chemistry (1903–07); [and] the new ophthalmological clinic (1907-09).[28]

These examples – and considerable work in the history of science – suggest that the university incorporated the natural sciences well before it incorporated the social sciences. The universalizing abstractions and experimental interventions of science, one might speculate, laid claim more easily to the entity nature than they did to the entity society.

In elaborated form, the same data appear in Figure 2, which depicts trends in faculty composition by branch of learning from 1915 to 1995. We have four data points on which to draw. The humanities trend-line is monotonic and steady – there were no discernible changes in that branch of learning's

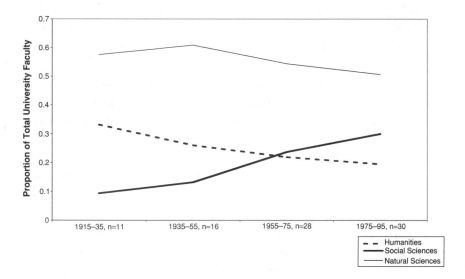

Figure 2   Changes in faculty composition by major branch of learning – British Commonwealth Universities, 1915–95.

rate of decline over the twentieth century. The trend-line for the social sciences was monotonically upward, but its slope ticked up slightly after World War II. The war stigmatized ethnic nationalisms and other exclusive corporate groupings and on the flipside gave rise to expressions of encompassing humanity (e.g., in the Universal Declaration of Human Rights, adopted in 1948). The war ultimately promoted, in other words, the universalization of society while raising the value of human cooperation and starkly demonstrating humanity's mutual interdependence. For all these reasons, the war may be responsible for the increased rate of expansion in the already rapidly expanding social sciences in universities worldwide. The natural sciences, meanwhile, enjoyed slight growth in faculty representation from the first to second time intervals before receding thereafter. Early in the twentieth century, the natural sciences were the locus of great hopes, verging on scientific utopianism. Following the stunning reality of the atomic bomb, much of that optimism fell away, as did the prominence of the natural sciences in the academic core.

In both the social and natural science cases, there seems to be a legible "war effect" on emphases in the body of university knowledge. Many analysts have posited the existence of this phenomenon, broadly conceived to break down the status quo and to open the academic core to renewal.[29] Fueled by repulsion from Nazi atrocities, crystallized by the victory of the liberal powers, and organized in such bodies as the United Nations and the Marshall Plan, the end of World War II appears indeed to have marked a sea-change in the global-institutional environment. In consequence it seems that processes long underway in world society shifted speed or even course, in sometimes dramatic ways.

Although a serious treatment of the war effect lies beyond the scope of the present analysis, its appearance here allows us to reiterate an important point. We do not see our theoretical perspective as operating to the exclusion of others. The evolution of cultural models took place concomitant with economic and political changes in world society during the twentieth century, and all of these together inform the university's priorities over time. The trend-lines observed in Figure 2 clearly suggest that the cosmological and ontological shifts that take priority in our argument interacted with pivotal world historical events in determining the timing and rate of changes in the academic core.

Faculty Composition in the Basic and Applied Divisions over Time

Going beyond the branches of learning, our argument predicts a redistribution of emphasis from the university's basic to applied divisions over the twentieth century. Given the common-denominator quality of the global-institutional frame, we expect the basic-to-applied shift to appear both generally and across knowledge domains, not only where particular economic and political needs and interests provided propellant. In other words, as there appeared computer degrees there should also have appeared degrees in racial and ethnic studies; and as there arose programs for the management of environmental problems, there should also have arisen programs for the management of interpersonal problems. Finally, our argument leads us to expect the basic-to-applied transition to occur not only in countries at particular levels of economic development or with particular economic characteristics. Alterations in globally institutionalized reality imply the reconstitution of universities along similar lines around the world.

With our expectations thus articulated, we turn to our results, listed first overall and then by branch of learning in Table 4. For the British Commonwealth countries in our main sample of universities, the table shows the average percentage of faculty in the university's basic and applied units at our earliest and latest time intervals (1915–35 and 1976–95), followed by the percentage change in each unit's faculty share from the first to last interval.

Table 4 Percentage of Total Faculty in the Basic and Applied Divisions for Universities in British Commonwealth Countries

	Faculty Percentage in 1915–35	Faculty Percentage in 1975–95	Percentage Change Over Time
Total Basic	59.7	45.7	−23
Total Applied	40.3	54.3	35
Humanities Basic	27.4	15.6	−43
Humanities Applied	5.7	3.9	−33
Natural Sciences Basic	28.5	17.7	−38
Natural Sciences Applied	29.1	32.9	13
Social Sciences Basic	3.8	12.4	223
Social Sciences Applied	5.5	17.6	220

The main findings are simple and striking. The so-called basic disciplinary fields lost substantial ground between 1915 and 1995 – declining from 59.7 to 45.7 percent of the university's total faculty. The applied fields developed in inverse proportion, increasing their average representation from 40.3 to 54.3 percent. The magnitude of the tradeoff was sufficiently large as to suggest that the basic-to-applied shift characterized universities worldwide over the twentieth century, not just universities in countries with particular economic characteristics. This broad rearrangement of academic-core priorities is as anticipated by our argument. With global-institutional reframing, reality's premises grew more favorable to the university's applied division, with humans gaining capacities to manipulate and to comprehend the universe, on a mass basis, in an era when university-society ties were gaining authority and legitimacy.[30]

Broken down one level of analysis, the data reveal that the basic-to-applied shift took place in two of the three main branches of learning. Table 4 shows that the percentage of faculty members working in applied humanities fields (which in practice means law) declined at a slower rate than the corresponding percentage in the basic humanities. The table also shows that the percentage of faculty members working in applied natural science fields actually rose, whereas the corresponding percentage in basic natural-science fields fell. Here, the applied/basic distinction is stark.

The exception again – as was true at the Université Catholique de Louvain – was the social sciences, where the basic and applied faculties both expanded massively and almost indistinguishably – exceeding 200 percent on both sides of the aisle. One factor behind the basic/applied equality in the social sciences may have been that, even in their so-called basic form, the social sciences – the newest of the three main branches of learning – originated in forms that were already highly rationalized or applied. From the outset, for instance, political science and economics were hitched rather tightly to collective social policies and benefits, whereas sociology was obviously oriented to social problems from its inception. "Social science has from its earliest beginnings aimed to administer and to change the world as well as to understand it. It did not spring forth from the head of humanity only, but from the body as well."[31]

We add a dimension of detail to these findings in Figures 3–6, showing trend-lines based on all four of our data points to elucidate issues of timing.

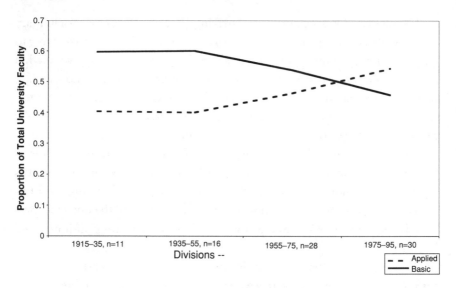

Figure 3 Changes in faculty composition by applied and basic divisions – British Commonwealth Universities, 1915–95.

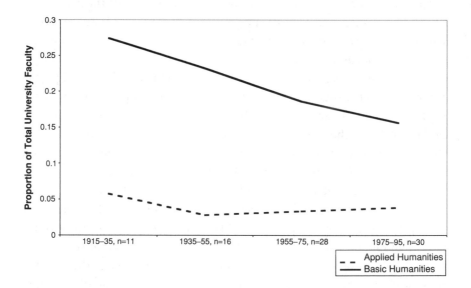

Figure 4 Changes in faculty composition in applied and basic humanities – British Commonwealth Universities, 1915–95.

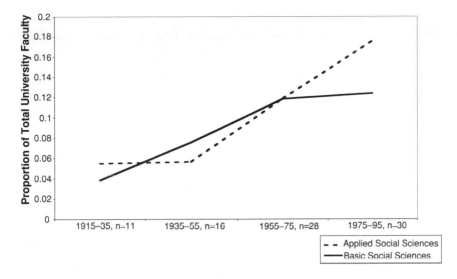

Figure 5   Changes in faculty composition in applied and basic social sciences –
British Commonwealth Universities, 1915–95.

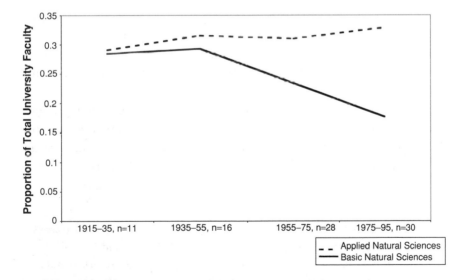

Figure 6   Changes in faculty composition in applied and basic natural sciences –
British Commonwealth Universities, 1915–95.

Overall, the basic and applied divisions' trajectories nearly mirrored each others (Figure 3), although the downward shift in the basic division's trajectory was slightly greater than the applied division's opposite shift. Both slopes changed around World War II, consistent with the notion that the war effort itself propelled the academic core toward applied pursuits. Among the branches of learning, we see that the basic humanities fell uniformly through the decades (Figure 4), whereas the applied humanities received a subtle uplift beginning mid-century (again around World War II). Meanwhile, Figure 5 reveals that the basic social science fields rose early and then flattened out, whereas the applied social science fields were flat early and then rose. If the current trends continue, the applied social sciences very soon will find themselves in the same boat as the applied humanities and applied natural sciences, out-competing their basic counterparts. Finally, Figure 6 shows that the basic natural science fields increased their university presence from interval one to two, but then took a sharp downward turn around World War II, yet again suggesting a war effect. The applied natural science fields, meanwhile, ascended steadily from the very first interval.[32]

Of course, it is important to note that the convention distinguishing applied from basic academic fields is problematic. The domains, after all, are massively interpenetrated. For instance, a dissertation in computer science might involve abstruse mathematical theory, even as a proper biochemist might pursue pharmaceutical breakthroughs. The line of division is somewhat artificial.

On the one hand, even the most applied endeavors (criminology, hotel management) are basic at heart, given universalism's defining and compulsory hold on university knowledge. Thus, the course description for Strategy in the Business Environment at Stanford University's Graduate School of Business was pitched in highly abstracted and generalized terms:

> Cases are set in both the U.S. and non-U.S. environments and illustrate how managers are called upon to interact with the public and governments in local, national, and international settings. Topics include integrated strategy, activists and the media, legislation affecting business, regulation and antitrust, intellectual property, Internet privacy, International trade policy, and ethics.[33]

Before being applied, in other words, the course contents had to be rendered as *knowledge*, in which particulars are linked to universals. Thus, Stanford's course offered all-purpose strategies for all kinds of contexts. Whether or not it is overtly tied to a direct application in society at large, university knowledge comes in nonsectarian packages. By the end of the twentieth century, nature and society were universalized so extensively that knowledge aimed even at the most concrete and specific social needs or problems could easily be postured in universalistic terms.

On the other hand, even the most basic university knowledge (mathematics, classics) is applied at heart – meaning it is rationalized around the human project, promising a minimum of understanding. In this sense, application begins at the moment of inquiry. In that instant, objects of study become linked to human endeavors. Thus at Humboldt State, one is not surprised to find courses in the philosophy of sex or the philosophy of racism. Although basic knowledge may be overtly oriented to the knowledge system itself, it is already deeply enmeshed in the highly rationalized and strongly purposive human project of comprehending reality, in which knowledge is itself a good.

Also despite its recent upsurge, it bears emphasizing that applied knowledge has long been a university standard. Generally speaking, the universities of Continental Europe originated around faculties of medicine, theology, law, and philosophy, even the last of which had the air of professional training for primary and secondary schoolteachers. More specifically, for example, applied emphases were already well evident at the University of the Cape of Good Hope in 1906, which offered degrees in land surveying, mining engineering, colony law, and so on.[34] Before its recent upswell in the academic core, applied knowledge had a long history in the university.

These qualifications aside, the larger finding remains. Worldwide over the twentieth century, there was a marked shift in university priorities, as knowledge sectors conceived to be joined more immediately to everyday social functions outgrew their counterparts. The monastic model for the university – separated from society, bounded from politics and commerce, and only thus pure – clearly lost resonance during the time period.

In overall terms, our findings here are consistent with expectations based on our argument. Following redefinitions of action and structure in the global-institutional frame, (a) the humanities lost relative ground, the social sciences gained relative ground, and the natural sciences almost held their own in the university, which itself grew exponentially, and (b) the applied disciplines expanded somewhat over the twentieth century in inverse proportion to the basic disciplines.

So far then, our argument offers a fairly reliable guide to changes in the university's academic core. Before proceeding onto finer-grained analyses, we pause here to consider several questions concerning our sample and indicator of academic priorities. First, we examine the robustness and generalizability of our findings across three university samples.

Comparing Findings across Three Samples of Universities

Although the foregoing evidence of faculty recomposition initially validates our global-institutional argument, it also sidesteps two important questions. First in the results detailed above, we have included in each time interval all the British Commonwealth countries with available data, meaning that our case base increased substantially over time. In the middle of the twentieth century, many (lesser developed) countries gained independence and first founded universities, only thus entering our data set during the second, third, or even fourth time intervals. This raises the question: Are the developments we observe in faculty emphases merely artifacts of a changing case base? We address this question by extracting a constant-case sample from the main one used above. The question then becomes simply, Does a sample of constant-case British Commonwealth universities exhibit trends similar to those from our main sample?

Second although all our arguments are formulated in global terms, the evidence presented above pertains only to the British Commonwealth (which, one should recall, comprises approximately 30 percent of the world's people and includes such diverse places as India, Fiji, and Mozambique). This is so for practical reasons, described in the Introduction. But it raises the question of generalizability. Do universities from the British Commonwealth exhibit the same changes as universities in general? For the three earlier time intervals, we are able to address this question by folding into our main sample additional data from the *Index Generalis* (for the first two time intervals) and the *World Guide to Universities* (for the third), both of which cast wide global nets. The

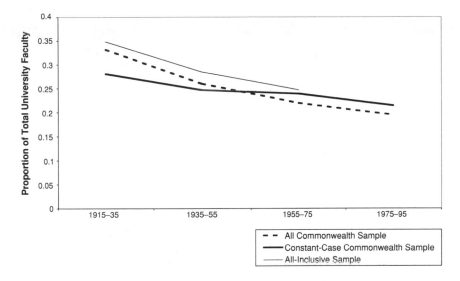

Figure 7   Changes in the share of university faculty in the humanities – three sample comparison, 1915–95.

question here is, Does an all-inclusive sample of universities, aggregating data from all three available sources, exhibit trends similar to those from our main sample?[35]

We answer both these questions in Figures 7–9, which show the average emphases given to each branch of learning over time by universities in the three alternative samples. Figure 7, to begin, presents humanists as a proportion of total university faculty for all three samples (constant-case Commonwealth, all Commonwealth, and all-inclusive). The trajectories are impressively consistent. In comparison to our main sample, the (much smaller) group of constant-case countries registered a more modest decline in the humanities over the century: Universities in this group both began with a smaller share of humanities faculty and ended with a higher share. Still just as in our main sample, the humanities demonstrated across-the-board recession. Meanwhile as compared to our main sample, the average proportion of humanists in the (much larger) all-inclusive sample began at a slightly higher point and declined at a slightly slower rate. Nevertheless just as in our main sample, the branch's fall was pronounced during the entire period. Generally then, Figure 7 supports our cause on two levels: It suggests

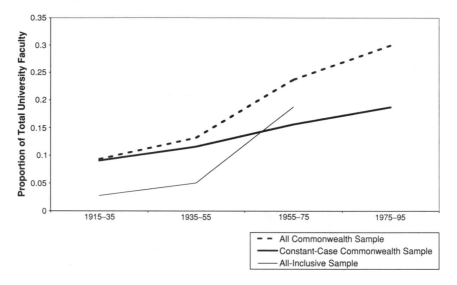

Figure 8 Changes in the share of university faculty in the social sciences – three sample comparison, 1915–95.

that the contraction of the humanities reported above is neither an artifact of a changing case base nor confined to British Commonwealth countries. The humanities lost standing everywhere.

Figure 8 takes the same approach to the social sciences, and as above, the three samples are remarkably consistent from one to the next. Social scientists from the constant-case Commonwealth universities experienced slower expansion in their average faculty representation than those from our main sample, but they nevertheless almost doubled their presence in the academic core between 1915–35 and 1976–95. Likewise, social scientists in the all-inclusive sample began with a lower proportion of total faculty and proliferated less quickly from time one to two but then proliferated more quickly from time two to three. Both alternatives exhibited strong and steady growth just as in our main sample. Once again, we are doubly encouraged. Figure 8 shows that regardless of sample – constant-case British Commonwealth, all British Commonwealth, or all inclusive – social scientists gained relative stature in the university over the twentieth century.

Finally, Figure 9 takes up the same two questions in regard to the natural sciences. Here, perhaps, the consistency is most impressive. The

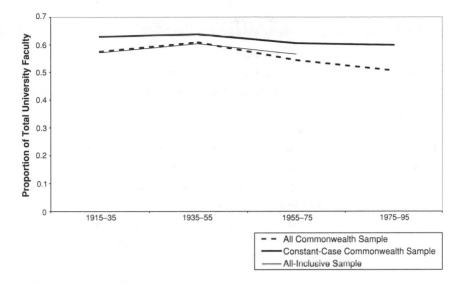

Figure 9 Changes in the share of university faculty in the natural sciences – three sample comparison, 1915–95.

constant-case sample both began at a higher intercept and changed less quickly, but consonant with our main sample, the constant-case universities showed a slight increase in average natural sciences representation from periods one to two, followed by decreases from periods two to three and then again from three to four. The two samples moved in the same directions throughout, and both showed a slight natural sciences retreat over the century. Meanwhile, the trend-lines for the main and all-inclusive samples are almost indistinguishable in slope or intercept. They overlap almost perfectly. As before, changes in the representation of natural sciences faculty follow roughly parallel paths regardless of sample.

In short, both questions raised above can be addressed to satisfaction. The original changes we observed were neither artifacts of a changing case base nor restricted to universities in the British Commonwealth. Similar changes appear in the constant-case and all-inclusive samples. These comparisons strongly suggest that the trends we document below with our main British Commonwealth sample are globally representative – occurring in countries new and old, from Namibia to France. To further test this claim, we next consider the issues of convergence and isomorphism.

Convergence toward Isomorphism?

Our assertion that British Commonwealth universities adequately represent the world population would be validated further were we to find convergence toward global isomorphism in the academic contents of universities around the world. There are two related questions. First, did universities from the British Commonwealth and universities generally converge on a common set of academic priorities over the twentieth century? Second, how much cross-national variation remained?

By the logic of most functionalist imageries, academic priorities should have diverged over the twentieth century. In one version of the story, divergence should have occurred as colonial-era universities sent down roots into domestic local labor markets and business sectors, state regulations and funding environments, and so on. In another version of the functionalist story, divergence should have occurred as the number of universities multiplied over the decades, heightening university-on-university competition and thus raising the premium on "product" differentiation and the incentives for academic-core distinctiveness. Our own theoretical imagery, by contrast, predicts convergence in academic emphases. As the global-institutional frame strengthened along with globalization generally through the time period, we expect that both world models of reality and world models of the university became increasingly prevalent and consequential, rendering bodies of university knowledge in all kinds of settings as more similar over time.

The process of convergence can be witnessed in many particular university settings. For instance, after Taiwan's retrocession to China in 1945, the new government took over Taihoku University and renamed it National Taiwan University. Being the first university in the country, National Taiwan "put emphasis on scholarly research . . . in humanities and social sciences, basic sciences, and applied sciences."[36] Given the global premise that universities are essential elements of all modern societies, Taiwan wasted no time in founding one according to world-legitimized standards – covering the three main branches of learning and both basic and applied fields.

Likewise, one sees convergence in motion in Sierra Leone in 2002. At that time, the President of Fourah Bay College recommended expanding the college's curriculum to include a "program in Mass Communication . . . [given that] it was generally agreed that lack of a proper school of journalism in the country was hindering the performance of the mass media, a very important sector of every democratic and developing society."[37] The rationales invoked for the new program at Fourah Bay all took the form of global generics: What is "generally agreed" about a "proper school" for "every democratic and developing society." In both Taiwan and Sierra Leone, we see the process of convergence underway.

More systematically, our data allow a brief investigation of the convergence/divergence question, at least between 1915 and 1975, for which we have faculty-composition data from three different sources. For both the main British Commonwealth and the all-inclusive samples described above, we first found the average percentage of university faculty located in each of the basic disciplinary fields at the first and third time intervals (1915–35 and 1955–75). We then calculated the sample-to-sample differences in average faculty representation on a field-by-field basis. Convergence is found when the difference in interval one is greater than the difference in interval three. The results of these efforts appear in Table 5.

The general answer to the convergence/divergence question appears at the bottom of the table. Across all the disciplinary fields, the total aggregated difference between the two samples was about twice as high during the earlier time interval than it was during the later (20.3 versus 8.2 percent). Over this sixty-year period, that is, the distance between the typical Commonwealth and all-inclusive academic menus more than halved. The findings indicate rapid convergence over the century.[38]

Among the three main branches of learning, the convergence was greatest in the natural sciences (from an aggregated difference of 10.8 to 2.0 percent), whereas the social sciences registered a slight divergence over time (from 1.9 to 2.2). By the 1955–75 time interval, both of these branches of science showed very high levels of global isomorphism, and the humanities were not far behind.

Turning now to individual disciplinary fields, we see that only six of twenty-two diverged over time. Between the Commonwealth and all-inclusive samples, for instance, the difference between the average percentages of biology faculty plunged from 3.4 to 0.1, between the average percentages of political sciences faculty dropped from 0.7 to 0.2, and between the average percentages of classics faculty fell from 2.0 to 0.3. Convergence was the rule of the day.

Table 5   Converging Emphases in Two Samples, 1915–35 and 1955–75:
Differences in Average Faculty Percentages by Disciplinary Field

	Differences between Average Faculty Percentages, 1915–35	*Differences between Average Faculty Percentages, 1955–75*
Classics and Archaeology	2.0	0.3
Philosophy	0.3	0.4
Theology	0.1	0.4
Art and Music	0.3	0.2
Linguistics and Philology	1.2	0.9
Western Languages and Literatures	2.5	1.5
History	0.2	0.3
Non-Western Languages and Literatures	1.0	0.0
Aggregated Humanities Differences	*7.6*	*4.0*
Sociology	0.2	0.2
Geography	0.3	0.8
Political Science	0.7	0.2
Economics	0.4	0.8
Anthropology	0.1	0.0
Psychology	0.2	0.2
Aggregated Social Sciences Differences	*1.9*	*2.2*
Astronomy	0.3	0.1
Botany	0.8	0.4
Zoology	0.7	0.5
Biology	3.4	0.1
Physics	2.0	0.2
Chemistry	2.1	0.4
Math	1.5	0.1
Geology	0.0	0.2
Aggregated Natural Sciences Differences	*10.8*	*2.0*
Aggregated Total Differences	*20.3*	*8.2*

The field that retained the largest sample to sample difference in the latter time period was Western languages and literature, at 1.5 percent. Presumably, decolonization and the more general horizontalization of world society over the twentieth century undermined the status of once-binding colonial cultures, thus inhibiting the convergence process (despite which there was marked convergence, from 2.5 to 1.5 percent).

The general findings from this probe speak unequivocally: Around the world, academic cores converged over the century, ending the period with very high levels of isomorphism in the sciences and only somewhat lower isomorphism in the makeup of the humanities. Thus, not only did the three different samples show similar patterns of change over time, as seen in the previous section, but universities also converged over time toward a common academic core.

For clarity and consistency in the next several chapters, we rely on the inclusive Commonwealth sample for our main empirical base. This sample has the triple advantage, described in the Introduction, of drawing from a wide range of countries and universities, avoiding extreme case-base jags caused by data-source changes, and being continuously available throughout the whole twentieth century. Given the reassurances above, it seems fair to say that this main sample of universities offers a reasonable representation of universities worldwide, and increasingly so over time.

Indicator Comparisons

Having affirmed the validity of our sample, we now turn to the question of our indicator. Are the contractions and expansions we find peculiar to our faculty-composition measure? Or do other indicators of academic-core emphases show similar patterns of change over time?

As earlier suggested, few measures of university priorities exist on cross-national and longitudinal bases. The faculty-composition measure constructed here is, to our knowledge, the only indicator of priorities available for a substantial number of countries during most of the twentieth century. But for many reasons, changes in faculty composition may not track well with other measures of the university's priorities. It may be overmuch, in other words, to conclude that there are fundamental twentieth-century revisions in the academic core based on only one indicator.

An alternative measure of composition – though only available for a large number of countries after 1965 – is disciplinary enrollments, collected and published by UNESCO. Drori and Moon analyze these data by branch of learning for sixty-six countries between 1965 and 1995. The authors find cross-national and longitudinal trends that resonate squarely with our own: "Most dramatically, tertiary education enrollments worldwide are contracting in the humanities and expanding in the social sciences." Also, they find that despite initial differences in disciplinary emphases across different types of countries (developed versus developing, communist versus noncommunist), "there is striking similarity in trends across these groups of countries."[39] Thus, this alternative student-enrollment indicator of emphases shows patterns of change that follow directly along lines of our own.

Ramirez and Wotipka, meanwhile, analyze this same UNESCO data, focusing on enrollments in the natural sciences and engineering relative to total enrollments between 1972 and 1992. Their results, like Drori and Moon's, articulate well with our results. As we do, the authors find "a slight decline in the world average science and engineering percentage (N = 73)."[40] Student enrollments in the natural sciences follow the same path as faculty recomposition.

In sum, to the extent that the data allow comparison, distributions of students and faculty run more or less parallel at the world level, showing large reductions in the humanities, large expansions in the social sciences, and small reductions in the natural sciences over recent decades. Although other indicators of academic priorities – especially measures of funding – would be useful and enlightening to have, it seems that the patterns we report are not peculiarities of our indicator but rather dependable guides to general shifts in the body of university knowledge.

Conclusion

Our main goals in this chapter were threefold. First we sought to describe and second to explain century-long worldwide shifts in the emphases accorded the three main branches of learning and the university's applied and basic divisions. We found that over the course of the twentieth century the humanities diminished in relative prominence as the social sciences expanded, whereas the natural sciences remained roughly constant. We also found increased emphasis on the university's applied divisions, not only overall but also within the natural sciences and humanities branches of learning. Altogether, our data show that to a greater extent than had been recognized previously, the marquee change in the university's academic priorities over the twentieth century was not the rise of the applied sciences but rather of the social sciences.

We explained the main revisions in the academic core with reference to fundamental transformations in the global-institutional frame, in which a revised theory of origins promoted amended conceptions of action and structure in the theory of being. These shifts in the features of reality reset the most elementary assumptions available as a platform for university activities and thus fomented the changes we observed.

Our third goal in the chapter was to test the robustness and validity of our empirical findings, both as regards our sample of universities and our indicator of academic priorities. Our sample comparisons revealed that the trends exhibited by our main Commonwealth data are roughly parallel to those exhibited by a small set of constant cases and a large set of cases cobbled together from all three data sources. Further explorations of the main Commonwealth and all-inclusive samples revealed substantial convergence over time in academic composition, leading toward global isomorphism. Finally, a comparison of faculty-composition trends with student-enrollment trends confirmed that both indicators moved along similar lines over recent decades. Altogether, these tests strongly suggest that faculty recomposition in the Commonwealth fairly represents worldwide changes in the academic core.

At the same time as they offer early support for our theoretical perspective, the findings reported here also challenge the standard functionalist accounts of university reconstruction. Of the three major changes we found in the body of university knowledge – substantially diminished attention to the humanities (down 41 percent), greatly enlarged attention to the social sciences (up 222 percent), and somewhat broadened attention to the applied division (up 35 percent) – only the last bends easily to needs-and-interests imageries. Furthermore, our observations of closely parallel movements among the alternative samples and converging academic priorities over time are difficult to reconcile with functionalist perspectives. Countries and universities differ sharply in congeries of needs and interests, along both economic and political axes. If these factors were decisive for academic-core revisions, they would militate against the appearance of the distinct global patterns we observed.

In contrast to the various functionalisms, our own approach asserts (a) that transformations in the academic core are first and foremost global phenomena; (b) that the body of university knowledge evolves as a whole, not on a part by part basis; and (c) that shifts in the global-institutional frame are critical to academic reconstruction in altering the supply of building blocks from default models of reality.

In regard to (a) the findings here speak in unison. We clearly show global trends in the distribution of emphases among the university's three main branches of learning and between its basic and applied divisions. There is undeniably some global process at hand. In regard to (b) our results suggest the fruits of considering particular priority shifts as components of a metamorphosing body of university knowledge. Common denominators seem to have simultaneously affected the three main branches of learning and the university's applied and basic divisions, and the individual changes make more sense in light of the whole. And vis-à-vis (c), our findings demonstrate that it is credible at least to claim that changing blueprints of action and structure help explain broad redistributions of academic emphases. The changes we observed are consistent with the expectations derived from our global-institutional argument. To further examine these issues, however, we will need additional evidence. Thus we proceed to a series of finer-grained investigations of discipline-level priorities within each branch of learning. To the extent that our emphasis on global-institutional reframing continues to make sense of the empirical data, our explanatory framework will gather support.

Notes

1. The language of "basic" and "applied" is conventional but misleading. All university knowledge is in some sense both (i.e., at once universalized and rationalized around the human project). (An alternative to the basic/applied distinction is the division of professionally from socially oriented sciences – see Schofer [1999] and Drori et al. [2003].). Nevertheless, we follow standard practice in designating fields

as basic if they are primarily oriented to knowledge for knowledge's sake. In Chapters 2–4, we limit our attention to these fields.

2. Including the Baccalauréat, Licence, and Doctorat degrees. From the 1930–31 Année Académique and the university's webpage at http://www.ucl.ac.be/.

3. According to Clark (1973), the social sciences only began to be institutionalized in French universities around 1880. Evidence suggests similar timing elsewhere.

4. cf. Soares (1999) on Oxford. Universities, like other organizations, are imprinted and exhibit founding-date differentiation accordingly (Stinchcombe 1965). But it seems likely that differentiation diminishes over time as modeling processes (like the one associated with the Bologna Accord in Europe) promote global isomorphism (Ramirez 2003; Lenhardt 2002).

5. In the United States, many curricular changes – minor in scale compared to those we are considering – generated dispute and foreboding in the past (Eakin 1999). A bitter 1890s debate pitted the Greek and Roman classics against controversial modern works by Dante and Shakespeare. Later, a 1920s storm raged over adding U.S. literature to the curriculum.

6. See Becher (1989).

7. From Workman (1994). See Bloom (1987) and Readings (1996) for related arguments.

8. The titles are from Kernan (1997), Szeman (2003), and Botton (1999), respectively.

9. The passage is from Brooks (1999), who challenges the views expressed, in contrast to Bok (2003), Gumport (1999), Slaughter and Rhoades (2004), and many others. Brint (2002b:231) writes convincingly of the "gradual shrinking of the old arts and sciences core of the university and the expansion of occupational and professional programs," but his purview is restricted to the United States.

10. The list is from Powell and Owen-Smith (2002:107). See Bain (2003) on Russian universities and the state. Applied studies have additionally been accused of inviting solipsism and threatening social fragmentation (e.g., Women's Studies), as in Schlesinger (1998). The applied division fell under sharper attack over most of the twentieth century, but the basic division was never immune to criticism. "People have complained about learning which lacks application to 'life' since ancient times" (Botton 1999:22).

11. The numbers are from the U.S. National Center for Educational Statistics, reported in Kernan (1997).

12. The degree and faculty data come, respectively, from the 1900–01 Imperial Tientsin University Courses of Study, the 1910–11 Pei-yang University Catalogue, the 1927–28 Yenching University Bulletin, and the 1904–05 Université de Toulouse Annuaire.

13. On Dilthey, see http://www.britannica.com/eb/article?tocId=9041479. On Tolstoy, see Miller (2001: 43). On Michelangelo, see http://www.hyperhistory.net/apwh/bios/b2michclangelo.htm.

14. In contemporary usage, societies are most often equated with nation-states. See Weber (1978), Meyer, Boli, and Thomas (1987), and Wallerstein (1984).

15. From the 1957–58 Korea University Bulletin.

16. From the 1967–68 University of Liberia Catalogue and Announcements.

17. Originally, the natural sciences were "considered a way of understanding God, through understanding the natural order that He had created." Thus the inscription atop the Lyceum of Natural History at Williams College reads, "Lo! These are parts of His ways." Rather than demystifying God, science "made the mystification of God more glorious because it uncovered a perfectly ordered world only God could create." Over the nineteenth century, however, religious justifications for science declined and by mid century they "all but vanished." See http://www.williams.edu/resources/sciencecenter/center/histscipub.html.

18. The quotations come, respectively, from the 1982–84 Beirut University Catalog and from Commoner (2002: 39). Mallard, Lamont, and Guetzkow (2004) argue that the branches of learning and disciplinary fields do not employ sharply distinct approaches to knowledge (contra Bourdieu 1984). Nevertheless, there are clear historical and institutional divisions separating that which typically counts as knowledge in the sciences from that which counts as such in the humanities.

19. The quotations are from the 1963–64 Universidad Central de Venezuela Catalogo de Cursos. The oppositions are drawn from Bourdieu (1984). On the struggling humanities, see Abrams (1997), Botton (1999), Bryson (2005), Kernan (1997), and Szeman (2003).

20. See Altbach (1998) on worldwide university massification.

21. The quotation is from Professor Bernard Tranel, in Adjari (2003:4).

22. Although our data cannot speak to the issue, anecdotal evidence suggests that the major expansion of the natural sciences in the university was underway by the mid-nineteenth century. For example between 1852 and 1875, the number of natural sciences books held by the Williams College Library grew by 199 percent. During the same years, humanities holdings grew by 139 percent, and social sciences holdings grew by 90 percent. See http://www.williams.edu/resources/sciencecenter/center/histscipub.html.

23. From the 1986–87 University of Adelaide Calendar.

24. See Kerr (2001) for the classic treatment of the university's penetration by society. Of course, the reverse process happened as well: Society was deeply penetrated by the university, most obviously in the form of credentialism (Brown 2001).

25. Clearly we would prefer to have even longer term data. Nevertheless, we believe that the 1915–95 period was sufficiently long and captured a sufficiently critical juncture in the process of global-institutional reframing to adequately test our argument.

26. The tables do not contain statistical tests of the differences in mean values given the nonrandom nature of the sample.

27. The decline suggests why those who decry the university's ruin are so often humanists. In future work, we hope to show that, even as the formal study of the

humanities declined in the university, the entire university organization reorganized around individualized humans (e.g., in pedagogical emphases on choice, participation, and active learning, as in Robinson [2005]). See Frank and Meyer (forthcoming).

28. On geometry, see http://plato.stanford.edu/entries/geometry-19th/. On the University of Tübingen, see http://www.newadvent.org/cathen/15083a.htm. Benavot (2004) finds roughly similar patterns in comparisons of the percentage of all countries requiring instruction in core subject areas in grades 1–8 at 1985 and 2000. Fewer countries require instruction in the humanities, more countries require instruction in the natural sciences, and many more countries require instruction in the social sciences.

29. For example, see Haraway (1989) and Wagner (2003). Bertrams (2004) and Geiger (1986) discuss analogous World War I effects.

30. The expansion of the applied division in universities worldwide coincided with and complemented the global expansion of socially oriented (as opposed to professionally oriented) international nongovernmental organizations, which used science for practical social benefits. See Schofer (1999).

31. From Porter (2003:13). Brint (2002b) also finds enrollment shifts in U.S. universities from the liberal to the "practical" arts, meaning occupational and professional programs. The shift is especially pronounced in the lower status tiers of the U.S. higher education system. Benavot (2004) compares the percentage of countries requiring instruction in several applied fields in grades 1–8 at 1985 and 2000 and finds inconsistent trends. For example, fewer countries required hygiene/health education in 2000, whereas more countries required environmental science/ecology; fewer countries required vocational education/ skills in 2000, whereas more countries required technology.

32. According to Brint et al. (2005), the shift toward the "practical arts" in the United States began during the 1930s. As suggested earlier, the rise of the applied natural sciences likely originated in the nineteenth century. In 1862, the Morrill Act established the U.S. land-grant universities, with emphases on agriculture and mining. By 1880 according to *The Cambridge History of Natural Sciences*, applied chemistry had already won the upper hand over basic chemistry. Further impetus for the applied natural sciences arose in the 1920s and 1930s, during which time science was considered to hold great promise for social progress.

33. From http://www.gsb.stanford.edu/academics/catalog/mbareq.html#PE230. See Frank and Meyer (forthcoming) for a discussion of the so-called knowledge society.

34. From the 1906–07 Cape of Good Hope University Calendar.

35. For the main sample of British Commonwealth countries, our case base increases from 11 to 16 to 28 to 30 over the four time intervals. The constant-case sample has a case base of six. The all-inclusive sample's case base moves from 54 to 71 to 64 over the first three time intervals.

36. See the university's website at http://www.ntu.edu.tw. Loya and Boli (1999) provide a general discussion of world standards. The contributors to Meek et al.

(1996) offer a variety of perspectives on convergence/divergence questions in higher education.

37. See Beecher (2002).

38. See the discussion of cross-national differences among universities in Ramirez (2003). Benavot (2004) shows convergence in median yearly instructional hours overall and in mean percentage of total instructional time allocated to mathematics in primary and lower secondary schools around the world between 1985 and 2000.

39. The original data come from the UNESCO *Statistical Yearbooks*. See Drori and Moon (2005).

40. See Ramirez and Wotipka (2001:233). Geiger (2004) finds that research has expanded more rapidly than faculty in U.S. universities over recent decades. The same is likely to be true globally, although to a lesser extent given resource constraints.

CHAPTER 2

The Humanities

In Chapter 1, we used a global-institutional perspective to make sense of dramatic worldwide redistributions of academic-core emphases – among the university's three main branches of learning and between its basic and applied divisions. We argued that long-term shifts in the global-institutional frame, particularly in redefinitions of action and structure, altered the premises of reality in world society and thus the platform of assumptions upholding university activities. Over the twentieth century, this process contributed both (a) to a sharp contraction of the humanities and an equally sharp expansion of the social sciences in university emphases and (b) to a redistribution of attention from the basic to applied divisions. We continue along this same path here, narrowing our empirical gaze to the disciplinary fields within the humanities.

As in the last chapter, our agenda is two-fold. First theoretically, we seek additional tests of the merits of our argument, tying the changing premises of global reality to worldwide shifts in the university's academic priorities. Second empirically, we seek to identify and explain relative change in the standings of the humanities fields in the university over time – concerning which there is a literature rife with distress signals but one short on systematic data.

We proceed thus to investigate the changing profiles of eight basic humanities fields: classics and archaeology, philosophy, theology, linguistics and philology, art and music, Western languages and literature, history, and non-Western languages and literature. All of these fields showed relative decline during the period of study, losing faculty shares in the world's universities over time. But some fields declined much more precipitously than others, a phenomenon we explain in terms of global-institutional reframing.

Background

In content and in form, the body of university knowledge changed extensively over the twentieth century. Much that was once routinely contemplated receded from academic focus, and much that was once rarely considered rose to the fore of university inquiry. Alterations in the humanities were especially wrenching. In the 1853 Terms of Admission to Yale University, the humanities indisputably played the leading role:

> Candidates for admission to the Freshman Class are examined in Cicero's Select Orations, the whole of Virgil, Sallust, Jacobs's, Colton's or Felton's Greek Reader, the first three books of Xenophon's Anabasis, Andrews and Stoddard's or Zumpt's Latin Grammar, Sophocles's, Crosby's or Kühner's Greek Grammar, Arnold's Latin Prose Composition to the Passive voice, (first XII Chapters,) Latin Prosody, Thomson's Higher Arithmetic, English Grammar, Geography, and Day's Algebra to Quadratic Equations.[1]

Needless to say, both at Yale and elsewhere, the humanities' leadership position was steadily lost over time, eliciting clamorous denunciations – against entrenched elitisms on the one hand (i.e., the domination of the humanities by European white males) and advancing disgraces on the other (e.g., Madonna studies, hip-hop, and comic books).

> Many academics continue to adhere to a vision of scholarship which appears baffling (and at times laughable) to otherwise sober and judicious people beyond the university walls . . . The doubts are not directed at all

sectors of the academy. It is those scholars in the humanities, in departments of English, history, philosophy, modern languages and the classics who are the chief targets of complaints.[2]

Even within particular humanities fields, tales of transformation were dramatic during the twentieth century – suggesting flux throughout the domain. From classics departments, for instance, came accounts of magic and folklore being taught alongside historically oriented training in Greece and Rome. From English departments, meanwhile, arrived evidence that popular song lyrics and the diaries of everyday people were encroaching on the territories of distinguished literary texts. In language studies, similarly, arrivistes such as Swahili and Sign Language were reported to be challenging the predominance of French and German (not to mention Latin and Greek). Religious studies, in parallel, were said to be ceding territory to New Age religions, as well as to unorthodox perspectives – environmental, feminist – on the old ones. By the end of the century, it seemed safe to say that universities housed more painting and less Art, more composition and less Literature, more singing and less Music. The Great Masters, by all accounts, had fallen from sway.[3]

In general, all that was once regarded as the high culture of Western civilization seemed to have lost out to matters formerly considered marginal and plebian at the same time as scientific, contextual, practice-oriented, and postmodern methodological innovations threatened formalist studies of the traditional canon.[4] Already by 1903, Durkheim's disciple Simiand had called on historians to renounce "their habitual 'idols' – individual character, singular events, and particular facts" in order that they might "construct facts of observation in such a way that they can be integrated into series that permit the determination of regularities and formulation of laws."[5] In status, in subject, and in method, thus, the humanities were transformed.

Commentaries on these changes were many and high pitched. Their intensity derived in part from what the university, quite broadly, is – the central repository of official knowledge in society, embodying all that can and should be publicly known. But in substantial measure, the shrillness of the commentaries related to features of the humanities in particular. More so than was true in the natural or social sciences – where the discarding of old materials and the embrace of new could be treated as "progress" in the discovery of "truth" – modifications to the humanities over the twentieth century seemed tantamount to changing the distinguishing features of human identity.[6] Thus often in strident tones, advocates of humanities reforms celebrated their empowering potential, whereas resisters deplored collapsing standards.

Even with emotions agitated to the point of a culture war, however, systematic research on the place of the humanities in the university languished. This was especially true of empirical studies at the macro level – across universities, countries, and time periods. Correspondingly and in consequence, theorizations of the humanities' decline remained underdeveloped. Without data to test the prevailing ideas, explanations became mired in rhetorical swamps, bogged down by default functionalist imageries.

Of particular salience for the study at hand was the void of field-by-field information over time. In Chapter 1, we observed a striking contraction of teaching and research in the humanities as a whole, but this overall portrait obscures any interdisciplinary variability. It seems likely, after all, that global-institutional reframing bore somewhat different implications for the individual fields in the humanities, resulting in significant differences in disciplinary viability.

Field-Level Implications of Global-Institutional Reframing

Throughout this book, we argue that basic features of the global-institutional frame – its master narratives of origins and being – comprise a crucial bed of assumptions on which university activities arise. As the globally institutionalized cosmology changed over the twentieth century, continuing its move from creationist to evolutionist imageries, and as this in turn helped motivate redefinitions of action and structure in world society's taken-for-granted reality, the bases for university teaching and research changed too.

We take this general argument as a springboard into our inquiry here, using it to develop expectations about which humanities fields fared better and which worse over the period in question. Our first step is to recapitulate the core revisions in the story of being, considering especially their likely impacts on the profiles of specific humanities fields in the university. Proceeding conservatively, we articulate only what seem to be the obvious implications of global-institutional reframing.

REDEFINITION OF ACTION IN THE GLOBALLY INSTITUTIONALIZED ONTOLOGY

As the imagined roots of reality withdrew from the soils of sacred creation and extended down into rationalized evolution over the twentieth century, actorhood was relocated in the system of everyday being. In the culture and organization of world society, blanket capacities to act and to know passed down from heavenly to human hands.

In the first and more general aspect of this change, humans supplanted divinities as reality's all-purpose actors. Whereas the ultimate forces of deliberate motion long had been seen to emanate from external spiritual realms, the shift at hand increasingly reassigned them to everyday women and men. In Chapter 1, we saw this change as weakening the humanities in total. The same transition is likely to have had specific effects on four humanities fields.

Most obviously, we expect that the contraction of divine action capacities carried negative ramifications for the status of theology, which studies the nature of God and religious truth. In 2004 at the University of Birmingham, for instance, the B.A. in theology focused on Christian texts, religious thought, and ethical teachings.[7] As the redefinition of action chipped away at God's authority and presence in public life, we expect that celestial matters retreated into private realms, undercutting theological pursuits in universities. In saying this, we do not mean to suggest that theological studies shrank from the world altogether – only that they shrank from the university and other public spheres. Neither do we suppose that theology's subject matters remained entirely fixed over the whole time period (one may now, for instance, enroll in A Mathematical Approach to God at Islamia University in Pakistan); we only suppose that the changes ran up against the definitional limits of the field. For all these reasons, we expect that the global deinstitutionalization of God's divine actorhood – the raison d'être of theological studies – stripped down the taken-for-granted latticework upholding theology in the university.

For some of the same reasons, we expect that classics and archaeology suffered from the relocation of action capacities in the global-institutional frame. As humans gained legitimacy and authority to shape their day-to-day worlds, the constraining powers of the past – be it the sacred past of creation or the mundane past of history – lost their muscle. At Harvard, for example, the classics department offered "general instruction and specialized training in Greek and Latin language, literature and culture, Medieval Latin, and Byzantine and Modern Greek."[8] Under reality's emerging assumptions, such matters came to seem highly esoteric. In a world where individual actors were thought to exercise free will – the capacity of rational agents to choose a course of action from among various alternatives – the distant past was simply the distant past. Thus, we argue that the redefinition of action dimmed the horizons for classics and archaeology in the university.

At the other end of the same axis, we expect that the rise of human actorhood brought into being new assumptions that favored the prospects of art and music faculties. These fields, more so than their counterparts, embraced the human doer from their inception. Already in 1915, the degree-examination for music at Dublin University assumed skilled and able student authorities, allowing them to choose between (a) the composition of a vocal cantata or string quartet or (b) the performance of Bach or Chopin. With their built-in connections to both Great Masters and individual mastery, art and music were well postured to evolve with the times, coming increasingly to focus on the abilities of student artists. Painting, sculpture, cello, and so on cultivated the actorhood of common persons, opening doors to self-actualization. Thus in 1982, Beirut University bowed to the traditional canon with five courses in art appreciation and art history. At the same time, however, Beirut offered two courses in design, three in ceramics, two in drawing, one in graphics, four in painting, and two in sculpture.[9] In these latter venues, students played the authorial roles – they made, they created, they designed, and they built, all with authority and legitimacy. Given such room for accommodation and change, we expect the academic prospects of art and music to have held up well over time, as capacities for action vested in humans.

It seems probable that history also won staying power from the redefinition of action in globally institutionalized reality. Insofar as historical narratives took form around human actor plot lines, and insofar as the availability of such plot lines exploded with global-institutional reframing, we see history as a potential beneficiary of this vector of institutional change. This held true in part given the field's porous boundaries, which allowed the discipline to broaden its gaze over time to include everyday persons as historical subjects and objects. At the beginning of the century when human actorhood was distributed more narrowly, history revolved around the elite. The questions for the 1915 Junior Examination at Dublin University concerned the caution and frugality of Queen Elizabeth, the Revolution of 1689, and the loss of the

American colonies. By the end of the century, by contrast – with action capacities attributed even to peasants, women, and children – the cast of historical characters and the collection of historical storylines had both multiplied.[10] Given its openness to human actors of whatever designation, we argue that history was well set to ride this wave of change through the twentieth century.

In addition to carrying these four clear implications for humanities disciplines, the reinstitutionalization of reality along the action dimension carried two, we speculate, more ambivalent ones. Both Western and non-Western languages and literature likely won advantage from the expansion of human action capacities, as both fields followed art and music in making the transition from the Masters to individual mastery. In 1999 for example, the University of Chicago introduced new actor-centric courses on Writing Styles, Writing Biography, Writing Description, and Writing Criticism – far cries from the traditional paeans to Milton or Chaucer. Still in comparison to music and art, departments of language *and literature* remained definitionally tied to the canon. Although "Art" classes could address artists as easily as Artists, "Literature" classes had no such latitude. Furthermore on the downside, literature and creative writing retained ethereal airs, holding within them the marks of divine provenance. A contemporary writer put it thus: "Imaginative writing is understood to be slightly mysterious. In fact it is very mysterious. A great deal of the work gets done beneath the threshold of consciousness, without the intercession of reason."[11]

Given these mixed signals, we see the reduction of divine and the enlargement of individual action capacities as having uncertain implications for Western and non-Western languages and literature. Although the contradictory forces probably wrought predictable changes within the contents of the two fields, at the whole disciplinary level, we guess, the effects canceled each other out.

Naturally, the redefinition of action in the global-institutional frame had repercussions throughout the university beyond academic composition. As divine action capacities diminished, for example, universities gradually ceased to require moral character references from prospective students, no longer compelled enrolled students to attend religious services, and severed official ties with religious bodies. Such movements arose concomitantly with the academic reorientations that are central to our study, being derived from much the same source.

We expect that the effects suggested here deflected upward or downward the overall negative humanities trend observed in Chapter 1. In other words, we expect that the consequences of global-institutional reframing were doubly depressing for theology and classics and archaeology, with the particular field-level negatives aggravating the general slide of the branch. Meanwhile, the field-level positives of art and music and to a lesser extent Western and non-Western languages and literatures should have counterbalanced the overall humanities trend.

In addition to conferring new-found general action capacities on humans, the ontological redefinition at issue here also gave rise to a more specific set of human capabilities in the realms of knowledge. Knowledge once was assumed to be mysterious and external – held in the minds of the gods and revealed in flashes of enlightenment at their choosing. Global-institutional reframing over the twentieth century removed most remnants of this orientation and issued humans greatly increased capacities to know. In the process knowledge came to refer to actively rationalized understandings, established by and for the benefit of everyday persons, under the rubrics of scientization and rationalization. We argued in Chapter 1 that this process exerted negative pressures on the humanities overall by removing cultural authority from singular inspirations (the brushstroke of Rembrandt, the melody of Verdi) and granting it instead to reproducible facts. The authorization and legitimization of the human knower also bore implications for three particular humanities fields.

First, the reassignment of knowledge capacities likely sapped fiber from the field of philosophy. This is so because philosophy's traditional stocks in trade – the studies of ethics, logic, aesthetics, metaphysics, and epistemology – lie in nonscientized and nonrationalized zones outside of human control. Korea University's 1957 Ethics course, for instance, discussed benchmark notions of "good, right, duty, justice, and happiness" that left little room for individual action.[12] Such benchmarks set fixed ideals against which to measure human life. Philosophy (from the Greek *philosophos*, lover of wisdom) entered the university in an earlier age when contemplation pointed the way to knowledge. In an age of active human experimentation and discovery, timeless philosophical standards lost their global-institutional supports. We therefore expect that the relocation of knowledge capacities from divine to human entities siphoned off attention from university philosophy.

Second, the activation of the human knower in the premises of world society likely lent strength to linguistics and philology. This is true because to an exceptional extent among the humanities, the study of language in the university lay open to scientization – slowly evolving from cultural and historical reflections over the twentieth century toward abstract and scientific investigations. Indeed though virtually every definition of the humanities includes linguistics among its component fields, definitions of linguistics place science foremost: "the science of language," "the science which concerns itself with the origin, development, history, relationships and structure of languages," "the scientific study of language."[13] In this guise, the active human knower was taken for granted in the field. Thus in 2002, Ohio State's Introduction to Linguistics emphasized not only "understanding the questions" but also "what sorts of evidence" must be gathered to "furnish satisfying answers."[14] The embrace of scientific grounding, we speculate, well positioned linguistics and philology to stay afloat over the course of global-institutional reframing.

By the same token, we expect that the elevation of the human knower in the culture and organization of world society contributed to the ongoing stature of academic history. As in the case of linguistics and philology, history demonstrated substantial methodological flexibility during our study period, easily making room for the new investigative authorities granted humans.[15] Prevailing historical standards increasingly demanded actively processed documentation and evidence from the field's practitioners and in the process the discipline lost much of its nineteenth-century philosophical bearing. Indeed no other humanities field drifted so near to the social sciences during the twentieth century, so much so that by 1963, the Introduction to History course at the Universidad Central de Venezuela was compelled to address the discipline of "history and its differentiation from the other social sciences."[16] Accordingly, we anticipate that history gained sustenance from the appearance of human knowers in socially constructed reality, enhancing its university stature.

Of course, this baseline redefinition of action in the global-institutional frame contributed to the reconstitution of the university along many dimensions, not just academic emphases. Pedagogical best practices, for example, increasingly demanded so-called active learning techniques, in which cognitively mobilized students participated in their own educations – conventionally in discussions and labs but then also in self-assigned exercises, self-graded work, and independent studies. Newer teaching styles put students in charge of their own "learning environments," assuming that they could and should discover knowledge for themselves. In a 2003 economics course at Chulalongkorn University in Thailand, for instance, "market experiments (laboratory economics) and seminar methods" were combined in order to create a participatory/discussion environment.[17] Such changes as these – likewise emanating from the transfer of knowledge abilities from God to individual humans – reinforced those we anticipate vis-à-vis academic emphases.

As before, we suppose that these three field-level effects – negative in the case of philosophy and positive in the cases of linguistics and philology and also history – combined together with the general humanities branch-level trend to produce the observed outcomes. Philosophy, thus, probably lost relative standing in the university somewhat faster than the average humanities field, whereas linguistics and philology and history likely declined at slower-than-average rates.

REDEFINITION OF STRUCTURE IN THE GLOBALLY INSTITUTIONALIZED ONTOLOGY

As the assumed origins of reality were reestablished over the twentieth century, the default models of structure were also reconstituted. The vertical hierarchies and fixed categories characteristic of creation increasingly gave way to horizontal assemblies and dynamic networks characteristic of evolution in the global-institutional frame.

In the first aspect of this shift, horizontal assemblies replaced vertical hierarchies – meaning that cybernetic-system models gained legitimacy and authority over top-down models in the premises of world society. We argued previously that this vector of structural redefinition gradually delegitimized graded rankings and thereby decentered the Great Works that traditionally anchored the humanities, weakening the branch's place among university activities. In addition to this overall humanities effect, the structural shift at issue here seems likely to have had particular impacts on five of the humanities disciplines.

To begin, we expect that the vertical-hierarchy-to-horizontal-assembly transition struck hard at the teaching and research bases of classics and archaeology. A "classic" (from the Latin *classicus*, the first rank of Roman citizens) provides a recognized standard of excellence to which others should defer. Well into the twentieth century, the preeminent standards of human excellence were located in Ancient Greece and Rome, the imagined birthplaces of high civilization. Of thirty-three classics courses at the University of Adelaide in 1986, for example, only two ventured beyond Greece and Rome.[18] The cultural hierarchy implicit in such a course distribution – and in the posturing of the field generally – became increasingly suspect with structural redefinition, deflating the prospects of classics and archaeology in the world's universities over time.

Along similar lines, structural redefinition in the global-institutional frame most likely weakened the body of assumptions propping up Western languages and literature. As long as the concept of superiority itself retained legitimacy, Western culture could be held as exemplary over others. As the notion of superiority was shredded, however, cultures were rendered into more equal companies. Thus even within the field of Western languages and literature the older structural models were replaced: By 2002, the Shakespeare offerings at the National University of Singapore had been joined by courses on postindependence literature and on postmodernism and postcoloniality.[19] Thus, with the decline of the vertical hierarchy as world society's default structural template, we expect that Western languages and literature lost some of their special charisma on the world stage, subsiding among academic priorities.

On the other end of this same teeter-totter, the re-institutionalization of reality in horizontal-assembly terms should have brought new-found attention to non-Western languages and literature. Here is the opposite of the previous effect. Horizontalization extended the figurative suffrage, such that formerly disenfranchised (i.e., non-Western) groups gained cultural standing in the university, coming to count more equally with Western groups. Multiculturalism was born. Already in 1967 the University of Liberia offered not only Beowulf and Shakespeare but also World Literature and African Literature, the latter making special efforts to "introduce works of Liberian authors."[20] By spreading authority and legitimacy to an expanding array of entities, the rise of horizontal-assembly structures in the framework of reality should have lifted university studies in non-Western languages and literature.

Additionally, we anticipate a dampening effect from this reconceptualization of structure on teaching and research in philosophy. Inasmuch as that discipline bended its knee to the Great Thoughts of Great Men through-out the twentieth century, vertical-to-horizontal restructuring should have undermined its place in the university. Even in 2005 at the University of Melbourne, Australia, a course entitled Moral Philosophy: Great Thinkers involved a "critical study of three of the classic works of moral philosophy: Aristotle's *Nicomachean Ethics*, Kant's *Groundwork of the Metaphysic of Morals*, and Mill's *Utilitarianism*. Students should acquire the competence and un-derstanding necessary to engage profitably with three of the most significant and influential texts in moral philosophy, and to appreciate what is distinc-tive and of abiding interest in these texts."[21] In the horizontal assembly, all thoughts – as all humans – are created as equals. Thus, we expect philosophy to recede among university priorities concomitant with this change in reality.

Theology, too, should have contracted in the academic core as the au-thority and legitimacy accorded vertical hierarchies disappeared over the time period. To worship – i.e., to honor with praise and devotion– is anti-thetical to the horizontal assembly. To deify – i.e., to exalt to the position of God – is directly opposed to the flattened community. Even the basic no-tion of God – a perfect, omnipotent, and omniscient supernatural being – runs flatly counter to the leveled congregation. These notions, all basic to theological studies, lost favor in world society, and thus we speculate that theology will have withdrawn from university prominence.

Finally, the ontological remolding of vertical hierarchies into horizontal assemblies likely worsened the prospects of art and music, which retained substantial holdings, as previously mentioned, in the stocks of Old Masters. Even the most professionally oriented programs – explicitly aimed at turning out painters, sculptors, violinists, composers, and so on – continued to devote substantial shares of their curricula to the singularly inspiring works of the likes of Monet and Picasso, Handel and Mozart. As relativized notions of talent, vision, accomplishment, and genius increasingly predominated in the culture and organization of world society, we expect art and music to have diminished in the academic core accordingly.

Needless to say, the restructuring of reality under discussion here carried implications for many aspects of the university, well beyond academic pri-orities. As horizontal models of structure diffused throughout society, for instance, many formerly excluded groups gained admittance to universities. Thus over the twentieth century, male and female enrollments moved rapidly toward parity around the world, even in the traditionally male-dominated fields in engineering and the hard sciences.[22] Changes of this nature complemented those underway in the body of knowledge, installing horizontal assemblies throughout the university.

As above, we expect that the specific field-level effects posited here combine with the general branch-level trend shown previously to yield each field's trajectory over time. For non-Western languages and literature, the field-level positive should have softened the overall humanities fall. By contrast for all the other five disciplines, the field-level negatives should have exacerbated the general humanities decline.

In the second aspect of structural redefinition, fixed categories were reconfigured into dynamic networks in the globally institutionalized ontology. Under the old assumptions – as in the sacred creation – reality's features were seen to fall into bounded domains, with established characteristics and preordained places. By contrast under the new assumptions – as in rationalized evolution – reality's order was reconceived into contingent and fluid webs of interrelationships. In Chapter 1, we argued that this dimension of global-institutional reframing threatened the humanities as a whole by melting away the boundaries granting special distinctions to humans and their culture. In addition to this general humanities effect, we see three field-level effects suggested in the fixed-categorical-to-dynamic-network reconfiguration.

In the first place, this shift in the baseline structural templates available in world society likely drew away emphasis from classics and archaeology, as the static boundaries traditionally demarcating the classical from the common and civilization from savagery came to be seen as malleable and permeable. By the time the Classics Department at the University of Wales diversified its course offerings in 2005 to include, for example, women in the ancient East and astrology in the ancient world, the battle for the old order had mostly been lost.[23]

In the second place, the fixed-category-to-dynamic-network structural change probably carried liabilities for linguistics and philology, justifications for which hinged on (a) the notion that different languages fixed categorical boundaries among groups of peoples and (b) the idea that the very capacity for language permanently separated humans from other animals. Recently of course, advanced communication capacities have been assigned to any number of species, from whales to ants and bees. Thus, we see perils for the study of linguistics and philology with the redefinition of the root structures of reality.

And finally third, the rise of dynamic-network models of structure in world society seems likely to have borne positive consequences for the field of history, the hallmark task of which is to recount stories of change among interlaced entities. Whether the topic was sixteenth- and seventeenth-century England under the Tudors and Stuarts or slave rebellions and uprisings in the pre-Civil War United States, historians over the twentieth century assumed the primary importance of an evolving and interacting world. Thus, as dynamic networks took root in the global-institutional frame, we expect that benefits redounded to history as a discipline.

Needless to say, this basic structural transformation can be related to many additional developments in the university during the time period, beyond the rearrangement of teaching and research priorities. One striking expression of the disappearing categorical order took form in the abolition of the fixed university curriculum – such that all students took the same courses – and the proliferation of electives (first introduced into the curriculum in the 1870s by Charles Eliot at Harvard).[24] The classical curriculum of old, with rigidly sequenced courses and tightly specified contents, gave way over the twentieth century to curricula that by nature were more varied, flexible, and interdisciplinary. Alterations of this sort accompanied faculty recomposition hand in hand.

In Figure 1, we pull together and summarize our guiding ideas concerning the university humanities. Recapitulating broadly, we argue that shifts in the globally institutionalized cosmology combined with shifts in the globally institutionalized ontology – i.e., in definitions of action and structure – to broadly repackage reality's undergirding premises, buoying the prospects of fields with more compatible assumptions while weighting down fields with less compatible assumptions. On both the action and structure fronts, we speculate that global-institutional reframing carried negative implications for classics and archaeology, philosophy, and theology: These fields should have lost the most relative standing in the university over the twentieth century. In contrast, on both the action and structure fronts, we see the reorientation of reality as bearing positive consequences for history – this discipline should have had the strongest of showings. As regards the other disciplines, our expectations are more mixed. Western languages and literature should fall

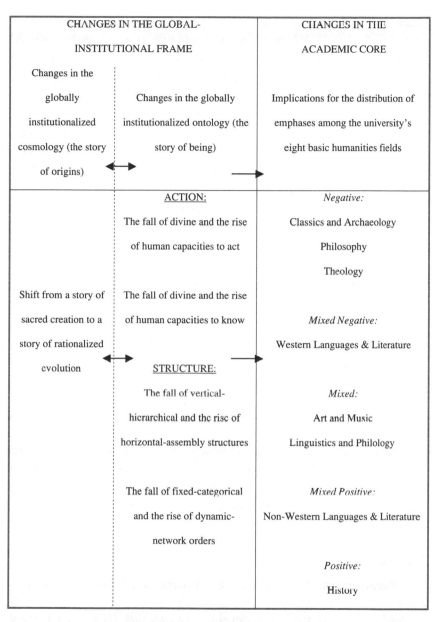

CHANGES IN THE GLOBAL-INSTITUTIONAL FRAME		CHANGES IN THE ACADEMIC CORE
Changes in the globally institutionalized cosmology (the story of origins)	Changes in the globally institutionalized ontology (the story of being)	Implications for the distribution of emphases among the university's eight basic humanities fields
Shift from a story of sacred creation to a story of rationalized evolution	ACTION: The fall of divine and the rise of human capacities to act	*Negative:* Classics and Archaeology Philosophy Theology
	The fall of divine and the rise of human capacities to know	*Mixed Negative:* Western Languages & Literature
	STRUCTURE: The fall of vertical-hierarchical and the rise of horizontal-assembly structures	*Mixed:* Art and Music Linguistics and Philology
	The fall of fixed-categorical and the rise of dynamic-network orders	*Mixed Positive:* Non-Western Languages & Literature
		Positive: History

Figure 1 Summary of argument and implications for the eight basic humanities fields.

on the lower end of the spectrum, having a neutral action effect and a negative structure effect. Non-Western languages and literature, meanwhile, should show the opposite result, having a neutral action effect and a positive structure effect. Linguistics and philology, and art and music, should fall right in the middle, having positive action but negative structure effects.

Of course, other theorists might set different odds on the various humanities fields over time. Were one, for example, to extrapolate from arguments hanging the humanities' ills on the neck of postmodernism, one might predict some of the worst outcomes for language and literature programs – both Western and non-Western. These disciplines arguably were hardest hit by subjectivism and fragmentation. Alternatively, were one to infer guidelines from those analysts who place globalization at the heart of the humanities' enervation, one might pick out history as the most susceptible to collapse, given its close disciplinary relationship with the imploding nation-state.

We emphasize that in many cases such forces collude and overlap with those inherent in global-institutional reframing. For instance where postmodernists see subjectivism and fragmentation, we place, respectively, the new-found authority of human actors and the demise of categorical orders. And what globalization theorists call nation-state implosion, we conceive of as the intensification of horizontal networks.[25] Of course, not all theories can or should be embraced within the arms of our own. We simply call attention here to theoretical common ground that might not otherwise be obvious.

Thus, we find before us the obvious questions: How well do our arguments stand up to empirical scrutiny? Do longitudinal and cross-national data on the composition of university faculty show changes in the humanities fields commensurate with our global-institutional imageries? We address these issues now.

Faculty Composition among the Basic Humanities Fields over Time

As in Chapter 1, we use data from the *Commonwealth Universities Yearbook* to document changes in the academic emphases of universities. The data present, for the growing number of independent British Commonwealth countries, the percentages of total university faculty employed in each of the eight basic humanities fields. Against the backdrop of a strong downward trend in the humanities overall, we foresee patterned global variations in the rates at which specific disciplinary fields endure in the university over the century. The assumptions of some humanities fields render them especially vulnerable to the vicissitudes of global-institutional reframing, whereas others seem better positioned to ride out the ontological storms. We investigate the field-level outcomes in Tables 1 and 2 and in Figures 2–4.

To begin, the first two columns of Table 1 show the relative percentages of university faculty engaged in each of our basic fields in the first and fourth time periods (1915–35 and 1975–95). Then in the third column, Table 1 offers a gauge of each discipline's century-long staying power; that is, the percentage change in its representation from first interval to last.

The initial observation concerning the data is a general one. Across the board, the disciplinary trajectories move in the downward direction. Not one of the humanities fields received heightened relative emphasis over the twentieth century; every one lost strength. Thus, it was not only the humanities overall but also each of its component fields that declined in the university through time. The negative consequences of global-institutional reframing appear to have been powerful and far-reaching.

Table 1   Percentage of Total Faculty in Each of the Eight Basic Humanities Fields for Universities in British Commonwealth Countries

	Faculty Percentage in 1915–35	Faculty Percentage in 1975–95	Percentage Change Over Time
Fields losing more than half their original shares			
Classics and Archaeology	4.5	0.6	−87
Philosophy	2.8	0.8	−71
Theology	4.3	1.7	−60
Fields losing about one-third of their original shares			
Art and Music	1.3	0.8	−38
Linguistics and Philology	0.8	0.5	−37
Western Languages and Literature	7.3	4.7	−36
Fields losing less than one-sixth of their original shares			
History	3.5	3.0	−14
Non-Western Languages and Literatures	2.3	2.0	−13

Nevertheless, the percentage losses varied greatly from discipline to discipline, from a high of 87 to a low of 13. At the bottom of the heap, with the largest reduction in relative prominence, was classics and archaeology, which hemorrhaged an enormous 87 percent of its original faculty share over the interval. This means that in the latest of the four time periods, the average percentage of university faculty performing teaching and research in classics and archaeology was little more than one-tenth what it was in the earliest period. Classics and archaeology, oriented primarily to the study of ancient Western civilizations, migrated to the remote periphery of the university knowledge system over these decades. Arguably, the decline occurred as the categorical hierarchies that go so far in defining classics and archaeology fell into noncompliance with global-institutional standards.[26]

Second among the sinkers was philosophy, which lost 71 percent of its average faculty share across our sample of British Commonwealth countries. Research and teaching in philosophy – the study of logic and reason within human (and especially Western) thought – slipped rapidly toward the margins of the university project over the twentieth century. From our perspective, the diminution followed from (a) the institutionalization of human action capacities over knowledge, which depleted the authority and legitimacy of philosophical dicta, and (b) the deinstitutionalization of vertical hierarchies, which fractured the pillars upholding the canon of Great Thinkers.

Not quite as sharp was the decline of theology, which gave up 60 percent of its former faculty presence. The study of God and religious thought receded toward the background of the academic core over the decades in question, leaving theology a comparatively minor university player. Possibly the field's deteriorating status was brought on by the redefinition of action that lowered God's presence in public life and by the redefinition of structure that delegitimated vertical hierarchies.[27]

All three of these disciplinary fields – classics and archaeology, philosophy, and theology – lost more than half their relative shares in the body of university knowledge during our period of study. And all three of the fields are fingered by our theoretical framework as having the weakest prospects over the twentieth century.

The next three humanities fields survived somewhat better, though their contractions were nevertheless striking. Each lost about one-third of its faculty prominence during the twentieth century. First among these stood art and music, which in the latest time interval occupied 38 percent fewer faculty than it did in the earliest. The decline was substantial if less eviscerating than those seen above. In one direction, art and music may have suffered from ongoing devotions to artistic Masters, who rest atop hierarchies deposed by global-institutional reframing. In the other direction, art and music probably benefited from reorientations around individual artistic practice, which promised to extend the range of human creativity. Indeed in a supplementary subdisciplinary coding, we separated the art and music faculty devoted to student practitioners from other art and music faculty. The former increased dramatically in proportional representation over the century. This finding is especially noteworthy in light of the across-the-board declines in the humanities' profiles. Together the counterbalancing Masters/mastery effects may have contributed to the comparatively moderate loss of standing registered by art and music over the time interval.

Next we find linguistics and philology, encompassing both more cultural and more scientific studies of language. This field shed 37 percent of its original faculty presence – another moderate outcome in view of the larger picture. Possibly on the one hand the prospects for linguistics and philology lifted upward when scientific additions to the methodological quiver increased the compatibility of language studies with expanded human action capacities. Possibly on the other hand the field suffered from its decaying assertion that language demarcates categorical boundaries between and around human beings.

Following thereafter we observe the contraction of modern Western languages and literature. The relative percentage of university faculty working in this disciplinary field decreased 36 percent over the period in question. Mainly focused on what are supposed to be cultural high points of the world's high civilization – the great languages, the pinnacles of literature – this field declined among the priorities of British Commonwealth universities but did not collapse. On the downside, the field may have been hurt by its commitment to canonical hierarchies, which form the very essence of literature.

The order of appearance here is not exactly what we anticipated for these three disciplines. We thought Western languages and literature would end up to be the weakest of the three – opposite where it is. In fact, what the results show is an exceptionally tight cluster of fields, equidistant from the hardest hit and least affected humanities fields. Again as previously emphasized, we do not suppose that our global-institutional variables operate in isolation from other causal forces. Perhaps, for example, Western languages and literature fared slightly better than we anticipated because of the growing importance of English as the world lingua franca.

Least dramatic of all were the outcomes for the two remaining humanities fields, both of which lost less than one-sixth of their starting faculty shares. History, which narrates the stories of nation-states and modern societies, showed quite a bit of staying power, declining just 14 percent over the twentieth century. The field's endurance may be owed in part (a) to the disciplinary credence it paid to the activated human as the propeller of social change and to its embrace of scientific methods, granting humans more rationalized control over knowledge production, and (b) to the articulation of its assumptions about social structure with emerging dynamic-network models in world society.

And finally with the best showing of all was the discipline of modern non-Western languages and literature, which draws attention to the oral and literary cultures of many formerly "peripheral" peoples of the world. This discipline showed more perseverance than any other humanities field, losing just 13 percent of its original faculty share. Perhaps the discipline derived strength from the rearrangement of reality into horizontal assemblies, which carried cultural authority and legitimacy to the (non-Western) corners of the Earth, spurring teaching and research in kind.

These last two disciplinary fields declined in prominence along with the rest of the humanities, but they exhibited a good deal more resilience than their brethren. And although we expected history and non-Western languages and literature to have the strongest showings among the humanities fields, we predicted the reverse order (although again here the percentage changes are virtually indistinguishable). Perhaps history's portability – applicable to every society everywhere – accounts for its slightly stronger-than-expected showing in our data.

Lest the trees obscure the forest, we recall here our main argument. We believe that the teaching and research emphases of universities are constituted in part of basic cultural materials – globally institutionalized stories of origins and being. With the long-term shift in the globally institutionalized cosmology – from sacred creation to rationalized evolution – came redefinitions of action and structure in the globally institutionalized ontology. These

Table 2   Number of Universities in Sample with No
Faculty by Disciplinary Field, 1986–95 (n = 28)

History	I
Modern Western Languages and Literatures	4
Modern Non-Western Languages and Literatures	9
Theology	11
Art and Music	14
Philosophy	14
Linguistics and Philology	15
Classics and Archaeology	18

changes in turn reframed the assumed reality in which academic emphases
took form, lending support to some disciplinary pursuits while withdrawing
it from others. The evidence detailed above shows a redistribution of emphases among the university humanities that is largely consistent with our
expectations: As anticipated, we witness the sharpest drop-offs in classics and
archaeology, philosophy, and theology, and as anticipated, we witness the
gentlest falls in history and non-Western languages and literature.

The results in Table 1 are strongly supported in Table 2, which shows the
total number of universities in our sample without any faculty representation in each of the eight basic humanities fields during the final decade of our
study, 1986–95. As our framework would predict, the fields of history and
non-Western languages and literature are the most prevalent, appearing in
the great majority of sampled universities. And also as our framework would
predict, the fields of philosophy and classics and archaeology are poorly represented, appearing in half or fewer of the sampled universities. Theology is
a little more common than we anticipated, perhaps reflecting the university's
medieval religious heritage. Linguistics and philology departments, meanwhile, are slightly less common that we expected, although the total number
of universities in our sample without any linguists or philologists increased
by just one 1986–95 decade. That is the best showing among the humanities
fields and contrasts at the other extreme with philosophy: The number of
universities without philosophy departments increased by seven. Overall, the
findings in Table 2 are broadly consistent with our expectations.

Figures 2–4 add a degree of nuance to the empirical picture presented in
Table 1. With four time points instead of the two, the figures reveal that our

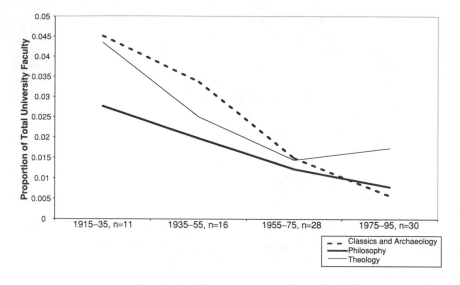

Figure 2 Humanities fields losing more than half their faculty share from 1915 to 1995.

eight humanities fields followed slightly different trajectories of decline over the twentieth century. Some fell earlier, others fell later, and some trailed off after early-century gains.

Figure 2 presents the three humanities fields that lost more than half their original faculty shares over the century. Two trend-lines in the figure – for classics and archaeology and for philosophy – show fairly steady reductions over time. Theology, however, shows a different pattern: a steep decline from the first through the third periods followed by a slight resurgence from the third to the fourth. If the withdrawal of divine actorhood spelled theology's long-term fall, the recent opening of the discipline to horizontal-assembly models of structure – with courses in Islam, feminism, etc. – may explain its minor revival.[28]

Figure 3 presents the three humanities fields that lost about one-third of their relative holdings over time. The figure shows that modern Western languages and literature, the topmost line, experienced a small surge between 1915–35 and 1936–55 before beginning its downfall. As long as it lasted, colonialism probably nurtured the study of Western culture, before a spate of mid-century independence movements (part and parcel of the restructuring of reality around horizontal assemblies) precipitated disciplinary contraction.

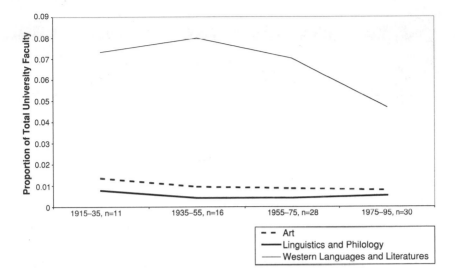

Figure 3 Humanities fields losing about a third their faculty share from 1915 to 1995.

The trajectory of art and music, for its part, floated steadily downward. And the trend in linguistics and philology headed downward across the first three periods, before showing a small up-tick at the end – arguably as more abstracted, universalized, and scientific understandings infused the older, more cultural study of language.

Continuing in this vein, Figure 4 shows the two most enduring humanities fields, which lost less than one-sixth of their original faculty shares over the interval. First, we see that history enjoyed a substantial relative expansion from the first through the third time periods before then falling off sharply. It may be that history's association with the nation-state – its traditional subject matter – was a growing liability toward century's end. (In Chapter 5, we explore such issues in detail in analyses of changes in the subject matters of history over the twentieth century.) Meanwhile, the field of non-Western languages and literature exhibited just the opposite pattern, with a long period of decline followed by recent resurgence. Here one sees roughly the mirror image of the trend-line for Western languages and literature, and perhaps for mirror-image reasons. Once the territories of the former periphery gained footholds in world society – in the course of structural horizontalization – their cultural materials gained standing in universities as well.

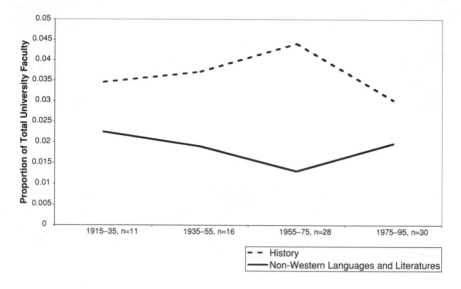

Figure 4   Humanities fields losing less than a sixth their faculty share from 1915 to 1995.

Thus, although the university humanities experienced all-encompassing deterioration over the twentieth century, there was substantial variation in both the severity and timing of descent by field. Our explanatory framework, hinging on changes in globally institutionalized reality, provides one toolkit for making sense of the disciplinary differences.[29]

Conclusion

From the perspective of the wailing wall, where the critics of the contemporary university often gather, the results presented in this chapter surely provide a new and darkly hued window onto the ruins of academe. There is no question but that the humanities beat a hasty retreat from the university over the twentieth century, and there is no question but that their departure left the university's academic core in substantially altered form. But hand wringing over the outcome, no matter how sincere, inhibits sober analysis of the university's reconstruction. Why – beyond rising philistinism – did the humanities decline among the priorities of the university knowledge system during our period of study? And why did some humanities fields decline so much more precipitously on a worldwide basis than others?

It is these questions we take up, with data on faculty composition and a broad explanatory framework. We argue that the body of university knowledge rests on the dynamic platforms of taken-for-granted reality – a globally institutionalized cosmology and a globally institutionalized ontology.[30] The humanities disciplines that were least vulnerable to reality's reframing were the ones that shared and were positioned to embrace compatible action-and-structure assumptions with the rising global-institutional frame. By contrast, the fields most exposed to hazards were the ones most tightly wedded – by disciplinary definition – to models of action and structure delegitimized and deauthorized by institutional change.

The findings here underscore the shortcomings of standard functionalist explanations of change in the academic core. Few such explanations would predict global trends of any sort, given their tendency to privilege local actors as the wellsprings of change. Few furthermore would see the connections underlying change in the various disciplines, again given their preference for case studies that only address single knowledge domains. Finally few of the standard functionalist accounts would grant any causal role to an evolving globally institutionalized frame, given the relative invisibility of these factors in local circumstances, where they tend to be upstaged by immediate needs and interests.

Thus in at least three ways, the findings reported above demonstrate the utility of a global-institutional approach to the university's ongoing reconstruction. In the first place, the data show unequivocally that vis-à-vis the basic humanities fields there are striking transnational trends in the teaching and research activities of universities. Although much of the literature gives pride of place to more local explanatory factors – national, university, and departmental level – the data we summarize strongly suggest that the academic priorities of universities also have significant global antecedents. This does not mean that local factors may be discounted altogether; it does mean that world-level factors should be considered along with them.

In the second place, the results from this chapter suggest the benefits of analyzing the humanities' fates in the university over time not as stand-alone phenomena but rather as components of an interconnected body of university knowledge – the whole of which is subject to global-institutional reforms. Although some unique variables certainly play into each discipline's rise and fall (e.g., history may carry on with relative success because the field is effectively marketed as a professional school prep degree), all such factors seem to be embedded within evolving world cultural models of reality.

Finally in the third place, the findings presented here illustrate the advantages of treating the global-institutional frame – specified in models of action and structure – as a constitutive factor in the body of university knowledge. Although power and domination, both economic and political, play all too certain roles in promoting revisions to the academic core, so too do the changing assumptions about reality, written into the cultural and organizational foundations of world society.

On this last point, of course, our case remains more plausible than proved. Still, the weight of supportive evidence is accumulating. In regard to the three main branches of learning, the university's basic and applied divisions, and now also the eight basic humanities fields, global-institutional reframing provides a dependable, parsimonious, and broad-ranging guide to rearrangements in the university's emphases.

From the humanities fields we now turn to the various social sciences in the university. In the course of explicating their developments over the twentieth century, we continue to hew closely to our two primary goals – to empirically document alterations in academic priorities and to further test the merits of the proposed theoretical perspective.

Notes

1. From the 1853–54 Yale College Catalogue of the Officers and Students.
2. From Botton (1999:19).
3. On the classics, see C. Smith (2000). An analysis of course offerings for English majors at twenty-five top liberal-arts colleges in the United States found that between 1964 and 2000, "Chaucer, Milton, Keats, Donne, Byron, and Pope, all [saw] their market shares plummet by 50 percent or more" (Eakin 1999:25).
4. See Abrams (1997).
5. See Revel (2003:393) on the relationship of history to the social sciences.
6. See Readings (1996).
7. See the university's website at http://www.theology.bham.ac.uk/undergrad/theology/. "Theology was once the keystone of the sciences. It lost its position during

the scientific revolution that began about 500 years ago. While the new mathematical, empirical and critical methods set off the explosion of knowledge that still engulfs us, the theologians were left behind." From http://www.naturaltheology.net/.

8. From http://www.fas.harvard.edu/~classics/.

9. See the 1982–84 Beirut University Catalog.

10. See the 1914–15 Dublin University Calendar. Wong (2004) demonstrates this dispersion of actorhood in a comparative analysis of the contents of history textbooks from China, Taiwan, and Hong Kong.

11. From Amis (2002:15).

12. See the 1957–58 Korea University Bulletin. Though the usage is now obsolete, "philosophy" once referred to the branch of knowledge dealing with the occult, magic, and alchemy. Of course, philosophy experienced some within-field change over the century, attempting to "shake off the stale air of academia" to render philosophy as "a practical resource in everyday life" (Lara 2004).

13. See http://www.google.com/search?hl=en&lr=&oi=defmore&q=define: linguistics for the definitions.

14. See http://www.ling.ohio-state.edu/courses/course_info/?course_no=601 for the course description.

15. The hybrid humanities/social sciences nature of history and linguistics is embodied in the fact that both appear not only in the Arts and Humanities but also in the Social Science Citation Index databases.

16. See the 1963–64 Universidad Central de Venezuela Catalogo de Cursos. On the changing character of history, see Revel (2003); Frank, Schofer, and Torres (1994); Frank et al. (2000); and Wong (2004).

17. From the course syllabus, posted at http://www.gsid.nagoya-u.ac.jp/sotsubo/MABE_GDM_2003.html. See also Braxton, Milem, and Sullivan (2000); Kuh, Pace, and Vesper (1997); and McEneaney (2003).

18. See the 1986–87 University of Adelaide Calendar.

19. See http://www.fas.nus.edu.sg/ell/mod_LIT_2002.htm.

20. See the 1967–68 University of Liberia Catalog and Announcements.

21. See http://www.unimelb.edu.au/HB/1999/subjects/161-007.html.

22. For example, see Ramirez and Wotipka (2001).

23. See the 2005 course listings at http://www.lamp.ac.uk/classics/undergrad.htm.

24. See Robinson (2005) on the twentieth-century rise of electives in the United States. Benavot (2004) finds a worldwide proliferation of electives between the 1980s and 2000s even at the primary-school level.

25. The contributors to Kernan (1997) largely follow the postmodern line on the decline of the humanities, whereas Szeman (2003) emphasizes globalization.

26. It bears repeating that the discussion here is of relative shares. Given the university's twentieth-century expansion, a department easily could have grown from ten to twenty members over the period and still have lost relative standing.

27. Theology's decline was almost certainly inaugurated earlier, at least in the nineteenth century. At Williams College, for instance, the number of library books on religion grew at a slower rate than books in general from 1872–75. See http://www.williams.edu/resources/sciencecenter/center/HistScioo/chapter1.html. Benavot (2004) finds analogous declines in the proportion of countries requiring instruction in religion and moral education between the 1980s and 2000s in grades 1 through 8. Cf. Reuben (1996) on the place of God in U.S. universities.

28. Theology has also adopted a more applied dimension. "Once a largely forgotten factor in social research, dismissed by those who believed that society would inevitably secularize and cast spirituality aside, religion is now a hot field of inquiry. . . . The bustling Center for Religion and Civic Culture at USC is a leading player in the new research efforts. Scholars there have examined religion's effects on health care, welfare, immigration and urban development" (Watanabe 2000).

29. Beyond the global trends on which we concentrate, there are undoubtedly interesting cross-national variations in the emphases accorded various humanities fields. For instance, one might expect philosophy to survive better in the European core or in religiously affiliated universities. Although we find these issues intriguing, we restrict our focus here to the world level, where the least empirical and theoretical work has been done.

30. This general argument extends Kuhn's (1962) central insight on the link between consensus and knowledge. Here we shift attention from scientific consensus to taken-for-granted reality.

CHAPTER 3

The Social Sciences

In Chapter 2, we demonstrated the ways that a global-institutional perspective sheds light on worldwide trends in the composition of university humanities faculties. We explained variations in the downward trajectories of eight humanities fields in terms of the changing global-institutional frame: shifts in the blueprints of action and structure struck hard at the foundations of classics and archaeology, philosophy, and theology even while they provided some relief to history and non-Western languages and literature. In this chapter, we continue along this same course, reorienting our gaze onto the basic disciplinary fields encompassed by the social sciences.

Our two-fold agenda remains as before. We aspire to evaluate further our theoretical argument, relating broad redistributions of university emphases to shifts in globally institutionalized reality. And we aspire to describe and analyze the flux within one particular knowledge domain over the twentieth century, here the social sciences.

Abstractly, the problem at hand is directly analogous to that considered in Chapter 2: The overall upward trend in the social sciences at the branch-of-learning level was not shared equally across its component parts, begging some account of the field-to-field variations. Practically, though, the problem is altogether different: Change in the social science fields resulted in relative expansion over the twentieth century. It thus provoked none of the hue and cry associated with movements in the humanities. On the contrary, the rise of the social sciences has been largely unnoticed by analysts, being at most quietly celebrated for bringing tools of observation, identification, description, experimentation, investigation, and theoretical explanation to bear on the study of society.

We begin the chapter by revisiting the global-institutional frame shifts that motivate our story, drawing out their implications for the six basic social science fields: sociology, geography, political science, economics, anthropology, and psychology. Over the twentieth century, we contend, redefinitions of action and structure established conditions more favorable to some of these fields than to others. To assess the argument's merits, we then present world-level descriptive data on the relative emphasis accorded each of the university social sciences from 1915 to 1995. Variations in rates of ascendance – which were quite extreme from field to field – are well illuminated by our global-institutional perspective.

Background

The entire body of university knowledge metamorphosed over the twentieth century, moving into many previously excluded domains of inquiry and pulling away from once prominent others. Among the new domains, perhaps none grew so much as the social sciences, which ended the period at the top-most end of the university's teaching and research agenda, having begun it, at best, on the distant margins.

Indeed, the social sciences took form in the university quite late relative to the other two branches of learning, owing largely to the fact that the social sciences' direct object of study – rationalized society – was scarcely conceivable before the modern era.[1] Under the old reality regime, it had not been obvious that the sum of human relations coalesced into an integrated entity, ruled by knowable laws, the investigation of which did not skirt dangerously close to zones guarded by the gods. Thus, the social sciences remained unrealized – outside the body of authorized and legitimized public knowledge.

By the end of the nineteenth century, however, the binding ties on the social sciences had loosened considerably.[2] The redefinitions of action and structure at the heart of our story had altered the global-institutional frame in ways that unblocked avenues leading toward the imagination of rationalized society – a manageable entity, open and amenable to scientific inquiry. At first slowly and then with increasing vengeance, the new "social sciences" appeared and gelled into university disciplines, becoming manifest throughout the world's universities. The fields coalesced around what were conceived to be modern society's defining entities and processes – public governance and order (political science), social prosperity and development (economics), society's relationship with nature (geography), modern and traditional social forms (sociology and anthropology), and the individual elements of society (psychology). All of these emerging fields shared a platform of common conceits, all of which were once regarded as hubris – that ordinary humans could discern and manipulate the rational scientific laws governing the abstract entity "society" in order to advance the common good. Such ideas were given their earliest formulations in the 1800s by Comte, Mill, and others, as reviewed in the Introduction. Their increasing plausibility in world society over time occurred in the course of global-institutional reframing, which thus granted authority and legitimacy to the university social sciences.

From the purview of the present, the social sciences' rise and institutionalization – no matter how rapid or deep – seems unproblematic and obvious, and thus it is largely invisible. Although many university denizens would guess correctly that economics and psychology, say, both exploded in prominence over the twentieth century, few would guess correctly that during the same period the addition of the social sciences comprised the university's single biggest curricular transformation. In retrospect, the social sciences' explosions appear as matters of fact, necessitating no query or investigation.

In part this is true because the branch's founding ideology contains an account of its own growth. The social sciences stemmed out of "the certainty of human perfectibility based on the ability to manipulate social relations." Their strength in the university thus increased because the social sciences met the needs of modern society, promising to enhance progress and justice for all.[3] "Liberal elites first formulated the social sciences in the late eighteenth century and . . . played a central role in sustaining these studies through the nineteenth century and establishing them as disciplines. Members of educated social strata, they embraced the Enlightenment ideal of modernity as a progressive and culminating stage in human history, grounded in individual liberty and guided by scientific social knowledge."[4]

For several reasons, however, such a prepackaged account of the expansion of the social science fields may be unsatisfying. At least, one may be struck by the paucity of empirical evidence for the account's core claim regarding collective goods or functional utilities. Whether the beneficiary is conceived to be society at large or some powerful segment thereof, it is difficult to pin down exactly which tangible goods have been delivered by the social science fields (world peace? improved health care? better wages?). The disciplines themselves suffer occasional crises of confidence, engaging in bouts of soul searching over their public payouts.[5] Whatever goods the social sciences claim to deliver, they are extremely diffuse in character and much easier to state rhetorically than to measure empirically. Thus, in terms of explaining the rise of the university's social science disciplines, the self-proclaimed functionalist imageries stand on tremulous ground.

We therefore offer an alternative approach to the social sciences' ascending presence in the university's academic core. In Chapter 1, we suggested that twentieth-century shifts in the global-institutional frame altered the premises of reality, reestablishing the subterranean foundations of university knowledge in ways that enabled the rise of the social sciences overall. Indeed as a whole, this branch of learning exhibited magnificent growth over the time period. But not each of the social science disciplinary fields flourished equally well. Some social sciences seem to have rocketed into world society, becoming university mainstays overnight. Others seem to have meandered more slowly and globalized less thoroughly during the century in question. It is this appearance of field-to-field differentiation that orients the present inquiry. Which fields benefited the most from the redefinitions of action and structure in global reality? And which fields benefited least? With these questions in our crosshairs, we proceed to detail our argument.

Argument

From our perspective, the facts, laws, and principles by which reality is conceived to come into existence (the cosmology) and also to operate (the ontology) make up a global-institutional frame, changes in which alter the knowable entities, relevant processes, and meaningful relationships that provide essential grist to university mills. The reframing of reality, in other words, fundamentally alters what can and should be covered by the body of university knowledge.

The task at hand is to apply this broad argument to the basic social science fields, focusing on the disciplines most common in our data sources.[6] Our strategy is to review very briefly the redefinitions of action and structure that anchor our argument and simultaneously to draw out their implications for the emphases accorded the various social science fields worldwide. As in previous chapters, we discuss only what seem likely to be the strongest ties from global-institutional reframing to the various disciplinary fields.

Redefinition of Action in the Globally Institutionalized Ontology

As the globally institutionalized cosmology changed over the modern period, remastering reality's origins from sacred creation to rationalized evolution, two reconceptualizations of action came in accompaniment. In the cultural scripts and organizational rules of world society, humans gained both expanded capacities to act and to know.

Taking the more general of these two first, humans gained expanded capacities to act over the twentieth century – i.e., to self-consciously cause intended effects – as divinities lost the very same. Over matters great and small, humans won imagined sovereignty from the gods, extending the rationalized tendrils of human management into formerly sacred domains. We argued earlier that such changes raised the possibility of "society" (a human collectivity able to specify its own ends and to manage the means to achieve them), giving impetus to the social sciences at large. The same changes also seem likely to have carried particular implications for four of our social science fields.

In the first place, we expect that the rise of human actorhood bode well for the field of economics by making sense of the "rational, or optimizing, economic agents" that came to dominate that discipline's imagination.[7] For instance, the most basic tool of microeconomics – the supply and demand curve – required the premise of the self-interested actor. Likewise, economic development was conceived around human action capacities, driving the "plans, policies, programs, and projects" aimed at "building institutional mechanisms" for the pursuit of progress and well-being.[8] Indeed, the strategic human calculator was taken for granted in virtually every economic process – buying, selling, producing, and trading – and every economic role – consumer, corporate raider, strike-breaker, and so on. Corporations displayed collective action capacities in unalloyed form, exhibiting the most extreme interests-maximizing features. Their highly stylized and often nefarious bottom-line orientations – operating in so-called free markets – almost caricatured the principles of actorhood. Given this pervasive presence in the discipline, the rise of the human actor in the global-institutional frame almost certainly facilitated the ascent of economics among academic priorities.

Second as humans were increasingly assigned the role of reality's default actors over the twentieth century, the shifting premises of world society seem likely to have fueled the fire of political science. As was true for economics, the apparatus of political science came to pivot to an exceptional extent on rationalized human action capacities (and thus like economics, political science proved particularly receptive to rational-choice theory). Absent the calculating human actor, such processes as revolutions, elections, putsches, and persuasion are all but rendered as inconceivable. Similarly absent the calculating actor, such entities as political parties, protestors, voters, and unions are all but stripped of meaning. Thus, at both individual and collective levels, the action assumption – by which humans are seen to be capable of intended and purposeful change – provided critical substructure to political science. Therefore, the relocation of action capacities from divinities to individual humans seems likely to have encouraged the field's expansion in the academic core.[9]

The activation of humans, third, should have offered limited benefits to the field of psychology. In modern societies, according to the rationale of the field, "individuals are required to be free," and psychologists thus are "obligated to correct or repair defects if they fail to cope on their own."[10] As human action capacities increasingly drove the operations of society and as their internal beings in consequence gained public salience, psychology should have gained standing in universities worldwide. But notice that the psychologized human is more detached structure than engaged actor; the human *actor* is better represented in economics. Furthermore notice the ongoing presence of divine action capacities vis-à-vis the individual interior. The psyche, formerly known as the soul, was released from divine control more slowly than the analytical objects of the other social science fields. In 1904–05, the description of Boston College's course in Psychology began as follows:

> PSYCHOLOGY: Life in General – Sensitive Life – the Senses, External and Internal – Sense-Perception – Imagination – Sensuous Appetite – Feeling. The Human Soul – the Simplicity, Spirituality and Immortality of the Soul – Recent Theories Concerning the Soul – Individuality and the Unity of the Soul – Union of the Soul with the Body – Locus of the Soul – Origin of the Soul – Animal Psychology.[11]

Even today, the psyche remains somewhat mysterious and under divine control. For instance, the terms we use to understand romantic love explicitly dismiss human sovereignty – we fall head over heels, swept away by forces beyond our control. Mysterious and divine action capacities thus remained to some extent present in psychology's direct object of study throughout the century. Accordingly when the subfield of psychology known as phrenology was denied university entry, it was not on the basis of "technical scientific issues" but on the basis of "religious ones: Phrenology was wrong because its monism was incompatible with the freedom of the will and the immortality of the soul."[12] Even at the end of the twentieth century, religious fundamentalists proclaimed, "Psychology is a subtle and widespread leaven in the Church . . . stealthily starving the sheep. It promises far more than it can deliver, and what it does deliver is not the food that nourishes."[13] In short, although we expect that the installation of humans as world society's master actors gave some impetus to psychology, we also expect that the field's liftoff in the university was weighted down by God's ongoing sovereignty in key psychological realms.

At the negative end of the spectrum, we speculate that the elaboration of human actorhood in the global-institutional frame will have depressing effects on the field of anthropology – the study of human culture. At McGill University in Canada, "Anthropology provides students with a unique opportunity to understand human cultural diversity – to compare our own culture with those which are remote in time, in geographic distance, or simply in terms of cultural difference."[14]

Because it is a feature of groups – the beliefs and values of the collective – culture is often opposed to action as an encumbrance on individual autonomy. Under the changing premises of reality over the twentieth century, individuals became the primary loci of action capacities, and we see a growing disarticulation as a result between that which is taken for granted in world society and that which is taken for granted in anthropology. The field's university status, we expect, declined as a result.

Naturally, the transfer of action capacities from divine to human hands wrought many changes in the university beyond those pertaining to teaching and research emphases. To take just one example, as individual action capacities were built into the foundations of world society, preferred pedagogical techniques moved sharply away from rote memorization and exact imitation, and the formal professor-centric lecture – before a passive, deferential, and silent classroom – lost legitimacy and authority.[15] Movements along these lines over the twentieth century coincided with and supported the academic reorientations we regard here as central.

We suppose that any field-level benefits accrued in the course of global-institutional reframing aggregated onto the social sciences' branch-level benefits witnessed in Chapter 1. This means that relatively speaking we expect economics and political science to be among the stronger social science fields, with a more middling result for psychology, and a weak result for anthropology.

In addition to infusing humans with all-purpose action capacities, the re-definition at issue here also infused humans with a more specialized kind of actorhood, in regard to knowing. Humans over the twentieth century developed substantially enhanced mastery over the acquisition and verification of knowledge (i.e., scientization) and also over the use and application of knowledge (i.e., rationalization). Increasingly in world society, the gods were forced to forfeit territories of understanding to the access and control of individual humans. In Chapter 1, we argued that this aspect of global-institutional reframing elevated the status of the social sciences among the branches of learning worldwide. Here we suggest additional ramifications, for two particular social science fields.[16]

Geography likely reaped higher-than-average benefits from the divine-to-human transfer of knowledge capacities, given its close historical association with applied endeavors, in which humans not only acquired but also used knowledge for collective benefits. Geography brings together Earth's physical and human dimensions, studying patterns and processes on the surface of the planet. In the late nineteenth century, geographers set about to produce "standardized knowledge of the planet" and "took up the project of building a unified science, founded on reason."[17] Early in the twentieth century, geography was associated with the exploration of the Earth – to know and to possess the nether regions – both via colonialism and via resource exploitation, as might be implied by an early-twentieth-century *National Geographic*. Later, geography became associated with such fields as urban planning and, increasingly over time, environmental protection. Geography's broad definition – to study the human-nature relationship – has allowed it to affiliate with a wide range of applied fields: It is the Department of Geography, Geology and Mineralogy at the University of Salzburg, Austria; the Department of Geography, Geology, and Planning at Southwest Missouri State University; and the Department of Geography and Environmental Studies at Carleton University, Canada. Because geography was peculiarly amenable to joining forces with applied fields, we expect that global-institutional reframing over the twentieth century gave the field substantial support.

Sociology, too, seems likely to have benefited from the relocation of knowledge capacities in the global-institutional frame. As proposed by Comte in the early 1800s, sociology involved the use of scientific methods to ascertain the laws of human development. It required the capacities to abstract and examine not only external matters – the economy, the polity, and so on – but also one's own social embedding, thus demanding highly elaborated notions of objectivity. To make empirical observations, to propose hypotheses to explain those observations, and to test those hypotheses in valid and reliable ways vis-à-vis a system that engulfed oneself were activities that assumed a sophisticated human knower, which became increasingly available over the twentieth century.

Of course, the baseline shift in the assumed locus of knowledge capacities favored transformation throughout the university, not just in academic emphases. Broadly speaking, for example, the whole mission of the university gained a new focus with the activation of humanity's knowledge capacities. Where the goal once had been to *preserve* eternal dispensations, it became instead to produce, to discover, to verify, and to apply the leading edges of knowledge. These latter goals assumed the sovereignty of the human knower.[18] Wider changes such as these reinforced those related to the academic-core reprioritizations on which we focus.

REDEFINITION OF STRUCTURE IN THE GLOBALLY INSTITUTIONALIZED ONTOLOGY

Alongside the twin revisions of action came twin revisions in structure in the global-institutional frame. As depictions of the cosmology were reconfigured around evolution rather than creation over the course of the century, structural models posing horizontal assemblies and dynamic networks supplanted those posing vertical hierarchies and fixed categories.

These reforms first entailed the reconfiguration of vertical hierarchies into horizontal assemblies. Losing authority and legitimacy were a set of old imageries depicting castes and clear pecking orders of beings, arranged by God and thus woven into nature's fabric. Gaining authority and legitimacy were another set of imageries envisioning interdependencies and ecological communities, emerging from evolution and interacting on a leveled ontological playing field. We claimed in Chapter 1 that this change had a positive impact on the overall social sciences by accrediting depictions of society as a congregation of juridical equals (e.g., the citizenry). Here we predict additional effects of vertical-to-horizontal restructuring on two particular social science fields.

The initial relationship we foresee is to sociology, which throughout this period was mobilized to uproot and eviscerate social hierarchies. In studies of class stratification, occupational mobility, racial prejudice, and so on, sociology ushered in the modern horizontal social structure, seeking both to promote equality and to extend incorporation and membership. Sociology's stance against vertical hierarchies, often traced to Marx, shows through in the description of the course, Principles of Sociology, held at the University of California-Berkeley in 2003: "[T]he class will examine core sociological ideas through the study of class, race, gender and sexuality in U.S. society. Once familiar with basic theoretical and empirical approaches used to explain unequal social outcomes, we will consider the ways in which the state, the educational system and the family have both perpetuated and resisted social inequality."[19] As the description makes abundantly clear, the horizontalization of reality in the cultural scripts and organizational rules of world society at large offered a baseline rationale to many of sociology's main study objects. Thus we expect that this structural transition fed sociology's global expansion, above and beyond the social sciences generally.

The second social science field for which we suggest a direct tie to vertical/horizontal restructuring is anthropology. In anthropology's case, the line is negative. This is so because anthropology formed around the logic of hierarchy. Although the field admitted the common humanity linking the civilized to the savage and the modern to the primitive, the inferior status of the latter was unquestioned. The human "races," as well, were graded in status. Ranked dichotomies, in short, provided the ideological substructure of the field. In the late 1800s, the discipline emerged by drawing together disparate intellectual "projects" around a touchstone concern with "the way in which human institutions and knowledge had developed from a savage to a civilized condition."[20] Almost 100 years later at the University of Auckland, hierarchical binaries still predominated: Anthropology I focused on the "beginnings of civilization," "primitive cultures," and the "impact of modern civilization on primitive cultures." Thus as vertical hierarchies were rearranged into horizontal assemblies, anthropology's structural assumptions grew increasingly problematic. The field's dichotomous foundations softened, and we therefore expect anthropology to have lost some of its stature in the university during this period.

Certainly the restructuring in our sights here bore wide-ranging consequences for the twentieth-century university, extending well beyond academic priorities. One such consequence appeared in the realm of grading practices. So-called grade inflation grew rampant, as grades themselves were repurposed. At the start of the century, grades served to vertically rank student achievements. By the end of the period, grades existed to "encourage better performance" and long-run "student effort."[21] From the restructuring of reality, a whole collection of changes followed in grading policies, in academic composition, and in the wider university.

As previously, we expect that field- and branch-level effects aggregated to yield the compositional trends we observe worldwide. This means we expect sociology to have been among the faster growing social science fields over the century, whereas anthropology should have ended among the slower growing fields.

In addition to the vertical-to-horizontal shift in the structural templates of world society, the ontological redefinition of structure also recast fixed categories into dynamic networks. That which took form in sharply demarcated and enduring orders (a la creation) was steadily reformed into elaborately interconnected and developing systems (a la evolution).[22] In Chapter 1, we drew no special connection from this aspect of institutional change to the social sciences as a whole. But at the field level of analysis, we anticipate several clear linkages.

One such linkage between reformed reality and university priorities tied fixed-category-to-dynamic-network structural transition to the field of geography. To the greatest extent among all the basic social science fields, geography throughout the twentieth century bridged the interstices of domains sharply demarcated by traditional categorical orders. Straight from its disciplinary origins, geography crossed the infinite chasm separating society from nature, depicting the two entities as intermeshed in a latticework of evolving systems. Thus, geographers exposed the interdependent circuitry of human prosperity, natural resource exploitation, and environmental protection. They drew attention to nature's material benefits, as well as to its sustenance of human life. The category-busting assumptions of geography were plainly evident in the two introductory courses offered by the University of the South Pacific, Fiji, in 1991. The first course emphasized the energy and water balance between people and their physical environment, whereas the second focused on human interactions with the Earth's surface, in agriculture, urban growth, and population change. Because geography by definition flouted creation's old boundaries, we expect that the ongoing process of structural reformation steadily brightened the field's prospects in universities worldwide.

We also expect there to be some benefits for economics during the period of inquiry, inasmuch as the market itself – an interconnected system in which buyers and sellers interact to exchange goods and services for money – came to provide the case *par excellence* of the dynamic-network structure. New journals in the field, such as *The Review of Economic Dynamics* and *The Review of Network Economics*, embodied the surging structural templates. Emerging concepts, such as uncertainty, liquidity, competition, and entrepreneurship, all relied heavily on the assumptions of a dynamically networked reality.

On the flipside, anthropology was perhaps disadvantaged by the fall of fixed-categorical structures, insofar as that field disproportionately relied on dualities in its basic intellectual apparatus. Anthropology conjured "the other" for its educated Western readership – modernity versus tradition, Western versus non-Western, hot versus cold, and so on. These

> essentialist stereotypes of the "us and them" variety continue to dominate anthropological discourse, appearing in the innocent guise of categories like "indigenous people," "migrants" or "modernity." Such categories continue to depend on largely unquestioned, and often unstated, binaries like indigenous/settler, migrant/mainstream, and modern/pre-modern, all of which are historically related to (and sometimes even identical with) the savage/civilised or simple/complex oppositions of yesteryear.[23]

With the deinstitutionalization of fixed categories in the baseline features of reality, we expect that anthropology lost its footing on a teetering bed of assumptions.

Also, we speculate that a bedrock assumption of psychology was hollowed by structural redefinition. The demise of fixed categories threatened to unravel the boundary of particularity around the human mind. The mind's facility for emotion, its range of perceptions, its capacity for self-consciousness, and the like stand without parallel under the assumptions of psychology. Courses on personality, intelligence, and even pathology at the Hebrew University of Jerusalem all rest on this premise.[24] There is still "little evidence that most apes use grammar in their communications, though one bonobo has attained at least a rudimentary grammar." Nevertheless, "in some highly specific situations, apes, sea-lions (*Zalophus californianus*), and dolphins (*Tursiops truncatus*) are able to comprehend the order of lexical items, and some apes and pigeons can reproduce certain simple series reliably."[25] In its assumption of abiding human difference, psychology invokes a structural model with declining authority and legitimacy, which should have darkened psychology's twentieth-century horizons in the academic core.

Needless to say, the structural shift under discussion here catalyzed many changes in the university in addition to fomenting alterations in teaching and research emphases. One way the structural change took form was in the opening of the university's doors to previously excluded social forces, ranging from social movement activists to community groups to for-profit corporations. Within older structural models, the university existed as a place apart, a pure ivory tower. As dynamically networked structural blueprints, however, increasingly gained default status, the desirability and legitimacy of external linkages greatly increased for the university. Such ties proliferated accordingly.[26] Alterations of this sort appeared hand in hand with shifts in faculty composition over the twentieth century.

The field-level effects outlined here should have aggregated with the branch-level effects discussed in Chapter 1 to produce average faculty rep-resentations over time. For geography and economics, we expect that the global-institutional frame shift bestowed a double positive, leading us to project these two among the faster growing social science fields. By contrast, for anthropology and psychology, we see the frame shift as yielding counter-vailing positive (branch level) and negative (field level) effects, leading us to project these two among the slower growing social sciences.

As regards the one remaining social science discipline, political science, we anticipate mixed effects from structural redefinition. The two dimensions of structural change likely pulled the field in opposite directions over the twentieth century, each canceling the other's impact. For instance in wars and the state, political science has direct objects of study that rather clearly assumed fixed-category models of reality, especially when contrasted with competition and markets. One might place political scientists on the losing side of the ontological battle accordingly. Then again in democracy and diplomacy, the field had direct objects of study from the dynamic-network storehouse. Given these emphases, one might place political scientists among the structural winners. All of these are meat-and-potato issues in political science, and their eclectic assumptions regarding structure suggest that the field remained more or less intact through the vertical-to-horizontal and category-to-network change. Of course, the reframing of reality may well have altered the internal composition of the field, say by enabling kings-for-commoners trades.[27] Nevertheless at the field level, we suppose that political science displayed no defining structural tendency.

In Figure 1, we pull together the main arguments from this chapter. We argue that reconfigured models of action and structure in the global-institutional frame reset the baseline features of reality and thus altered the

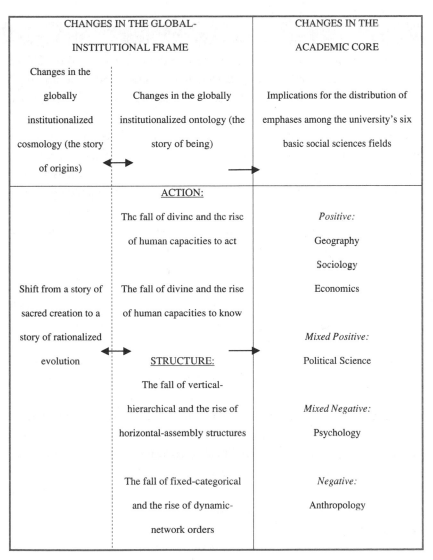

CHANGES IN THE GLOBAL-INSTITUTIONAL FRAME		CHANGES IN THE ACADEMIC CORE
Changes in the globally institutionalized cosmology (the story of origins)	Changes in the globally institutionalized ontology (the story of being)	Implications for the distribution of emphases among the university's six basic social sciences fields
Shift from a story of sacred creation to a story of rationalized evolution	ACTION: The fall of divine and the rise of human capacities to act	*Positive:* Geography Sociology Economics
	The fall of divine and the rise of human capacities to know	*Mixed Positive:* Political Science
	STRUCTURE: The fall of vertical-hierarchical and the rise of horizontal-assembly structures	*Mixed Negative:* Psychology
	The fall of fixed-categorical and the rise of dynamic-network orders	*Negative:* Anthropology

Figure 1 Summary of argument and implications for the six basic social sciences fields.

supply of building blocks available to university studies. On both action and structure dimensions, the process bore positive implications for three fields – geography, sociology, and economics – and we thus expect to find these fields exhibiting relatively faster rates of expansion as overall shares of university activities. For political science, we foresee a positive action effect and a neutral structure effect, whereas for psychology we see a neutral action effect and a negative structure effect. We expect these two fields to land in the middle of the social sciences in terms of academic recomposition. We see anthropology, meanwhile, as subject to negative action and structure implications, leading us to anticipate its placement as the weakest discipline over our inquiry period.

Undoubtedly other theorists would place different bets on the social science fields over the century. Were one to argue, for example, that the United States was in the position to dictate worldwide academic emphases, given its superpower status after 1945, which was further consolidated after 1989, and its related centrality in the field of higher education, one would likely reverse the places of geography and psychology in the scheme above. In the 1970s, as is well known, geography entered the doldrums in the United States, as nature came to appear thoroughly utilized, tamed, and vanquished (so it seemed). Psychology, meanwhile – enabled by the country's enduring Anglo-Protestant culture – showed strength in the United States throughout the postwar era.[28] From this perspective, it seems that psychology, not geography, should have won the better position in the global-academic standings.

Alternatively were one to hitch the global prospects of social science fields to nation-state agendas – given, after all, that nation-states founded and fund most of the world's universities – one would predict the strongest twentieth-century showings for the fields most salient to the state's twin goals, security and development. By this logic, political science and economics should have led the pack in growth, whereas anthropology and psychology – the most remote from state concerns – should have brought up the rear. At the field level, this alternative framework makes predictions in line with our own. It stumbles, however, in the face of the converging academic priorities reported earlier. Were nation-states really driving the process, as actors defending their interests, differentiation and specialization should be more readily apparent in the composition of academic cores around the world.

We now test our ideas on cross-national and longitudinal data describing changes in the overall composition of university faculty by social science field. The compelling questions are two-fold. First what are the empirical facts of change? And second, how well are they predicted by our global-institutional argument?

Results

As in previous chapters, we draw here on data from the *Commonwealth Universities Yearbook* to study transformations in the university's teaching and research priorities between 1915 and 1995. For the growing number of British Commonwealth countries, the data present the percentages of total university faculty working in each of the six basic social science fields over time. Against the foil of a powerful upward trend in the emphasis accorded the social sciences on the whole, we expect some social science fields to enjoy more rapid global expansion than others. The results appear in Table 1 and in Figures 1 and 2.

Table 1, first off, provides a measure of each social science's growth relative to its starting point over the twentieth century.[29] The first column of the table shows each field's average percentage of total university faculty in the 1915–35 time spell. The second column shows the same percentage for the 1976–95 spell. The third column, then, gauges the former in relation to the latter, showing percentage growth over the century.[30]

What is immediately striking in Table 1 is that without fail the social science fields gained prominence in the academic core over the twentieth century. Just as we saw an across-the-board retreat among humanities fields, so we see an across-the-board advance among social science fields: Every one rose on average among the university's teaching and research priorities

Table 1   Percentage of Total Faculty in Each of the Six Basic Social Sciences Fields for Universities in British Commonwealth Countries

	Faculty Percentage in 1915–35	*Faculty Percentage in 1976–95*	*Percentage Change Over Time*
Fields gaining more than double their original shares			
Sociology	0.1	2.2	2,100
Geography	0.4	2.9	616
Political Science	0.8	2.0	148
Economics	1.7	3.8	124
Fields gaining less than double their original shares			
Anthropology	0.2	0.4	97
Psychology	0.7	0.8	11

in our main British Commonwealth sample. The benefits of the global-institutional frame shift, apparently, were widespread for the social sciences, not only fueling expansion in the branch overall but also in each of the branch's component fields.

Nevertheless even as this is true, widespread growth did not translate into equal growth across the social science fields. In fact on a discipline-by-discipline basis, the percentage changes over time varied enormously, from a stratospheric 2,100 percent growth to a more pedestrian 11 percent growth. Expansion thus occurred at very different rates.

Greatest among all gainers was the field of sociology, which began in our timeframe all but invisible in British Commonwealth universities but then leapt forward over the ensuing decades. By the end of the twentieth century, the average sociology faculty in our sample had grown 2,100 percent, having started with the smallest of all faculty shares. Centrally oriented to studies of inequality, social problems, and the concerns of the welfare state, sociology became a mainline university pursuit in the course of this stunning growth. Perhaps the field's good fortunes owed in part to global-institutional reframing, in which the increasing adoption of horizontal-assembly models of structure offered enhanced authority and legitimacy to sociology's focal emphasis on equality. Maybe also sociology's good standing was thanks in part to the thick elaboration of human knowing capacities, with which the global-institutional frame shift offered an increasingly well-crafted platform from which humans could turn the scientific eye unto themselves in society.

Second among the faster growing social science fields was geography, which grew by 616 percent growth over the century – remarkable by any standard. Research and teaching in geography – the study of humanity's place in nature (and vice versa) – moved to the university's center stage during these years. The field's rapid advance was likely facilitated by the ontological redefinition of structure, which bridged the categorical divide formerly separating humanity from nature and thus provided an academic base for emerging environmental studies. Also, geography may have benefited from the revision of action, given its close association with a variety of applied endeavors, in which the knower was not only allowed to acquire knowledge but also to use it.

Geography's strong global showing is bound to surprise some, given the field's quiescent reputation in the United States (only now reviving). The result shows one benefit of our global sample: Where goes the United States does not always go the world. On one side, the country's exceptionalism surely relates to the extreme extent to which nature is conceived to be rationalized in the United States – thoroughly brushed and braided so as to be useful in meeting human needs – and on the other side to the aggrandized theory of actorhood that characterizes American society. At both ends of the equation, the United States is positioned to dismiss geography more readily than the average country. Thus, patterns of cross-national variation show that the industrialized Protestant countries, such as Canada and Australia – having less in the way of nature and more in the way of actorhood – undertake relatively little geography, whereas Sierra Leone and Papua New Guinea place among the countries with the most geographers.[31]

Political science follows next after geography, growing on average 148 percent from the first to the fourth time periods. The field's expansion was less phenomenal than that seen for sociology or geography, but that owes in part to the fact that political science was already moderately well represented in the university at the beginning of the twentieth century (second highest among all social sciences at 0.8 percent). Thus, political science places among the stronger social science fields. The field is focused on security and the administration of public affairs, and its increasing prominence may have been driven in part by the fact that it assumes a wide array of human actors and action capacities, which themselves proliferated with the redefinition of action in the global-institutional frame.

On the heels of political science in Table 2 followed economics: Its share of the university's total faculty grew 124 percent during the period. Although this expansion again seems modest compared to that enjoyed by sociology and geography, it is again related to the discipline's faculty presence at the outset (unequaled at 1.7 percent), such that as above we place economics

Table 2   Number of Universities in Sample with No Faculty by Disciplinary Field, 1986–95 (n = 28)

Economics	1
Geography	2
Sociology	3
Political Science	5
Psychology	13
Anthropology	19

among the stronger fields. Economics depends heavily on human-action-capacity assumptions – individual actors serve as the main engines driving the rationalized economy – and in this way the redefinition of action may have contributed to the strong showing of economics in universities world-wide. Perhaps also the restructuring of reality into dynamic networks assisted economics by legitimizing the process- and relation-based characteristics of the market that provide the field's daily bread.

The one discrepancy we find here between the expectations derived from our argument and the social science standings we observe is the slightly higher than expected placement of political science, which our scheme ranked below sociology and geography (as observed) and also economics (contrary to observation). Were our data to begin in 1850 rather than 1915 – so as to include the very first appearances of the social science disciplines in the university – we might find the results we anticipated.

All four of the preceding social science fields more than doubled their faculty shares over the century in question, and all four ended up with a minimum of 2 percent of all faculty slots in the final time period (Table 2, second column). Neither anthropology nor psychology could claim the same.

The stronger of the two fields is anthropology, which expanded 97 percent from the first interval to the last. Although in the grand scheme of things this outcome is excellent, it is among the weakest of the social science fields, and it came on top of a relatively low starting share of 0.2 percent. Even by the 1976–95 period, after nearly doubling its university presence, anthropology occupied on average only 0.4 percent of university faculty positions in our sample, leaving it the smallest of the social sciences. Anthropology, in short, remained marginal in the university throughout the twentieth century. With the global-institutional frame shift, the hierarchical and categorical structures bundled into anthropology's foundations lost their taken-for-grantedness, weakening anthropology's base and seemingly inhibiting the field's growth in the university. For example, following independence in Africa, "anthropology was demoted to a sub-discipline of sociology in many African universities, and some institutions did not include it in their teaching and research programs ... [A]nthropological research in Africa was mainly conducted by European and American Africanists to a greater extent than was the case in the other social sciences. During the 1970s ... the perception of anthropology remained a negative one."[32]

Falling in last place, finally, appeared the discipline of psychology, which registered a minimal 11 percent growth over the twentieth century, barely increasing its average faculty presence from 0.7 to 0.8 percent of the total. Throughout these decades, psychology stayed at the periphery of university endeavors. The positive effect we posited from the activation of human individuals seems to have been hamstrung by negative forces. The individual interior, or soul, seems to have resisted widespread scientization. Furthermore, the field's commitment to the conceit of human uniqueness grew stale over the decades, as fixed-categorical structures gave way to dynamic networks. The latter effects also may have hampered psychology's success in the world's universities.

As was true vis-à-vis geography, the results for psychology are surprising from the purview of the United States, where psychology is a clear winner among the social sciences. Once again, the results demonstrate the benefits of our global sample. Cross-national research shows that the field of psychology is prominent only in the liberal Anglo-Protestant countries, where prevail the world's tightest links between the individual being and the public good.[33]

These results are broadly consistent with the expectations derived from our theoretical framework. We expected psychology to have a better showing than anthropology, but we expected to find these two fields at the bottom of the social sciences heap.

Our division of the social science fields into faster- and slower-growing groups is confirmed by Table 2, which shows the total number of universities in our sample without any faculty representation in each of the six fields. As one would predict both from our argument and from the results in Table 1, sociology, geography, political science, and economics are all commonly represented in universities throughout the British Commonwealth, whereas barely more than one-half have any psychology and barely more than one-third have any anthropology.

Stepping back now, recall that our main argument roots university reconstruction in the global-institutional reframing of reality. Changes in globally institutionalized reality underlie the worldwide rise of the social sciences in the university, and they also underlie variations in the trajectories of specific social science fields. In particular, we argue that redefinitions of action and structure over the twentieth century improved global-environmental conditions for four of our six social science fields while worsening them for psychology and anthropology. Individual field-level effects combine with the overall branch effect discussed in Chapter 1 to produce the observed trends. The outcomes presented here, although broad brushed, lend additional support to that garnered by our argument in the previous two chapters.

In Figures 2 and 3, we take one further step by adding the two intervening time points and showing each field's trajectory over time. Some indicate fairly steady rates of growth, whereas others exhibit more jagged patterns of change.

In Figure 2, we display the two social science fields whose original shares less than doubled over the whole time period. Psychology showed regular but incremental growth: Its relative faculty share crept upward from period to period, perhaps constrained by the field's categorical boxing of humans and its connection to territory still partially controlled by the gods. Anthropology, by contrast, reveals a jagged growth pattern, made bold by the scale of the figure. Between 1915–35 and 1936–55, anthropology stayed essentially flat: So-called modern society was itself in crisis during these conflict-filled decades, and the study of "traditional" society languished. Between 1936–55 and 1956–75, by contrast, anthropology's faculty share shot upward, as the

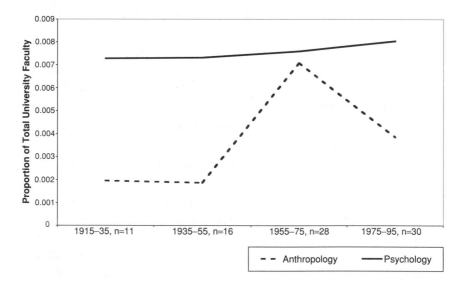

Figure 2   Social science fields gaining less than twice their faculty share from 1915 to 1995.

promise of modernization drew attention to the newly decolonized periphery. In the final period, however, the modern/premodern hierarchy itself grew suspect. With the redefinition of structure in terms of horizontal assemblies in the culture and organization of world society, anthropology's foundations seem to have crumbled, the field's faculty share declining accordingly.[34]

In Figure 3, we continue in this direction, depicting the trend-lines for the four social science fields that more than doubled their original faculty shares over the twentieth century. Economics and political science experienced quite similar growth trajectories. The faculty shares of both fields grew slightly from periods one to two, then rose rapidly from periods two to three, before flattening out from periods three to four. It may be that the human action assumption central to both fields became turbocharged in the post-World War II era with the victory of the liberal powers and the subsequent emphasis on individuals. Geography, meanwhile, showed considerable growth from the first through the third intervals, before tapering off slightly. Throughout most of the century, the field seems to have been catalyzed by its dynamic networking of human and natural systems, ultimately leading to environmental studies and earth sciences – suggested by our research but not demonstrable with our data. Sociology, finally, ascended slowly at first

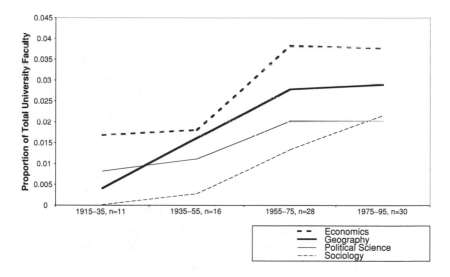

Figure 3   Social science fields gaining more than twice their faculty share from 1915 to 1995.

before taking off in the later periods of the century. As human knowledge capacities multiplied and as the world was reconfigured both conceptually and politically around the rule of equality contained in structural models of horizontal assembly (e.g., in the United Nations), sociology's university stature fired upward.[35]

Along all these empirical pathways, our expectations are generally borne out. The social science fields all enjoyed growth over the twentieth century – in stark contrast to the humanities fields. Nevertheless, they flourished unequally, and changes in the global-institutional frame provide a reliable guide to the variations and explanation thereof.

Conclusion

From our perspective, the composition of university teaching and research reflects a good deal more than the best available approximation of truth, as a few idealists still maintain. It also reflects more, we believe, than functional responses to the needs of society or the demands of the influential. A functionalist might plausibly claim that those fields in the social sciences offering greater immediate benefits to the wealthy and powerful fared better over the twentieth century (these would include economics and political science, obviously, but also geography, in its associations with natural resource exploitation and colonialism, and sociology, as the science of modern rationalized society) than did those that offered fewer (anthropology and psychology). What troubles the account, however, is the location of such studies in the encumbered, inefficient setting of the university, where proprietary claims on knowledge are heavily restricted. The interests of the wealthy and powerful obviously could be pursued more precisely and freely in private domains, where rules of objectivity and universalism do not prevail.

Alternatively, we argue that university activities are constituted within an evolving global-institutional frame, in which redefinitions of action and structure – underway throughout the modern period – gave rise to society and thus fomented the expansion of the social sciences generally. The same frame changes reestablished the premises of world society in ways that improved the prospects of sociology, geography, political science, and economics more so than psychology or anthropology.

The divergence among the various social science fields – with some experiencing much more vigorous average growth in our sample than others – may thus be linked to differential implications of global-institutional reframing. This causal picture of change in the academic core is simplified and general, of course. But given a literature short on theory and shorter on data, we believe our explorations here offer solid starting ground for future analyses. To some extent at least, university faculties seem to rest on global-institutional substructures.

Returning to our three animating themes, the social science findings presented here provide further validation and support for them. First, the distinct trends we observe in faculty composition over time – not only vis-à-vis the social science fields but also the humanities fields, the branches of learning, and the applied and basic divisions – leave little doubt that there are global wellsprings of university reconstruction. Second, the accumulated evidence of the last three empirical chapters now unambiguously suggests that the various knowledge domains march to a common drummer, such that the domains are usefully conceived as components of a single body of university knowledge. Third, it seems increasingly plausible – given our success in anticipating many sweeping changes in the menu of university activities – to claim that revisions in the global-institutional frame have a central role in reconstituting the academic core over time. Redefinitions of action and structure, in particular, have proven to be able guides to the changing roster of university teaching and research priorities.

We move onward, then, to the natural sciences, in which social influences are given little play. To the greatest extent among the domains of knowledge, the priorities and emphases of the natural sciences fields are thought to represent state-of-the-art facts, rather than globally institutionalized realities. In this sense, the natural sciences pose the greatest challenge yet to our explanatory scheme. With data in hand, we explore the possibilities.

Notes

1. See, for example, Clark (1973) and Mazlish (2000).
2. See Porter (2003) and Porter and Ross (2003) on the social sciences in the nineteenth century.

3. The quotation is from Wallerstein (1991: 147), who situates the social sciences in the history of modern society and critiques their capacities to deliver promised benefits. On progress and modernity, see Huntington (1968).

4. From Ross (2003:208).

5. See Drori et al. (2003). The recent excitement over "public sociology" – which is charged with taking "sociology out of the classroom and laboratory to directly impact social change and decision making in the public sphere" – has precisely this character. See http://pubsoc.wisc.edu/.

6. We focus here on the so-called basic social sciences, oriented to knowledge for knowledge's sake. We consider the "applied" social sciences, such as business and education, in Chapter 1.

7. See Morgan (2003:279).

8. From the 1982–84 Beirut University Catalog. See Chabbott (1999) on development as a national goal.

9. The same cannot be said for law, which operates in conjunction with political science but builds from more humanistic foundations, concerned with collective morality.

10. From Ash (2003:274). See also Rose (1996).

11. From the 1904–05 Boston College Catalogue.

12. Notably, such resistance arose not from members of the religious community but from members of the Académie des Sciences. From Goldstein (2003:149).

13. From http://www.rapidnet.com/~jbeard/bdm/Psychology/psych.htm.

14. From the department's website at http://www.mcgill.ca/anthropology/.

15. For preschoolers, the emergent curriculum is now in fashion, in which the children choose what to study.

16. All the social science fields are extensively scientized and rationalized. This is so despite the fact that some fields are clearly more quantitative than others: Although quantitative methods sometimes now seem to be a measure of scientism, the association is of recent derivation and unrelated to science's definition.

17. See Robic (2003:382).

18. See Ramirez (2002).

19. See http://sociology.berkeley.edu/courses/schedules/FL03UGCD.pdf.

20. See Kuper (2003:358).

21. See Bulterman-Bos et al. (2003:344).

22. One result of restructuring along this dimension is a post–World War II shift in primary school curricula from history and geography to a new integrated subject category, "social studies." See Wong (1991).

23. From Morton (1999:243).

24. See Hebrew University of Jerusalem Courses of Instruction 1974–1975: pp. 99–100.

25. From the abstract of Animal Language and Cognition Projects by Carolyn Ristau of Massey University, New Zealand. See http://www.massey.ac.nz/~alock/hbook/ristau.htm

26. See, for example, Slaughter (2002).

27. See Bendix (1978). In Chapter 5, we investigate the changing subject matters of history.

28. See Frank, Meyer, and Miyahara (1995) on cross-national variations in psychology. For several decades, the United States has dominated the market for doctorates. Professors who are trained in the core bring the core's academic values back home. In 2004, for example, fourteen of the twenty-one professors of psychology at Thailand's premier Chulalongkorn University received their highest degrees in the United States.

29. Recall that the tables do not contain statistical tests of the differences in mean values given the nonrandom nature of the sample.

30. We set the floor at 0.01 in the 1915–35 time period to provide a reasonable basis for comparison.

31. We believe geography languishes in the United States because (a) nature is largely harnessed in the United States and (b) under harnessed conditions the study of society-nature relations takes place mainly in applied sciences, such as agriculture and environmental studies.

32. From Sichone (2003:478).

33. See Frank, Meyer, and Miyahara (1995).

34. Analyses of cross-national variations found that old countries do relatively more anthropology than new ones on average. New countries, of course, prefer to see themselves as civilizations on equal footing with the old.

35. Figures 1 and 2 show that the trajectories of the basic social sciences in the university flattened out toward the end of the century, strikingly so compared to mid-century and even early-century expansion. In Chapter 1, we showed that by the last time interval, the locus of growth had migrated from the basic to applied social sciences – to business, education, and so on.

CHAPTER 4

The Natural Sciences

In the preceding two chapters, we turned a global-institutional eye toward the striking distributions of teaching and research emphases in the humanities and the social sciences. Within both branches of learning, deep shifts in ontological conceptions of action and structure led to the decline of disciplines premised upon a top-down view of the world (classics, anthropology) and the ascendance of disciplines embodying a bottom-up view (non-Western languages and literatures, sociology). In this chapter we turn our attention to the final of the three great branches of the twentieth-century university: the natural sciences.[1]

Again, we proceed with a two-fold agenda. We first articulate the relevant portions of our theoretical argument, which holds that redefinitions of action and structure in globally institutionalized reality manifest themselves in the shifting teaching and research emphases of the natural sciences. Following this, we proceed to an empirical investigation of the shifts we observe in this domain of knowledge over the course of the twentieth century.

We restrict our discussion in this chapter to the so-called basic natural sciences – that is, those disciplines that purport to investigate the natural world for the sake of knowledge alone. We include in this category the disciplines of astronomy, biology, botany, chemistry, geology, mathematics, physics, and zoology. Although undeniably the products of these fields' investigations have been – perhaps with increasing frequency – put to work in applications as mundane as a better mousetrap and as terrible as an atom bomb, we distinguish these fields theoretically from those that are fundamentally premised upon the harnessing of natural science for particular applications. This latter category includes such fields as medicine, agriculture, and engineering.[2]

Drawing this theoretical distinction allows us to see clearly that, as we reported in Chapter 1, the overall flat trend in the proportion of university faculty devoted to the natural sciences is the result of a tenuous balance – growing faculties in the applied natural sciences counterbalance shrinking faculties in the basic natural sciences. When we look at the basic natural sciences, we see a picture that resembles the declining humanities much more than it resembles the ascendant applied and social sciences.

Background

Although many research universities today exist as a confederation of diverse faculties ranging from communications to veterinary medicine, at the center of the typical university is generally a faculty of arts and sciences, comprising the core humanities, natural sciences, and social sciences (as, for example, at Boston University and Harvard University). Although some universities separate these faculties – for example, the University of Oslo maintains a Faculty of Arts, a Faculty of Mathematics and Natural Sciences, and a Faculty of Social Sciences – the two great pillars of the modern university's mission are the investigation of the great achievements of humans (the arts) and of God (the sciences).

As we noted in Chapter 2, the decline of the humanities in the university has been mourned and remarked upon widely. The presumptive beneficiaries in this zero-sum game are the sciences. A typical elegist wrote, in a letter to the *New York Times*, of "the decline of the humanities in an age of scientific breakthrough."[3] A panel convened in the 1980s by the National Endowment for the Humanities complained that "students can easily obtain bachelor's degrees knowing FORTRAN but not French or world history or Mozart."4 In contrast to the withering humanities, it seems, stand the sciences: well funded and flourishing with their promises of concrete developments in the store of knowledge as opposed to the arts' nebulous "understandings." Indeed, we have already demonstrated that these are not empty fears: Over the course of the twentieth century, the humanities experienced a genuine proportional decline – although the lion's share of the faculty proportion lost by the humanities was gained by the *social* sciences, rather than by the natural sciences.

The widespread concern expressed at the decline of philosophy and the classics is notable for its absence in regard to the natural sciences. Although few would be surprised to learn that the relative sizes of various disciplines in the sciences have shifted over the past decades, it seems somehow inappropriate to mourn the demise of, say, zoology or botany. If a discipline in the natural sciences loses support in the academy, we assume it must be commensurate with the ongoing search for objective truth. That is, if biologists multiply while botanists become scarce, we account for the shift not in terms of trendiness or political correctness but rather in terms of moving nearer to the concrete facts – just as neuroscience supplanted phrenology, biology supplanting botany must be a consequence of the discovery that biology's model of the world is somehow more accurate in an absolute sense than is botany's. *Prima facie*, this is attractive reasoning. The products of scientific research became stunningly conspicuous in the twentieth century; if biologists provide us the wherewithal for genetic engineering and botanists do not, we tend to take this as evidence that the biologists are on to something and hence deserve their prominence vis-à-vis their taxonomically oriented brethren.

Historians of science, however, long ago demonstrated that scientists' supposedly objective interpretations of the natural world are as susceptible to influence by the winds of cultural change as is the Supreme Court's supposedly objective interpretation of the Constitution. As Kant noted, when one beholds the world, one fits one's observations to preexisting forms and preconceptions. Along with historians of science, however, we argue that these mental schemes are not fixed but rather evolve through history – and along with sociological institutionalists, we add that many mental schemes are contained not only in human minds but also in social structures: distilled in cultural assumptions and organizational rules. Specifically, we link redistributions of emphases among the natural science fields to shifts in the global-institutional frame. In the remainder of the chapter, we elucidate theoretically and empirically our argument and show that interdisciplinary shifts in the natural sciences are consistent, in their underlying logic, with the interdisciplinary shifts we have already documented in the humanities and in the social sciences.

Argument

To briefly restate our core argument, we believe that the teaching and research emphases of universities worldwide at any given point in time are the manifestation of a globally institutionalized cosmology – a vision of world origins that is built into rule-like assumptions and taken-for-granted rules. As this cosmology shifted over the modern period, it prompted movements in core features of the globally institutionalized ontology. Revised action templates extended human control into new territories, both general and specific to knowledge. And revised structure templates reshaped vertical hierarchies into horizontal assemblies and fixed categories into dynamic networks. The root models of reality changed.

With this change, disciplines relatively inconsistent with the new global-institutional frame suffered throughout the university. As we have already shown, this shift led to a dramatic decline across the humanities and a surge in the social sciences. Although the natural sciences are typically presumed to be the very embodiment of the modern worldview, in fact, we suggest that the basic natural sciences in their fundamental assumptions about the universe are more similar to the humanities than is commonly assumed. Correspondingly, we expect to see a decline in the share of the university devoted to these disciplines – particularly in those most tied to the outdated blueprints of action and structure.

Classical and medieval cosmology viewed the world in the manner of an Aristotelian hierarchy, created and motivated by God from base materials, such as rocks up through plants and lower animals to man (with room below for lower orders of man, such as women and slaves), and continuing beyond common men to great men, such as priests and rulers, then to angels and other divine beings, and finally to God Himself. Both the humanities and the basic natural sciences came into being as intellectual tools for the investigation of this hierarchy; the social sciences (and the more applied natural sciences), by contrast, are of relatively recent vintage and embody quite different assumptions.

The humanities are charged with the study of the top of this hierarchy – God, other divine creatures, and higher men, such as philosophers and artists. The fundamental premise of the humanities is that there are Great Men and Great Works, superior in merit, exemplary in accomplishment, and revelatory in insight – beyond the reach of average individuals. For example, theologians read the Bible, philosophers read Aristotle, and scholars of literature read Dante – all with the presumption that these works are uniquely important and telling of the human condition. (The social sciences, by contrast, would regard these documents as merely products of a particular time and place – at best, reflective of the conditions in which they were produced.) This is a view of the classical hierarchy from the top down.

The basic natural sciences also arose to study this hierarchy, but from the bottom up. By rigorously observing and categorizing the incidence and behavior of mundane phenomena, such as rocks, ferns, and fish, natural scientists might hope to gradually reveal the universe in all its divine order. Although the view of the hierarchy looks different from the bottom than it does from the top and necessitates a different methodology, in both directions the ultimate object is the same: to map a picture of a static, rigidly ordered creation so as to better understand our place in it.

In her historical study of primary-school science textbooks, Elizabeth McEneaney captures this aspect of the scientific enterprise. Based upon a multinational sample of textbooks, McEneaney concludes that "before World War I, science was depicted as fact-oriented and taxonomic rather than broadly processual.... Commonly, the textbooks march through a panoply of local species of flora and fauna, with fairly regular sketches and an occasional photograph of the species under study."[5] The enterprise was framed as almost theological: "The depicted science involved a kind of filling-in-the-blanks in a god-given taxonomy. In this sense, expertise is located in the deity, and his work is merely revealed to human practitioners of science."[6]

Ultimately, however, McEneaney finds – consistent with our argument – a fundamental shift in the global-institutional frame over the course of the century. Whereas science early in the century (and before) was about discovering the world as God had created it and thus doing tribute to His genius, science today is about empowered individual actors manipulating a dynamic, horizontal universe. McEneaney finds this dramatic shift manifest in a new-found emphasis on the child's interests as the drivers and virtually sole justification of his or her scientific activities. "Primary school science (as embodied in textbooks) has transformed from an inert body of facts to principles for action and participation by individuals...In short, the main pedagogical imperative of contemporary primary science is both to cultivate agency in students *and* to construct a cultural field in which students believe they can exercise this agency."[7]

To recap, there has been a redefinition of action and of structure. *Actor-hood* has been relocated increasingly from God down through professional scientists and ultimately to all individuals, even young children.[8] Instead of passively observing a universe created at Genesis and thus ordered forever-more, individuals are now active participants in a dynamic universe. *Structure* is no longer conceived as a static vertical hierarchy, but rather as a dynamic horizontal system, unified in shared processes rather than in a divine order. These shifts, combined, have led to a model of reality that is consistent with the idea of humans actively manipulating their natural environment. This is not to say that God has been excommunicated from the institutionalized ontology; rather, the mark of His (much depersonalized) hand is seen in low-level processes as opposed to high-level taxonomies. This makes it legitimate for humans to reorder the visible universe; the *processes* rather than the *manifestations* are taken to be the ultimate level of reality. Therefore, we should expect that those disciplines that are more consistent with the altered global-institutional frame should retain a greater share of universities' finite resources than those that are not.

As noted earlier, we are restricting our discussion in this chapter to what might be termed the basic natural sciences – that is, those natural sciences that are not founded upon practical applications (though, as noted, their findings may well be used in an applied context). These disciplines include astronomy, biology, botany, chemistry, geology, mathematics, physics, and zoology. We have chosen these eight disciplines both because of their substantive similarity – all involve the investigation of the world with no *a priori* premise of application to technology – and because they are by common practice grouped together in university faculties, as well as in sociological and historical accounts. Three of these disciplines – astronomy, botany, and zoology – are definitionally tied to the outmoded global-institutional frame. Others – biology, chemistry, physics, and geology – are relatively adaptable to the modern cosmology, whereas the final one – mathematics – is uniquely suited to the modern worldview. We thus expect these disciplines' fates to have diverged accordingly over the course of the century.

Astronomy, botany, and zoology are all fundamentally premised upon the observation and classification of discrete, static fields of phenomena. They assume, in other words, a reality structured around fixed categories and vertical hierarchies, in which action capacities are restricted largely to external spiritual realms. "Naturalists who laid flora and fauna away in specimen cabinets and astronomers who recorded the positions of the stars and planets were accumulating a factual variorum of the Creator's imprint on the universe."[9]

Among the three disciplines, astronomy is the very paradigm of the observational science. Although we have sent men to the moon and robots to Mars, for all practical purposes astronomical phenomena are completely removed from human manipulation – we can do no better than to gaze at the stars and to map their movements. Among the natural sciences, astronomy is perhaps uniquely close to the humanities, with ties to classic works in art and philosophy. Although this orientation has earned astronomy an esteemed position within the university and unique "marquee value" in popular culture at large, we do not expect that this will translate into actual faculty resources. The subject matter of astronomy is, virtually by definition, excluded from human interaction or intervention, and this is true for not just the lay astronomer but also the professor. This remove is manifestly inconsistent with an emphasis upon empowered individuals effecting change in a dynamic universe. Structurally, too, astronomy embodies older models. Just as the justification for the discipline of anthropology erodes as the chasm between the civilized and the primitive dissipates, so does the justification for the discipline of astronomy erode as the gulf between the heavens and the earth evaporates. Substantively, in fact, astronomy has become nearly a branch of physics, in which the dynamic interrelations of earth and the universe are taken for granted.[10] Thus, although we would not expect any members of a university community to deny the symbolic value of the astronomical enterprise, we expect that over the long run astronomy's share of universities' teaching and research resources will decline.

Botany is a similarly classificatory science – indeed, Enlightenment astronomer William Herschel saw himself as a "celestial botanist."[11] Like all fields, botany has moved to incorporate redefined models of action and structure – the Botanical Society of America (BSA) now highlights the processual aspect of the field and the crucial importance of human action. Botanists, the BSA's Web site notes, might "study interactions of plants with other organisms and the environment.... Botanists study processes that occur on a time scale ranging from fractions of a second in individual cells to those that unfold over eons of evolutionary time."[12] Nonetheless, the field's identity – unlike that of biology – is fundamentally tied to its observatory and classificatory origins. The discipline's seminal founders include Gaspard Bauhin and Carolus Linnaeus, each of whom meticulously observed and classified thousands of plants. Modern botanists produce and refer to vast encyclopedias of leaf shapes and root systems. A frankly defensive document published by the BSA explicitly argues for the value of a comprehensive understanding of the plant kingdom as opposed to the "narrow training" of biologists.[13] Thus, the continued health of the field of botany is contingent upon the persistence of the notion that an understanding of universal processes is inferior to detailed knowledge of specific plant species. This is a direct parallel to the position of anthropology vis-à-vis sociology; we expect that as the global-institutional frame moves *toward* process and *away* from the discrete, static morphologies on which the discipline of botany was founded, there will be a relative decline in botany faculty size – just as we have observed in the case of anthropology.

Zoology, finally, is botany's analogue in the animal kingdom. The very fact that botany and zoology are discrete fields is a sign of their link to the outmoded cosmology, with its notion of static, hierarchical kingdoms as opposed to evolving and integrated systems. Although biologists conceive of life as a fundamentally unified process that cannot always be readily classified into one kingdom or another, zoologists and botanists maintain their traditional boundaries (with the occasional border dispute over such organisms as bacteria, algae, and fungi). As botanists devote themselves to the observation and cataloguing of plants, zoologists map the diversity of animal life. Zoology courses currently being offered at the University of Toronto include

Introductory Animal Physiology, Field Ornithology, and Comparative Endocrinology of Invertebrates.

Although zoology, like botany, has recently begun to position itself as a dynamic, process-based science, it finds itself in a similar quandary – the more it emphasizes ecology and the universal processes of life, the more it calls into question the validity of its own existence as a field. Historically, zoology and biology have been separated by a profound theoretical rift; many prominent zoologists went to extensive (though ultimately futile) efforts to prevent biology from emerging as *the* authority on the nature and workings of evolution.[14] It is telling in this respect that Toronto's zoology courses include a number of courses that explicitly invoke biology (Developmental Biology I, Biology of Fishes, Biology of Mammals). The zoological cosmology – entailing a rigid hierarchy of categorically distinct species created by God and observed by man – is losing legitimacy to the newly dynamic institutionalized worldview, in which humans are an integral and active part of an ever-changing natural ecology. Thus, we expect that zoology will lose relative standing in the university over the century's course.

Biology, chemistry, physics, and geology – like astronomy, botany, and zoology – are about the observation and understanding of the fundamental workings of the universe. They differ from the latter three disciplines, however, with respect to their assumptions regarding both actorhood and structure. The latter group of disciplines presumes that their practitioners are passive observers of a fixed, categorical, hierarchical universe – the former group, on the other hand, presumes a practitioner who is an active experimenter, discerning the nature of dynamic processes that underlie and connect previously separated categories of existence (as in the animal kingdom and the plant kingdom). Although such disciplines such as medicine and engineering are premised upon an even more active (indeed, *intervening*) practitioner, the disciplines of biology, chemistry, physics, and geology are all – in comparison to astronomy, botany, and zoology – relatively amenable to the process-oriented, human-centric model of nature currently institutionalized in world society. Therefore, we expect that all four of these disciplines will demonstrate greater persistence throughout the century than the hierarchy-oriented disciplines discussed above.

Geology might seem to be grouped more appropriately with the fundamentally classificatory sciences. Indeed, we do expect geology's footprint in the university to shrink over the course of the century – though not as precipitously as that of astronomy, botany, and zoology. Although the typical individual's experience with geology probably involves a lot of classifying rocks, geology has long assumed a world in which humans are sovereign actors – drilling for oil, say, and mining for gold. The discipline furthermore has always been deeply concerned with the ongoing processes shaping the Earth.[15] Although plate tectonics is a relatively recent development in the field – only formulated in the 1960s – geology has long operated with a hybrid model of structure: fixed categorical (i.e., types of rocks) as well as dynamic network (i.e., the physical development of the Earth). Geology's founders from Herodotus on down have concerned themselves not simply with the classification of earth phenomena but also with ongoing processes from silt deposition to fossil formation. As the globally institutionalized frame has come to portray our planet as a dynamic system, geology has been well positioned to be the disciplinary location for studies of the newly conceived ecosystem.[16] The field has close relationships with other earth sciences, such as geophysics and oceanic science, as well as with the social science of geography. Like the more narrowly classificatory sciences, we do indeed expect geology to lose ground to lower level sciences, such as physics and chemistry. With its relatively substantial historical focus upon human intervention and process, however, we expect that geology's openness to studies of a dynamic, interconnected ecosystem will slow its decline.[17]

Biology, like botany and zoology, focuses upon the study of living things. Whereas botany and zoology, however, are historically premised upon the study and classification of whole organisms, the science of biology embraces all aspects of the workings of life – even extending to human beings. This catholic approach has positioned biology to evolve over the course of the century (continuing a process that had begun centuries earlier) from the study of discrete organisms to the study of webs of life, as well as cells and subcellular processes.[18] The introductory biology course at Canada's University of Victoria, for example, covers "biological chemistry, cellular diversity, membrane structure and function, energy transduction, DNA replication, mitosis and the cell cycle, meiosis and sexual life cycles, Mendelian genetics, gene expression, evolutionary theory, and diversity of prokaryotes, protists, plants, and fungi."[19] We expect that the field's emphasis upon universal processes will bolster biology's position in the university relative to its category—and hierarchy-oriented siblings, as structural blueprints of fixed hierarchies give way to dynamic networks. The fact that modern botanists and zoologists profess deep interest in these dynamic processes and claim a sort of intellectual jurisdiction over them indeed strengthens our argument – these low-level processes *could be* and indeed *are* studied under the aegis of the historically hierarchy-oriented disciplines. The eclipse of those disciplines, we argue, will come about not because they are shown to be scientifically wrong so much as the fixed, hierarchical model of reality upon which they are premised has lost legitimacy. The process-oriented approach of biology, in addition to being consistent with a cosmological shift from hierarchy to process, is also consistent with a shift from divine to human actorhood – for example, Victoria's current course offerings in biology also include Economic Entomology ("the variety of measures available for pest control will be emphasized"[20]) and Plants and People (a look at "economically important plants and their products, sources of food, shelter, clothing, drugs, and industrial raw materials"[21]). Biologists care not only about what things *are*, independent of humanity, but also about how things *work*, in relation to humanity.

Chemistry's approach – and, increasingly, its subject matter – is fundamentally the same, as manifested in the recent ascendance of biochemistry.[22] But chemistry moves one step further in the decategorization process. Where biologists bridge the gulf between plants and animals, chemistry builds the further bridge between organic and inorganic. We expect that the universalistic, process-oriented approach of chemistry – the science concerned with the workings of matter at the atomic level – will be highly conducive to its persistence over the course of the century. Compared to any of the sciences discussed above, chemistry has grown in scope and ambition, with dozens of subfields ranging from analytical chemistry to organic chemistry. With this range at its disposal, modern chemistry sees itself as *the* foundational science. Cambridge University's chemistry department, for example, tells prospective students: "We like to think of chemistry as the 'central science,' as a knowledge of molecular structures and properties is crucial in our understanding of large parts of science, from semiconductors to proteins and from the composition of interstellar clouds to the human genome. By studying chemistry you will acquire a wide range of skills and learn about ideas and concepts which address all the important questions in modern science."[23] This all-embracing worldview is natural for a discipline that traces its historical roots to attempts to explain a wide range of natural phenomena by recourse to a few simple laws of behavior and makes the field a prime candidate for such industrial dabblings as a course taught at Cambridge by a team of scientists from Amoco ("the chemical industry is one of the most successful parts of British industry and, unlike much of commerce, an understanding of fundamental scientific principles and the application of technology lies at the very heart of the business").[24] As the institutionalized power to *know* and *do* shifts from God to humans, chemistry should claim university resources unavailable to its disciplinary brethren that are premised upon the eclipsed model of actorhood.

Arguably the processual science *par excellence*, however, is physics. Physics, the discipline concerned with the behavior of matter, hoists an even broader umbrella than does chemistry. *Any aspect* of the behavior of matter – from the coherence of subatomic particles to the paths of the planets – is in this discipline's scope, flouting traditional categories and collapsing traditional hierarchies.[25] The Department of Physics at Morocco's Mansoura University, for example, includes research groups studying solar energy, electronics, glass, nuclear physics, optics, and physics theory.[26] Among the natural sciences, physics is perhaps most frequently joined in interdisciplinary ventures (as in geophysics, biophysics, and astrophysics), as well as being put to industrial application. Far from conceiving of the universe as a static hierarchy, physics seeks universal laws that should apply to all matter (including human matter) and that are to be discerned by active human investigators.[27] The only basic science more compatible with an integrated, dynamic view of the universe is mathematics, as discussed below. Thus, we expect that among the basic natural sciences, the relative decline of physics will be less significant than that observed for any other science save mathematics.

Mathematics is, among the natural sciences, perhaps uniquely well suited to revised templates of action and structure. In the newly institutionalized scheme, all phenomena are fundamentally interconnected and fundamentally similar, behaving in accord with basic natural laws.[28] "Many modern physicists and philosophers (Albert Einstein being a notable example) maintain, with the early Pythagoreans, that nature is 'essentially' mathematical."[29] In virtually every natural science, basic or applied, advanced studies require additional mathematical training, and the same cannot be said for physics or chemistry. Although mathematics has long been a pillar of the university, understanding the contemporary cosmology *requires* mathematics in a way that the outdated cosmology did not. Mathematics provides an abstract key to the universe, which humans can comprehend and therefore manipulate. In the past, understanding human behavior meant understanding theology and natural law; today, understanding human behavior means building statistical models[30] – for this reason, statistics has been called the most important development in twentieth-century mathematics.[31] In the past, understanding the natural world meant painstakingly observing and cataloguing plants and animals; today, it means simulating the atmosphere with supercomputers. Modern universities understand this well: The Web site of the Department of Mathematics at the Universidad Nacional de Columbia speaks of the discipline's power to illuminate "the most general structures of logical thought," which can be applied to a "diversity of fields."[32] Although pure mathematics may bleed faculty to departments of applied mathematics and computer science, we expect that this foundational importance of mathematics to the currently institutionalized cosmology will slow or perhaps entirely prevent its decline over the century's course.[33]

Although we have emphasized that certain fields are particularly well adapted to evolve in a manner compatible with the broad shift in the globally institutionalized and ontology that we have described, it is worth restating that – as shown in Chapter 1 – we do observe decline across the basic natural sciences. Despite all the new interdisciplinary openness to real-world applications, the basic natural sciences (again, as opposed to the explicitly or implicitly applied natural sciences) remain one step removed from the remodeled reality, which is a dynamic assembly motivated by human volition. To some extent, the basic natural sciences have a direct object of study that is external to human society and thus beyond manipulation. That universe may become less static and more dynamic, less hierarchical and more horizontal, and seen to be fundamentally ordered at ever-lower levels, but the basic natural sciences remain at their heart an ivory tower enterprise – and pride themselves as such. Whereas such disciplines as engineering and medicine aim to understand the natural world in the direct, mundane service of the human community, the basic natural sciences remain officially aloof from human application and intervention in the natural world. Even in their most progressive guise, they retain the spark that has long animated scientific exploration – the empirical quest for the ultimate nature of reality.

As Stephen Hawking noted in conclusion to his astrophysics blockbuster, *A Brief History of Time*, "If we discover a complete theory, it should in time be understandable by everyone, not just by a few scientists. Then we shall all, philosophers, scientists and just ordinary people, be able to take part in the discussion of the question of why it is that we and the universe exist. If we find the answer to that, it would be the ultimate triumph of human reason – for then we should know the mind of God."[34]

It is in such sentiments – widely if implicitly shared among scientists in these disciplines – that we see most clearly the philosophical link between the humanities and the basic natural sciences. The ultimate basis of this philosophy in a waning global-institutional frame has led to a slow but inexorable decline in the basic natural sciences' position in the university – though, we hypothesize, with interdisciplinary differences in slope that vary by the extent of each discipline's philosophical ties to the outdated models of action and structure. Our hypotheses are presented visually in Figure 1.

Empirical Trends in the Natural Sciences

As in the previous chapters, we display and discuss the results from the full case base of the *Commonwealth Universities Yearbook*. These results appear in Tables 1 and 2 and are graphically presented in Figures 2 and 3. In reporting and discussing our results, it is worth emphasizing that we are not arguing that the official disciplinary classification of faculty members' activities maps cleanly onto their concrete research activities. As we discussed in the Introduction (and demonstrate in the next chapter), our argument accounts for *intra*disciplinary shifts, as well as interdisciplinary shifts – thus, "zoology" in 1915 and "zoology" in 1995 are in practice somewhat different from one another. Official classifications, however, are precisely our object of interest – thus, the indicator and the variable are one and the same. We argue that when it comes to academic disciplines, a name says less about the substantive nature of work in a given field than about the *framing* of that work: the story the discipline's practitioners tell about their history and their role. Kay refers to this storytelling as a discipline's "representational practice" – with each natural science laboring "under the conviction that its own representational practice grasps the essence of life."[35] In this respect, the fate of zoology and the fate of "zoology" are one and the same.[36]

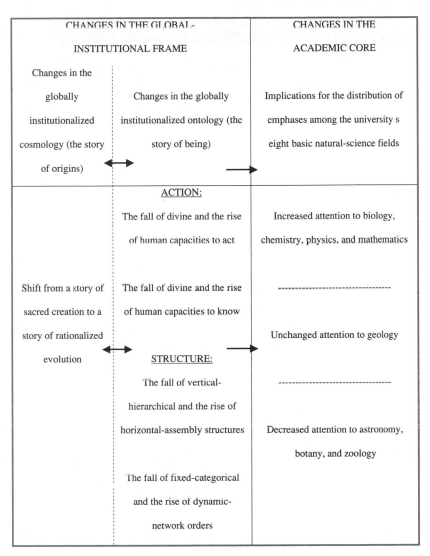

Figure 1 Summary of argument and implications for the eight basic natural-science fields.

As we hypothesized, the sciences experiencing the steepest declines are those primarily oriented toward the passive observation and classification of static entities. Botany and zoology, as Table 1 and Figure 2 show, decline in near-lockstep – from 2.7 percent and 2.4 percent of university faculty, respectively, to 1.0 percent and 1.1 percent.[37] Over the century's course, each

Table 1   Percentage of Total University Faculty in Eight Basic Natural-Science Fields for Universities in British Commonwealth Countries

	Faculty Percentage in 1915–35	*Faculty Percentage in 1976–95*	*Percentage Change Over Time*
Geology	1.3	1.2	−6
Mathematics	4.7	3.6	−24
Chemistry	5.8	3.8	−34
Physics	5.0	3.2	−35
Biology	5.5	3.1	−44
Zoology	2.4	1.1	−54
Botany	2.7	1.0	−64
Astronomy	0.1	0.01	−89

of these disciplines lost more than half its faculty presence, as their respective endeavors became more marginal to the modern university's mission. To put it another way, early in the century about one in thirty-five faculty members was a botanist; by the century's end only one in a hundred was.

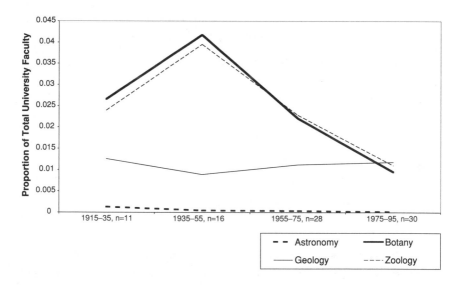

Figure 2   Natural science fields employing less than 4% of university faculty in period 1.

The decline of astronomy is even more stark, particularly given that these data reveal its foothold in the university to have been surprisingly tenuous to begin with – a fraction of 1 percent of the total faculty. These figures may be somewhat shocking in light of the massively disproportionate amount of public attention paid to astronomy. From the aforementioned Stephen Hawking to Carl Sagan – long an institution of public television – astronomy enjoys a romance with the public and has long boasted an unusually large number of amateur practitioners.[38] Our data suggest, however, that this public allure does not translate to faculty resources. As the ontological assumptions of the academy have shifted toward the processual and human-centric, we expect (although our data cannot definitively answer this question) that what astronomy is taught is increasingly shifted under the umbrella of physics (as is the case at Manchester, for example). Although this might mean that the incidence of astronomy teaching and research is underestimated in our data, the result is not a mere artifact – as we have repeatedly emphasized, the label placed upon research in a given area is a telling indicator of the institutional underpinnings of that research. If a professor researching, for example, star clusters is called an astronomer in the nineteenth century and a physicist in the twentieth, this suggests that we have reconceptualized his or her very enterprise in accordance with the newly institutionalized models of action and structure. Further, this result – like that obtained for psychology – highlights the value of a wide-reaching sampling scheme. Surely, astronomy would seem to enjoy a greater share of faculty were we to turn to U.S. universities (for example, our World Guide data reveal that as late as 1971, astronomers comprised 0.8 percent of faculty at the University of Wisconsin at Madison and 1.2 percent of faculty at Harvard); our global data, however, reveal that astronomy is inessential (or, at best, highly marginal) for most universities.[39]

Table 1 and Figure 2 show that geology has demonstrated considerable staying power over the century's course. Its relative decline, in fact, is the least dramatic of any natural science: In the earliest time period for which we have data, about 1.3 percent of university faculty were geologists, and this percentage had barely declined by the final time point. What this means, as Figure 2 shows, is that a field with only half the faculty share of both zoology and botany early in the century now has a greater faculty share than either of those fields. This result is something of a surprise, as geology (unlike, say, chemistry or physics) assumes by definition a categorical order, wherein the physical matter of the Earth may be clearly designated. Still, the field accommodates human actorhood (often in the form of natural resource exploitation) and assumes basic dynamism. As the dynamic, integrated model of the natural world gained currency over the century, geology proved itself most readily adaptable to the ecosystem model and has been buttressed accordingly.[40]

Although the field of geology was relatively open from the beginning to such adaptation, this is a case in which the widely noted mid-century boost in national security funding interacted with shifting global-institutional currents to produce the robust field of geology we observe today. "The ascendance of geophysics" – as opposed to "geology" in the more traditional, classification-heavy sense – "was not primarily the result of prior intellectual success. Rather, it was the result of an abstract epistemological belief in the primacy of physics and chemistry, coupled with strong institutional backing for geophysics premised on its concrete applicability to perceived national-security needs."[41]

Turning to Figure 3, we again see a graphic representation of the broad decline in the basic natural sciences. The four disciplines included here – all

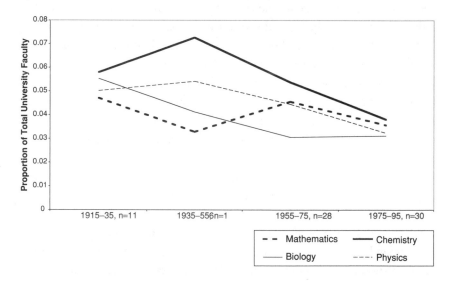

Figure 3   Natural science fields employing more than 4% of university faculty in period 1.

disciplines that occupied a greater share of university faculty in the first time period than any of the four discussed thus far – without exception experienced significant decline in faculty share over the century's course. Again, however, the differences in slope are telling.

Among these four, biology experiences the steepest decline, losing a full 44 percent of its share between the first and last time periods. Biology is primarily an experimental science and thus consistent with current globally institutionalized assumptions regarding the locus of action. But – in contrast to chemistry, physics, and mathematics – biology assumes that a categorical boundary can and should be drawn around life,[42] a premise of declining legitimacy. Biology's intermediate decline is thus consistent with our argument that fields most unequivocally premised upon fixed hierarchies rather than dynamic assemblies and upon divine rather than human actor hood should find themselves worst off in the wake of the quickly shifting cosmology. Recall, however, that we observe even more dramatic losses for zoology (−54 percent) and botany (−64 percent) – sciences with the same fundamental subject matter as biology but with more explicit emphasis on classification, hierarchy, and passive observation; rather than dynamic processes and active experimentation.[43]

Even more abstracted and process oriented than biology are the disciplines of chemistry and physics, and we are not surprised to find their losses less significant than those experienced by biology, botany, or zoology. Both chemistry and physics lose approximately 35 percent of their faculty share – a full third, but proportionately less than higher level fields. Again, the relevant axis of difference is adaptability to the new cosmology – chemistry and physics are both relatively compatible with a vision of a horizontal, dynamic universe, encompassing humanity and driven by universal processes (rather than its alternative – a static, rigidly hierarchical universe for humans to observe but not affect).

Finally, among these four disciplines the losses of mathematics are least dramatic. Over the century's course, the share of university faculty studying mathematics went from about 4.7 percent to about 3.6 percent – a loss of about one-quarter of the discipline's original share. This relative persistence has meant that a discipline once eclipsed by chemistry, biology, and physics now has a stronger representation on university faculties than any basic natural science save chemistry (which it trailed, at the close of our observation

Table 2   Number of Universities in Sample with No
Faculty by Disciplinary Field in 1986–95 (n = 28)

Mathematics	0
Chemistry	1
Physics	1
Biology	8
Geology	9
Botany	14
Zoology	14
Astronomy	27

period, by only 0.2 percent and which now may have fully eclipsed). This discipline, with its emphasis upon abstract principles and universal laws underlying all observable phenomena and its widespread application to all manner of human interventions in the natural world, has emerged as probably the dominant basic natural science in the university.[44]

Table 2 presents an alternate perspective on these same data. Among universities at the end of our observation period, departments of mathematics, chemistry, and physics were all but universal: These three core disciplines have all but *become* the basic natural sciences. If a university is to exist as a legitimate enterprise, it virtually must cover these areas. Biology and geology are somewhat less prevalent, but still established in the clear majority of universities. Botany, zoology, and astronomy, by way of contrast, are purely optional. Although the *Commonwealth Yearbook* may be slightly misleading in suggesting that astronomy is at the utter vanishing point, all of our sources confirm that astronomers are very much a relative rarity.

As we noted earlier, observers are much more lax in the case of the natural sciences (as opposed to the humanities) to characterize shifts in teaching and research emphases as other than a teleological procession toward a universal "truth." These data, however, seen in conjunction with the data we present elsewhere in this book strongly suggest that observed shifts among and within the natural sciences are best understood in the context of broad shifts in the globally institutionalized reality. As our fundamental models of structure and action shift, disciplines across the university rise or decline in accordance with their underlying assumptions about the universe. Those disciplines that emphasize a static hierarchy of being that is merely observed by humans – disciplines ranging from theology to anthropology to zoology – see their faculty shares relatively decline; whereas those disciplines that emphasize a dynamic, integrated system of being that is actively manipulated by humans – disciplines ranging from history to sociology to mathematics – see their shares relatively increase.[45]

Conclusion

Harvard's venerable Museum of Comparative Zoology, founded in 1859, is a museum not only of animal species but also of an entire eclipsed worldview – hundreds of specimens of taxidermied birds, fish, and mammals are arranged by species behind glass cases, the natural world in perfect order, for humans to observe and catalogue but not to tamper with. Ageless, unchanging glass replicas of plant species are arrayed in careful botanical order; guidebooks tell of heroic Harvard professors roaming Africa's savage jungles in search of the perfect gorilla specimen to shoot, stuff, and triumphantly display among its fellow primates. The museum's unifying cosmology is manifestly that of a past age – boundless diversity for humans to capture, classify, and gawk at. The net impression is one of an awesome natural world full of powerful, exotic, scary creatures ordered by a divine logic operating beyond the scope of human intervention.[46] Further, the clear presumption of the exhibit design is that the act of knowing involves merely observing rather than experimenting. The visitor is there to be told what scientists have discovered about the order of the universe, not to discover anything him- or herself.[47]

The newly constructed Science Museum of Minnesota presents a powerful contrast, embodying the new cosmology of process and human empowerment. Its *raison d'être* is to involve and empower the individual in a dynamic universe. Interactivity is pervasive – even the dinosaur skeletons are outfitted with levers that allow visitors to move the beasts' jaws. An exhibit on local waterways emphasizes rivers' historical utility (children can play inside an actual tugboat and operate a toy lock-and-dam) and unified ecosystem (visitors can assemble a puzzle representing the web of life). An exhibit on physics emphasizes the discipline's broad relevance to phenomena from the weather (make your own tornado) to music (play a violin and watch the harmonic waves the sound produces) to geometry (manipulate pendulums connected to a pen that draws figures for the visitor to sign). The museum's programs "strive to open minds, not just fill them."[48] This is our new vision of the natural world, and as it has risen to globally institutionalized dominance, academic disciplines incompatible with mind-opening empowerment in an interconnected ecosystem operating by universal laws have lost prominence in the university and elsewhere.

The manifestation of this shift in museums is evidence of the breadth of the global-institutional reordering our data show has occurred among university disciplines. Again, although we emphasize adaptation by selection (with faculties of eclipsed disciplines being proportionately trimmed), we argue that *intra*disciplinary change – to the extent it is permitted by disciplinary definitions and interdisciplinary boundaries – has been occurring as well. The shifts we discuss have occurred in fractal manner, manifest at levels both macro (founding of institutes and universities) and micro (shifts in syllabi and course offerings). As our vision of the natural world has shifted toward the dynamic and interconnected, the very notion of discrete disciplines has begun to erode. Nonetheless, the vast majority of basic natural science research at universities continues to be done under one of the eight disciplinary headings discussed in this chapter. Disciplines less amenable to the cosmology as currently institutionalized have declined particularly steeply, but each of these disciplines has suffered for its fundamental focus upon the passively observing (even if through experimentation) human actor – as opposed to the actively manipulating human actor presumed by the applied natural sciences.

Throughout this discussion, we have made reference to the vast and informative literature on the history of science. In addition to informing our historical discussion, prior work by sociologists and historians of science has firmly established the validity of our suggestion that shifts among disciplines are caused by something more than a march toward objective truth. The natural sciences, thanks to this prior work, "are no longer seen as possessing a special epistemological warrant which makes their sociological analysis irrelevant."[49] We hope to contribute to these literatures both theoretically (by drawing attention to a level of analysis and to the usefulness of the institutional literature in sociology) and empirically (by contributing much-needed macro-level data on a subject of wide interest). That is, we hope both to answer some long-standing questions in the literatures and to enable the asking of new questions.

It may be suggested that our approach – specifically with respect to the natural sciences and the applied sciences – over-theorizes a shift that might be explained more parsimoniously by reference to the historical coincidence of two world wars, each of which drove governments to fund and otherwise promote applied science at the expense of basic research. Certainly we acknowledge that this mechanism played a role, as has been widely noted by historians of science.[50] We do not, however, believe that this fact challenges the validity or usefulness of our argument. For one thing, the applied/basic tension has always been present in scientific research – from the very first astronomical observations for use in navigation, the promise of application to practical problems has always been an impetus for science and thus was not new to the wartime period or any other. At the same time, whether their aim was to map divine creation or to uncover the unifying principle of physics, researchers in basic science have long felt threatened by the mundane projects of their peers in the technical sciences.[51] Empirically, arguments for the significance of the war years are challenged by the fact that the natural sciences that seemed most clearly to grow during that period are botany and zoology, which have few obvious military applications and which go on to plummet precipitously (Figure 2).

What we empirically observe as a decline in many of the basic natural sciences and a rise in many of the applied sciences is best understood, we argue, not as a historical coincidence but as one manifestation of profound shifts in the globally institutionalized cosmology. From this perspective, the basic natural sciences represent the corner of the university associated with the humanities – historically and symbolically central as a project to find God's fingerprints in the cosmos, but out of place in a world that places actorhood on the shoulders of humans, rather than their Creator. For fundamentally applied scientific research to become central to the project of the university, the university had to make ontological room for a field of human endeavor once regarded as deeply suspect.[52] Exigencies of war are not sufficient to explain the shifts we observe – applied scientific research could have taken place in government laboratories or under the auspices of industry. Only once globally institutionalized reality shifted to make the study of industrial applications legitimate knowledge could this study be sited in universities. Further, our own theory accounts for shifts across the university faculty – even among fields in the humanities, where the decline of classics and philosophy and the ascendance of hands-on arts training cannot be explained by global conflict.

This leads to the cumulative conclusion of Chapters 2–4: The strength of our theory is manifest not only in the shifts among the branches of learning and between the basic and applied divisions (which we reported in Chapter 1) but also in the lower level shifts among the disciplines within each branch of learning. Although we have discussed and acknowledged the important field- and institution-specific mechanisms that have driven change in the university, the results we have presented in these three chapters taken together lend powerful support to our argument that these mechanisms interact with (indeed, are often manifestations of) shifts in globally institutionalized models of action and structure. Our theory – which encompasses rather than contradicts mechanisms previously discussed in the literature – has unique value in its scope and range, generating testable hypotheses across a substantively wide range of disciplines. These hypotheses are strongly supported by our longitudinal worldwide data on faculty composition. In the following chapter, we test our theory at yet another level of analysis: the shifting focus and framing *within* a discipline.

Notes

1. Much material from this chapter appeared previously in Jay Gabler and David John Frank. "The Natural Sciences in the University: Change and Variation over the Twentieth Century." *Sociology of Education 78: 183–206 (2005).* Copyright © 2005 by the American Sociological Assocation.

2. Supporting this distinction is the fact that a number of the universities in our sample report faculty members in such fields as applied biology or applied chemistry. We do not observe professors of applied engineering or applied veterinary medicine, such labels being redundant.

3. See Krantz (1985).

4. See "Living in a Fishbowl." 1985. *New York Times*, December 1, Section 1, p. 22.

5. See McEneaney (2000:6).

6. See McEneaney (2000:18–19).

7. See McEneaney (2000:16).

8. See Gabler (2004).

9. See Kevles (1979:7).

10. See Rosner (2002:197).

11. See Smith (2003:160).

12. See http://www.botany.org/newsite/botany, 2003.

13. See http://www.botany.org/bsa/millen/mil-int1.html, 2003.

14. See Mayr and Provine (1998).

15. Geology's assumptions in this respect have long placed it in a controversial position among creationists who posit a relatively young and static Earth (Rosner 2002: 96).

16. The first use of this term appearing in the Oxford English Dictionary dates only to 1935.

17. Indeed, Schofer (2003) uses geology as a case study of the very process of international institutionalization that our argument highlights.

18. See Rosner (2002: 95).

19. See http://web.uvic.ca/calendar2001/CDs/BIOL/190A.html, 2003.

20. See http://web.uvic.ca/calendar2001/CDs/BIOL/313.html, 2003.

21. See http://web.uvic.ca/calendar2001/CDs/BIOL/334.html, 2003.

22. In these data, biochemistry and biophysics are merged with biology. Although biochemistry and biophysics together do grow significantly over the course of the century, even together they remain only a fraction of the size of their "pure" parent disciplines. In the first time period under consideration, for example, biochemistry and biophysics together are only one tenth the size of biology; by the final time period, together they are one-fifth the size of biology.

23. See http://www-teach.ch.cam.ac.uk/introcourses/faq.html, 2003.

24. See http://www-teach.ch.cam.ac.uk/introcourses/part2/PartIIpublicity03_4.pdf, 2003.

25. The fact that both chemistry and physics can claim – with some legitimacy – to be *the* foundational science highlights the fundamental distinction between these disciplines and such as zoology and botany, each of which explicitly neglects an entire "kingdom" of being.

26. See http://www.mans.eun.eg/facscim/PhyDept/index.htm#Introduction, 2003.

27. "It is often thought that if the theories of physics are true, they must fix the behavior of all other features of the natural universe" (Cartwright, Psillos, and Chang 2003:27).

28. See Boyle and Meyer (1998).

29. See Cartwright, Psillos, and Chang (2003:23)

30. Porter (2002).

31. Rosner (2002: 200).

32. Translated by authors from http://www.matematicas.unal.edu.co/academia/programas/index.php, 2003.

33. In predicting persistence rather than decline in the faculty share of mathematics, we are predicting a trajectory quite different from that of philosophy – a discipline similar to mathematics insofar as it has attempted to define itself as a universal *tool*, rather than a specific body of knowledge. The reasons that philosophy has failed at this definition while mathematics has succeeded are not all obvious – mathematics, after all, has historically carried a strong whiff of divine order – and the contrast would make a fascinating case study. For our purposes here, we note only that mathematics was far better positioned from the beginning to be a universal tool with practical applications; philosophy has historically been relatively wary both to discard its late greats and to embrace practical application.

34. Hawking (1988:193).

35. Kay (1993:16). Note the distinction between *representational practice* and *object of study* – although zoology and botany study different categories of objects, their representational practices are very similar to one another. Conversely, though botany and biology study the same objects, their representational practices are very dissimilar from one another.

36. Fisher notes increasing philosophical distaste for disciplinary boundaries, which is consistent with the ascendant global-institutional order that emphasizes systems and overarching principles. Even, however, if "differentiation is more of interest to funding bodies than to philosophers" (Fisher 1990: 867), the disciplinary boundaries are so deeply institutionalized that they refuse to evaporate.

37. Although the long-term trajectory of both fields conforms to our expectations, it is interesting to note that we observe a clear (though short-lived) rise in the prevalence of both fields between the first and second time points of our observation. This increase may be an artifact of the birthing process of biology; as attention and funding poured into genetics and the related activities that became foundational to modern biology, much of this work initially took place in departments of botany and zoology. By mid-century, however, biology had triumphed as a frame and a location for these research activities (Mayr and Provine 1998) – in addition to their emergence as standbys of agricultural and medical research.

38. Knight (2003:79). In fact, the motives behind the establishment of prominent official observatories have often had to do more with symbolism than with science (Bennett 1987; Smith 2003:159).

39. Cross-source checks do suggest that astronomy may be an exceptional case in which the *Commonwealth Yearbook's* data reporting procedures may be depressing the discipline's apparent standing. Despite this anomaly, our argument and substantive findings remain the same: Available data from the *Index Generalis*

and *World Guide* confirm that astronomy has always been nominally among the smallest of the natural sciences and, further, experienced steep decline over the century's course.

40. Although professors of geology have been combined with professors of geophysics for conciseness, we initially coded them separately, expecting to witness the ascendance of the latter discipline. We did indeed witness a rise – we observe *no* faculty members in geophysics in the 1916–35 time period, but by the 1976–95 time period we observe twice as many geophysicists as astronomers.

41. Oreskes and Doel (2003:539).

42. cf. Biglan (1973).

43. Smocovitis (1996) and Mayr and Provine (1998) describe biology's tortuous path to acceptance as a unified science amounting to more than "a shotgun marriage of botany and zoology" (Simpson et al. quoted in Simpson and Beck 1965: v). Even, however, as biology gained traction on those outmoded disciplines, its practitioners felt threatened by chemistry and physics. Our data suggest that these concerns were well founded.

44. Philosophers have argued that their discipline is similarly universal in ambition and potential application. In the words of the American Philosophical Association, "the enhancement of our understanding of matters with which thinkers of great intelligence and sophistication have long been wrestling, which do not admit of definitive resolution and yet have far-reaching implications, is both challenging and central to the academic enterprise" (http://www.apa.udel.edu/apa/governance/statements/research.html, 2003). In actual substance, however, we argue that mathematics has found itself much freer to shed its emphasis on great thinkers of the past than has philosophy; accordingly, mathematics is seen as being more readily applicable to a broad variety of disciplines in the modern university.

45. As we have noted, we found broad consistency among our source bases with respect to overall patterns and trends. One discrepancy worth noting was that, through 1955–75, biology, chemistry, and physics performed even more strongly in the non-Commonwealth cases – marking upward progress where we observe a downward trend in the Commonwealth cases. Unfortunately data on these non-Commonwealth cases are not available for 1975–95. Despite these differing slopes, support for our theory is to be found in the fact that the two samples are converging on a common absolute distribution of disciplinary representation. Further research would shed helpful light on this question.

46. New York City's American Museum of Natural History, an institution of the same vintage and founded on similar principles, notoriously extended this logic to "primitive" human beings (Haraway 1989). Though now updated to eliminate some of the cultural hierarchy, the museum's anthropology exhibits retain much of their original flavor and demonstrate the deep sympathy between anthropology and zoology. We argue that it is far from coincidental that these outmoded disciplines are seen

to similarly founder in comparison to their peer disciplines in the social and natural sciences, respectively.

47. McEneaney (2000) notes that an intervening step between divine actorhood and human actorhood highlights the role of the scientific "expert" – note the parallel to the role of the "expert artist" in the humanities.

48. See http://www.smm.org/getinvolved/donorsandsupport/, 2003.

49. Pinch (1990: 87).

50. Rowe (2003:129), Smith (2003:166).

51. Shinn (2003).

52. "For years, technical students at Harvard and Yale lived in different buildings from the rest of the undergraduates, went to different lectures, sat apart in the college chapel, and earned degrees that Harvard and Yale proper held in suspicion if not disdain" (Kevles 1979: 9).

CHAPTER 5

The Subject Matters of History

In Chapter 4, we completed our examination of disciplinary recomposition within the branches of learning with an investigation of world-level changes in the emphases accorded to eight natural science fields over the twentieth century. In terms of faculty composition, we found proportional declines across all eight of the fields. But decline for some fields involved a slight waning (geology, mathematics), whereas for others it verged more nearly on collapse (astronomy, botany). Our global-institutional argument steered us well through the field-to-field variations. As expected, transformations in action and structure proved to be far more deleterious to some natural science disciplines than to others.

Here we ratchet down another level of organizational analysis and proceed forward along our path.[1] Having begun our inquiries among the branches of learning and the basic and applied divisions, and then having narrowed our lens to query each branch's disciplinary fields, we now tighten our gaze again and focus in on subject-level matters. Did twentieth-century changes in the global-institutional frame reconstitute academic priorities *within* disciplinary boundaries at the same time as they raised and lowered relative standings at the branch and field levels?

To answer these questions, we had to choose a discipline for subject-level analysis. For two main reasons, we settled on history. First it is a substantively interesting case. History is linked to the most troubled zone of the university – the humanities – and yet its durability over the twentieth century was outstanding, as it declined only slightly in average faculty share. Did history adapt to new conditions, even as environmental changes selected against the humanities at large? Second the story-telling qualities of the field give it practical advantages, meaning that the changing subject matters of history are relatively accessible – i.e., relatively easy to observe and to measure – as compared to most other disciplines. Thus among the many options, we chose to delve into the subject matters of history.

As in previous chapters, our starting point is the two-fold evidence culled from case and comparative studies suggesting that history's composition changed over our study period and that the changes followed discernible patterns, such that some subjects rose among the priorities of history whereas others fell, even on a global basis. Our first goal is to pin down these changes – empirically demonstrating the global recomposition of history over the twentieth century – and thus to introduce systematic data into a discursive stream replete with feelings but scarce of findings. Our second goal is to use the data as a further testing ground for our theoretical argument – this time at a lower level of organizational analysis – tying broad changes in globally institutionalized reality to long-term revisions in the academic core.

We set off toward these goals by considering the likely impacts of the global-institutional frame's master transitions on five dimensions of history: units of analysis, areas, time periods, subnational groups, and special subjects. Then we test for the expected trends in teaching and research emphases, using data assembled from a global sample of course catalogues that chart the changing makeup of university history between 1895 and 1995.

Background

Although world-level research on historical subjects is small in supply, comparative work in the domain has called attention to the pliability of history's subject matters.[2] In extreme instances, an era is quietly disposed of or a war is forgotten. More typically, different groups of characters are included or excluded and various events laid bare or shrouded. Although the discipline of history is definitionally bound to provide a realistic accounting of the putatively objective development of society, *what* and *who* count in society and how that entity is conceived to develop turn out to be highly variable matters.[3]

To illustrate history's malleability in regard to subject matter, consider that in 1909–10, the history department at Kansas State University offered courses in ancient, medieval, modern, constitutional, industrial, English, French, modern European, and American history. One course description, for American Nation, offered a rationale for such a subject portfolio: "The roots of our American history and institutions are found in the history and institutions of European nations, especially in that of England. In order really to understand American history you must know European history. This is one of the chief reasons . . . for our study of ancient and modern history."[4] The logic inherent in the course description poses a sacred thread linking the realities of the American present to the "birthplaces of civilization" in ancient Europe.

By 1990, Kansas State's history curriculum seemed to operate on different premises, having grown to encompass a broader and more differentiated array of historical subjects. Although the department retained courses analogous to those appearing earlier, it offered as well (1) access to a geographically broadened world, including histories of India, Latin America, Russia, Southeast Asia, and Mexico; (2) classes on the very recent past, such as War in the 20th Century and the Rise and Fall of Nazi Germany; and (3) courses emphasizing a newly variegated picture of American society, manifest in the History of the Indians of North America, Black American History, and Women in American History.[5] Between 1910 and 1990 at Kansas State, the composition of history – its subject matter content – clearly shifted.

Some comparative evidence from secondary-school textbooks hints that history's composition was reestablished elsewhere during this period as well. A study of how history was taught in Japanese, East German, and West German schools in the post-World War II decades finds that the subject portfolio moved in directions similar to those seen at Kansas State. For instance, "The 'great men' approach to political history gradually disappeared in West Germany from 1945 to 1995. A more differentiated attribution of agency seems to particularly 'take off' in the early 1970s with the introduction of... general attention to social systems and to sub-national actors in history."[6]

Along some of the same lines, a study of secondary-school history textbooks from China, Taiwan, and Hong Kong documents a substantial reshuffling of historical subject matters over roughly the same decades. For example, the likes of emperors and dynasties were forced increasingly to make room in the historical arena for workers and professionals. In many countries, it seems, history experienced nonrandom recomposition over the twentieth century.

Motivated by work in this vein, we set sail in this chapter to explore global trends in the teaching and research emphases of history. Our effort is both empirical – to document the trends – and theoretical – to explain them.

The literature has not addressed this issue directly, but two general approaches may be applied. In the first, changes in the subject matters of history are understood as responses to new societal needs. For instance one might say that given the imperatives posed by an increasingly multicultural society, the history department at the University of Notre Dame recently embraced the theme of unity in diversity, which is "evident in the concern of many members of the department with what the colloquy refers to as 'human solidarity,' matters of political participation, and of social and political justice as they are mediated by national, cultural, racial and gender identities."[7] In the second view, history's contents may be conceived as reflecting the demands of powerful constituents (students, corporations, funders, etc.). For example, the emergence of the women's movement may be tapped to explain expanded attention to women among the subject matters of history.[8] Both frameworks represent a broad stimulus-response functionalism.

Although reasonable on the surface, needs-and-demands views on disciplinary revisions imply substantial cross-national variation in what counts as history (and also sociology, biology, industrial engineering, and so on). There are, after all, extreme country-level differentiations in the quality and quantity of both societal needs and loci of power, and by the logic of functionalist frameworks these variations should translate into extreme differentiations in disciplinary composition. Therefore if a needs/demands argument characterizes the primary causal force behind subject reprioritization, global trends in teaching and research emphases should be invisible, overwhelmed by local variations. We test this possibility below.

By contrast if the arguments made throughout this book are operative down at the university's subject levels – beyond the branch, division, and field levels, where we have already observed effects – then worldwide trends in disciplinary composition are to be expected. From our perspective, the onset of modernity inaugurated long-term revisions in the globally institutionalized cosmology and ontology, which together recast the basic characteristics of reality – its taken-for-granted depictions of action and structure. These changes renewed the assumptions that form the academic core's most basic building blocks, shifting the tectonic plates on which university knowledge rests worldwide.

Although our focus here is specifically on the subject matters of history, case study and comparative evidence from other disciplinary fields implies that any one of those fields could be discussed in terms of our framework. For example during the post-World War II period in the United States, prioritized subject matters in the field of economics grew increasingly abstract and technical, data oriented, and statistically complex. Simultaneously on the flipside, economics lost most of its substantive orientation (e.g., on railroads and banks).[9] Also in the United States around the same period, the substantive contents of English literature moved away from two old linchpins, the canon and literary masterpieces. On the premise that literature should reflect and authenticate diverse voices in the American mosaic (a melting pot no more), a wider variety of texts and a broader range of authors came to qualify as English literature even while some of the oldest and whitest Anglo males lost their validations. Dafoe and Dryden were nearly forgotten in the process while Toni Morrison and Amy Tan grew prominent.[10] Such changes as these in the subject matters of economics and English – and no doubt subtler ones in mathematics or neurology – could be held up to the global-institutional light.

For the moment, however, those analyses will have to wait. At hand are the contents of history, parts of which we anticipate rose in prominence over the twentieth century as other parts fell. We expect the pattern of observed changes to fall in line with global-institutional reframing. We set out to assess our suppositions accordingly, with the subject matters of history in our sights.

Argument

In Foucault's elegant formulation, historical eras differ not only in what people think but also in what people find thinkable.[11] Throughout this book, we have built around this general theme, arguing that global-institutional reframing resets key parameters around what is thinkable – or what at least is publicly claimable in world society – and what therefore becomes incorporated into the body of university knowledge.

At the base of the global-institutional frame is a theory of origins, a master genesis implicit in the culture and built into the organization of world society. Over the whole modern period the institutionalized cosmology eased away from traditional creationist imageries and moved toward rationalized evolutionist ones. This process of change, which sped up considerably in Darwin's wake, spurred revisions (also long underway) in the globally institutionalized ontology along its dual action and structure dimensions.

Redefinition of Action in the Globally Institutionalized Ontology

Jointly with the reorigination of reality came a two-part change in the essential elements of action. To an increasing extent over the century, the ability to bring about, as well as the ability to know about, traded hands in the global-institutional frame.

In the first part of this move, the capability to author reality – to bring about change with independence and volition – descended from divine to human realms. Humans became the all-purpose doers in the cultural scripts and organizational rules of world society. In previous chapters, we drew causal connections from the redefinition of action to the university's branches, divisions, and fields of learning. It seems likely that the renewal of action also brought about world-level changes in the subject composition of history.

Along the time dimension to begin with, as humans increasingly inherited action capacities from divinities, we expect that history moved away from studies of the far distant past (ancient heritage) and became more "presentist" in orientation (contemporary function). Under conditions of divine actorhood, preeminent meaning was located in the period of ancient origins during which the divine plan for the universe was revealed and final destiny was born. To understand one's self and one's world – to comprehend the present – required one to delve into the distant past. Christians study the book of Genesis not to learn about the ancient world but to understand their present universe. As sacred creation and divine actorhood faded from the public accounting system over the twentieth century, meaning waned from the ancient past, and we expect that historical interest in the period declined accordingly.

On the other side of this equation, we suppose that university history also grew more presentist during the twentieth century as global reality became unhitched from divine harnesses, to be shaped by human hands. As action-loaded humans exerted their rationalized wills, they continuously changed the state of existing reality. In the midst of such dynamism, meaning could only be fixed in the present moment. Understanding one's world and self came to require comprehension of current events and immediate affairs. Thus, we expect that action's twentieth-century handoff pulled historical attention toward contemporary matters.

Then along the spatial dimension – for many of the reasons just articulated – we suppose that the remastery of action stripped historical interest from Greece and Rome. These mythical places served as the imagined centers of ancient Western civilization, and they retained their preeminent salience in history only so long as it could reasonably be assumed that past heritage determined present configuration. As humans came increasingly to be self-made beings operating in a self-created present, Greece and Rome lost their signifying powers, and thus we expect they fell among the subject priorities of history.

The redefinition of action in the global-institutional frame also meant that capacities to comprehend reality – to discern and know its characteristic features – increasingly passed down from the heavens, such that over the course of the twentieth century humans obtained more keys to knowledge (scientization) and more keys to its application (rationalization). This ontological development, like the first, altered the taken-for-granted premises at the heart of world society, stripping sense from some historical subject matters and giving plausibility to others.

Along history's time dimension, we expect that the elaboration of human knowledge capacities drove up teaching and research interest in the contemporary period. As humans gained the powers of understanding, they simultaneously acquired the responsibility to use those powers as self-conscious agents of change. Thus through these decades, humans found themselves charged with administering growing swaths of reality. This rearrangement of assumptions should have raised the legitimacy and authority of contemporary subject matters in history in which humanity's sovereignty over knowledge promised to benefit the common good.

Meanwhile along the special subject dimension, we expect that the reassignment of knowledge capacities in the global-institutional frame permitted historians to venture out beyond the ken of concrete facts and material entities to speculate on the underlying processes and inner workings of society. As questions of meaning were released from heaven's clasp, heightened human powers of understanding raised possibilities for more highly abstracted and theorized event narratives. Historians, we expect, began to consider systematic rules and generalized principles (such as "national development") in their accounts of society. Asserting the new muscle, one German intellectual declared around 1900, "Historical science . . . must replace a descriptive method by a genetic one which tries to formulate general laws."[12] We thus expect that global-institutional transformation introduced more process-oriented and social-scientized subject matters into the field, as exemplified by economic history.

In sum during our study period, we suppose that the twentieth-century relocation of action capacities in the global-institutional frame drew historians away from stories of sacred unfolding and toward stories of rationalized functioning. We foresee several specific impacts on historical subject matters: reduced academic emphasis on Greece and Rome and on the ancient period generally, and increased emphasis on the contemporary period and also economic history – all in universities worldwide.

Of course, a wider range of subject matter variables would allow us to pursue additional lines of inquiry. For instance, although the kings-to-commoners theme is clearly implicit in much of our discussion, our data do not allow us to investigate the extent or timing of that change or subtler questions, such as which commoners were included and which excluded from the emergent everyman historical narratives. Some comparative work on the subject suggests such changes were dramatic.[13]

REDEFINITION OF STRUCTURE IN THE GLOBALLY INSTITUTIONALIZED ONTOLOGY

Just as action was redefined as evolution trumped creation in the globally institutionalized cosmology, so also was structure. Logics of horizontal assembly supplanted logics of vertical hierarchy, and logics of dynamic network replaced those of categorical order.

This change meant first that over the twentieth century the floor-line assumptions of equality and interconnection on which horizontal assemblies were premised came to be increasingly plentiful in the cultural scripts and organizational rules of world society and thus grew generally available in everyday life. Already we have seen the effects of this structural shift on the university's major divisions and fields. For the subject matters of history, we suppose the change also bore several consequences.

Along the unit of analysis dimension, this structural redefinition seems likely to have brought about demotions of the major colonial powers from the corner offices of history. As long as reality took form as a vertical hierarchy, it could be maintained that history was made by the colonizers to be read in the colonies. Imitation and deference were matters of course. With the deinstitutionalization of vertical hierarchies, however, the assumptions bracing up this system quickly vanished, and the colonial empires themselves collapsed. One result, we expect, is a retreat in the historical study of colonial powers throughout the world's universities.

Logically extending this argument to the area dimension, we expect that by the time the United States achieved global dominance after World War II, horizontal-assembly models of structure already were implemented in the global-institutional frame to the point that sovereign status was decentralized. Even the recently independent countries of the former periphery claimed social honor and identity. Such changes voided the translation of military and economic hegemony into history-making and history-having monopolies, as had occurred automatically for England and France. The process inhibited the United States (or any other country) from assuming a command position in the story of society. It was not the only place that mattered, regardless of its geopolitical and economic supremacy. We thus expect no rise in the academic priority of the United States during our study period.

Also along the area dimension and again extending the previous argument, we suppose that vertical-to-horizontal restructuring eventuated in a substantial aggrandizement of the historical relevance attributed to the world's former peripheries. As reality's structural templates leveled, the arrangement of world society flattened both literally and conceptually. The axes of hierarchy (e.g., the old imposition of high over low civilizations) barring most countries from historical agency grew obsolescent and in their places unfurled claims asserting fundamental equality. Every independent country (at least independent *de jure*) was granted dominion over its own history. Thus as the countries of the former periphery came to count in world society, we expect to observe decentralization and particularly de-Westernization in the subject composition of history.

Then finally along the dimension of subnational groups and by much the same logic, it seems likely that global-institutional reframing favored the proliferation of historical roles for peoples formerly marginalized in society. Women, peasants, minority ethnic and religious groups, lesbians and gays, children, and others should therefore have gained entrée into historical narratives. New equalities shone light on the ways these groups contributed to the heritage of society (often by redefining what were formerly marked as subversive activities into contributions), and they revealed particular histories of oppression. The twin processes should have fomented the rise of new subgroup histories in the university's academic core.

Structural redefinition in the second of its senses involved a shift in the premises of world society that removed the old fixed boundaries characteristic of creation – man is man and ape is ape and never the twain shall meet – and replaced them with the active bridges characteristic of evolutions. Under the new institutional regime, a welter of interconnections fused reality's elements into a single universal system. In the preceding chapters, we witnessed some consequences of this structural remodeling on academic emphases at higher levels of analysis. Here we lengthen our argument's reach down into the subject matters of history.

Beginning with the unit of analysis dimension, we expect that the restructuring of the global-institutional frame diminished the historical attention paid to particular nation-states. At the beginning of the twentieth century, history "enjoyed particular legitimacy . . . for it had served the construction of national identities."[14] With structural transition, however, the very idea of any social group as a bounded entity, with history of unique development, lost tenability. Nation-states fell into webs of interrelationship. Under the new body of assumptions, no nation-state was truly set apart, and thus no nation-state's story could be told without pervasive reference to its wider system of embedding. Thus we expect that over the twentieth century particular nation-states were reduced in the historical imagination.

By the same token and along the same dimension, we suppose that supranational cultures and regions, including histories of international relations and the world as a whole, grow increasingly prominent in university history curricula. As ontological reframing released societies from the strict categories of traditional orders, unit boundaries were conceived to decrease, whereas interlocks were imagined to proliferate, yielding a rise in social expressions of interconnection and oneness. For instance, principles of human rights across national boundaries appeared, as did intergovernmental organizations (especially the League of Nations and then the much stronger United Nations) along with massive numbers of international nongovernmental organizations.[15] There even materialized notions of a global village and a planetary holiday (Earth Day). All such developments distilled and elaborated theorizations of interactive interdependence across a unified world. Thus we argue that structural redefinition spurred heightened attention to supranational, international, and world histories in the subject matters of the field.

Next along the dimension of subnational groups, we expect that the fixed-category-to-dynamic-network ontological shift brought about increasing academic devotion to the various subfacets of society, which itself was refashioned into a mosaic. Under the rules of the old categorical order, nation-states appeared monolithically, their fissures covered over by citizenship. In emerging dynamic-network models, by contrast, differentiation crept into view. Society's components took on more definite form, as did the bands of interdependence connecting them. Thus, citizenship identity became one among equals, falling into line with race, class, gender, and sexual orientation.[16] The reauthorization and relegitimization of structure, in short, enabled the realization of subnational groups in society, heightening their profiles in university history.

Finally along the dimension of special subjects, the fixed-category-to-dynamic-network transition propelled social-scientized histories into the academic foreground. This is so because such histories brought focus to the common and connective tissues bridging societal divides. Generic abstractions grew paramount over concrete particulars, calling forth comparisons and generalizations. Histories of revolution replaced, say, the history of the French Revolution, and histories of science replaced, say, the history of Islamic science.[17] As the regime of assumptions regarding structure shifted in world society over the twentieth century, we expect that social-scientized histories (such as economic history, with its focus on modernization and development) rose in relative academic emphases globally.

Overall, we argue that redefinitions of structure in the global-institutional frame – such that vertical hierarchies and fixed categories were reconfigured into horizontal assemblies and dynamic networks – altered the taken-for-granted platforms of reality upon which history's subject matters were constituted. The shifts bore unfavorable consequences for several subject matters, including histories oriented to ancient Greece and Rome and the ancient period generally, those narrating the tales of colonial powers and other particular nation-states, and histories of England and the United States. By contrast, we argue that the consequences of global-institutional reframing were favorable for several other subjects in history, including those focused on the contemporary period, the former peripheries of the world, and subnational groups; supranational, international, and world histories; and economic history. We predict that the disfavored subjects lost relative standing in the portfolio of historical subject matters and that the favored subjects gained standing. We outline our argument, from cosmology and ontology to history, in Figure 1.

Of course, data beyond that provided by university course catalogues would present other opportunities for exploration. Many of the currently fashionable subject matters in history – environmental history, history of science, history of sexuality, etc. – are missing from our data set, given their recent vintage, but they would be interesting to consider within the purview of global-institutional reframing. For instance, one could link the emergence of the history of childhood to the extension of actorhood to children and to their elevation in status in the flattened social structure. In the current global-institutional environment, children can do more and what they do counts more than it did in the past.[18] In this and other ways, the effects of global-institutional structural reform almost certainly extended both within and beyond historical subject matters, and even beyond history itself. Any of

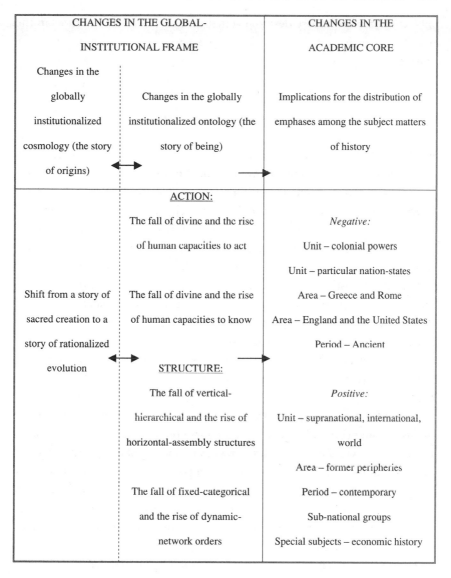

CHANGES IN THE GLOBAL-INSTITUTIONAL FRAME		CHANGES IN THE ACADEMIC CORE
Changes in the globally institutionalized cosmology (the story of origins)	Changes in the globally institutionalized ontology (the story of being)	Implications for the distribution of emphases among the subject matters of history
Shift from a story of sacred creation to a story of rationalized evolution	ACTION: The fall of divine and the rise of human capacities to act The fall of divine and the rise of human capacities to know STRUCTURE: The fall of vertical-hierarchical and the rise of horizontal-assembly structures The fall of fixed-categorical and the rise of dynamic-network orders	*Negative:* Unit – colonial powers Unit – particular nation-states Area – Greece and Rome Area – England and the United States Period – Ancient *Positive:* Unit – supranational, international, world Area – former peripheries Period – contemporary Sub-national groups Special subjects – economic history

Figure 1 Summary of argument and implications for the subject matters of history.

the university's disciplinary fields could be analyzed within our framework. In this sense, history provides no more than a testing site, where unusually vivid transformations in subject matter translate into exceptionally clear results.

With all of this in mind, we now turn to the empirical evidence. The primary question of interest is how well our expectations concerning the subject matters of history describe actual data on academic priorities in the world's universities over time. Our first step here is to describe how we collected such data.

Data on the Subject Matters of History

As described in the Introduction, we test our subject-level arguments on data culled from 335 course catalogues from 89 countries dating from 1895–1994.[19] The data present the proportions of the total number of history courses rooted within each of five domains, selected for their demonstrated importance in previous studies of the field. A given history course's unit of analysis, first, designates the societal entity that is its direct object of study. Its area, second, specifies the territory on which a course may focus. Time period, third, distinguishes the historical era of interest. Fourth, a course may be organized around a particular subnational group, such as women. Finally, a course may be organized around a professional specialization, such as economic history – we call these special subjects in shorthand. Certainly, one could identify other interesting domains in the subject matters of history, but we believe these five are central to the field and highly relevant to our arguments.

Naturally, a particular history course may register in several content domains simultaneously. For example, a course on Women in Contemporary England scores in the nation-state category of unit of analysis, in the England category of area, in the contemporary category of time, and in the gender category of subnational groups. Sometimes, a course scores in more than one category per domain. For example in area, a History of Latin America and the Caribbean would receive a half-point in Latin America and a half-point in the Caribbean.

For each university in our sample, we found the proportion of total history courses devoted to each subject matter within each twenty-five-year interval. For instance in the 1895–1924 period, a university that offered three Middle-East-based histories out of thirty total courses received a 0.10 score in the Middle East area category – 10 percent of its history courses focus on the Middle East. We then averaged these numbers across university cases to yield the average world-level proportions presented below.

Table 1   History Courses with Specified Subject Matters as Percentage of
Total History Courses, 1895–1994 – Those Expected to Lose Emphasis

	1895–1919	*1920–44*	*1945–69*	*1970–94*
Units of Analysis:				
Histories of the Colonial Powers	33	11	4	3
(never colonized countries excluded)	n = 8	n = 16	n = 37	n = 42
Histories of Particular Nation-States	39	33	30	24
(outside the home country)	n = 16	n = 28	n = 54	n = 55
Areas:				
Histories of Classical Greece & Rome	10	6	5	4
(Greece and Italy excluded)	n = 23	n = 35	n = 60	n = 66
Histories of England	14	6	4	2
(England excluded)	n – 23	n – 35	n – 60	n – 66
Histories of the United States	3	3	2	2
(United States excluded)	n = 23	n = 35	n = 60	n = 66
Period:	18	15	11	10
Ancient History	n = 24	n = 36	n = 61	n = 67

Changes in the Subject Matters of History over Time

The variables that result from the endeavors described above allow us both to
describe the substantive changes that characterized the field of history over
the twentieth century and also to test our global-institutional arguments at a
lower level of organizational analysis. The relevant data appear in Tables 1–3.

To begin, Table 1 summarizes the results for history subjects expected to
lose relative stature over the twentieth century. First, we anticipated proportional declines in the histories of two units of analysis: colonial powers and particular nation-states. The hierarchical assumptions at the heart
of colonialism and the categorical assumptions at the heart of autonomous
nation-statehood both collapsed with the redefinition of structure in the
global-institutional frame.

Indeed the data do show that, at the beginning of the twentieth century,
the former colonies placed very high priorities on the histories of their colonial powers (note that the colonial powers themselves are excluded from the
sample). On average, 33 percent of all history courses dealt in some way with
the colonial powers. As the century unfolded, however, and as the colonial

system was dismantled, this proportion plummeted more than tenfold to 3 percent. The colonizing nation-states lost their special prominence in history curricula as horizontal-assembly structures took hold in world society.

Particular nation-states also receded as main vessels of history over the twentieth century. The average proportion of the university history curriculum organized in terms of specific nation-states (outside the home country) declined from 39 to 24 percent. With the embedding of nation-states in extended networks of interdependence, stories of society seeped over the edges of tightly bounded nation-state units.[20] Both trends then – concerning the historical profiles of the colonial powers and particular nation-states – resonate with our guiding imageries.

Second, we expected to witness declines in the teaching and research priorities accorded three different areas: Greece and Rome, England, and the United States. Histories of Greece and Rome, we argued, moved backstage with the deactivation of the gods and the activation of humans, a process that drew emphasis away from distinguished heritage and pushed it toward present function. Histories of England and the United States, meanwhile, should have faced heightening barriers over the interval as taken-for-granted assemblies displaced taken-for-granted hierarchies as reality's default structures in world society, denying hegemons historical supremacy.

As hypothesized, the average proportion of university history courses devoted to Greece and Rome fell sharply between 1895 and 1994, declining from 10 to 4 percent. Stories of charismatic genesis, in the hallowed birthplaces of civilization, receded from worldwide view, as present human actions overtook past divine actions in the ordering principles of the global-institutional frame.

Likewise, histories of England and the United States descended as historical subject matters. England stood at the apex of the nineteenth-century world, wielding considerable military and economic power and serving as the model of a civilized national society. Its importance was duly noted: Worldwide, the average share of university history devoted to England was 14 percent in the 1895–1919 spell. Very rapidly, however, England's leading role diminished. By 1970–1994, England occupied only 2 percent of history's subject matters, a drop that well reflects vertical-to-horizontal restructuring.

Still England's decline could have followed from its loss of hegemony, rather than global-institutional reframing. Therefore it is remarkable to see that the United States, even as it gained immense economic and political importance, failed to take England's place at history's center. The United States began the twentieth century with 3 percent of the average university history curriculum and then actually ceded ground, ending the century with 2 percent. The new structure of reality – depicting the world not as a vertical hierarchy but as a horizontal assembly – restricted the cultural lionization of the United States. The country's "secret" was stored in the abstract terms of the social sciences (industrialization, economic development, etc.), rather than in a unique historical trajectory. All three of these subject-level trends in the area domain – concerning Greece and Rome, England, and the United States – prove to be compatible with our initial expectations.

Third, we foresaw the withdrawal of historical emphases from the ancient time period. According to our argument, the significance of the far distant past should have faded away as humans usurped divine action capacities in the global-institutional frame.

In fact, the average proportion of the university history curriculum focused on the ancient period fell steeply over our 100-year period, sinking from 18 percent in the years 1895–1919 to 10 percent in 1970–94. The transition from divine to human actorhood depleted the legitimate meaning that could be stored in primordial origins: Humans were masters of the present. Again, the numbers ring true with our predictions. Altogether the results in Table 1 suggest that what counts as history underwent fundamental change over the twentieth century, in directions hypothesized by our global-institutional argument.

Turning next to Table 2, we summarize the results for those subject matters predicted to gain historical significance over the twentieth century. In the first place, we regarded as likely a rise in supranational, international, and world units of analysis. These embody the assumptions of the dynamically networked (as opposed to the statically categorized) reality that became institutionalized during the period of interest.

In point of fact, there was a large rise in the emphases placed on these broader units of analysis in the subject matters of history.[21] At the beginning of the twentieth century, with vestiges of the old models of structure still imposing categorical divides, a mere 5 percent of the average history curriculum focused on world, international, and supranational entities. However, over our 100-year time interval, that percentage rose four-fold. By the last period,

Table 2   History Courses with Specified Subject Matters as Percentage of Total History Courses, 1895–1994 – Those Expected to Gain Emphasis

	1895–1919	*1920–44*	*1945–69*	*1970–94*
Unit of Analysis:				
Supranational, International,	5	18	16	21
and World Histories	n = 24	n = 36	n = 61	n = 67
Areas:				
Eastern Europe	1	1	2	3
(countries in region excluded)	n = 18	n = 29	n = 55	n = 61
Latin America and Caribbean	0	0	1	2
(countries in region & colonizer	n = 23	n = 29	n = 49	n = 57
excluded)				
Africa and the Middle East	2	2	2	3
(countries in region and colonizer	n = 22	n = 31	n = 40	n = 38
excluded)				
Far East	2	2	3	3
(countries in region and colonizer	n = 18	n = 30	n = 51	n = 58
excluded)				
Period:	27	25	29	38
Contemporary History	n = 24	n = 36	n = 61	n = 67
Sub-National Groups:	0.3	2.2	1.9	3.3
Histories of Sub-National Groups	n = 24	n = 36	n = 61	n = 67
Special Subject:	1.6	1.5	1.3	2.4
Economic History	n = 24	n = 36	n = 61	n = 67

more than 20 percent of history courses on average depicted society in these more expansive terms. A world level of reality, interdependent and whole, became increasingly real with the dynamic networking of institutionalized reality. The findings follow suit with our expectations.

In the second place, we expected to observe an ascent in the teaching and research priority allocated to areas formerly regarded as peripheral in world society. Under the rules of the deinstitutionalizing vertical-hierarchical structure, historians could legitimately ignore such remote entities as lacking both civilization and modernity. Under the rules of the institutionalizing horizontal-assembly structure, by contrast, the peripheries came to command equal access to the world historical stage.

Indeed among the subject matters of university history, four "peripheral" zones – Eastern Europe, Latin America and the Caribbean, Africa and the Middle East, and the Far East – all enjoyed more academic-core visibility at the end of the twentieth century than at its beginning, even though they still remained minor presences. With the horizontalization of reality in the global-institutional frame, the West lost its civilizational crown, and other global regions achieved ontological standing, on average doubling their representation in history. The effect on historical subject matters was immediately obvious in the former colonies. For example, "following independence, two main political concerns shaped historical scholarship in India – (1) the assessment of colonial rule and of the anticolonial struggle, and (2) the shaping of an historical consciousness of modern nationhood."[22] The results for all four of these formerly peripheral areas line up with our presuppositions.

In the third place, we anticipated expansion in histories of the contemporary time period. This supposition follows from the idea that, as humans wrested from the gods the capacities to comprehend and rationally act within reality, immediate matters at hand gather increasing salience. These immediate matters represent both the current state of a changing world and the possibilities for collective betterment.

Contemporary history, in fact, rose substantially among the subject priorities of university history. Between 1895 and 1919, 27 percent of all history courses on average took up contemporary matters. Between 1970 and 1994, the figure was 38 percent. The redefinition of action in the global-institutional frame granted humans new-found powers to change their worlds sensibly, such that progress replaced tradition as society's signature orientation. The process brought new emphases, as predicted, to the contemporary period.

In the fourth place, we expected to see relatively greater numbers of histories of subnational groups, such as ethnic minorities. These subject matters should have benefited both from vertical-to-horizontal restructuring in the culture and organization of world society, which enabled the recognition of once-subordinated groups, and from categorical-to-network restructuring, which encouraged the differentiation of citizens into distinct but interdependent communities.

The data show just such an increase. With the procession of the twentieth century, the total coverage of subnational groups in university history expanded a substantial eleven-fold, from 0.3 percent to 3.3 percent. With structural redefinition, racial and ethnic minorities, indigenous peoples, women, class, and religious groups all became aspects and vessels of the differentiated social system and thus all experienced enhanced roles in university history. The findings are consistent with our initial expectations.

Finally in the fifth place, we thought economic history would show upward movement in the teaching and research emphases of university history. In part the expansion of human knowing capacities, facilitating the abstraction of history's concrete facts into abstracted theories, should have generated this kind of specialization. In part economic history should have followed in the wake of category-to-network restructuring, which drew attention to the common and interconnecting tissues that bind societies together.

In truth, economic history showed marked expansion over the twentieth century, rising from 1.6 to 2.4 percent of historical subject matters between our first and fourth time intervals. Economic histories increased as the theorization of past events became possible with the shift from divine to human sovereignty over knowledge and also as shared and interlinking threads among societies grew salient with structural redefinition in the global-institutional frame. Our argument suggests a rise, as observed in the data. Altogether, the results in Table 2 lend credence to our global-institutional arguments. The subject matters of history changed along the predicted lines.

To ensure that the findings presented above are not merely the artifact of a changing case base (which in substance involves the inclusion of more non-European countries over time, as universities and their course catalogues become more common around the world) rather than global-institutional reframing, we also show results yielded from a constant-case data set. These data appear in Table 3. In order to retain a reasonable number of cases, we reduced the number of time periods from four to two: 1895–1944 and 1945–94. Across the board, the constant-case results exhibit the same upward and downward movements as the all-case results, although the magnitudes of changes among constant cases are typically less pronounced. Our findings, in short, are not artifacts of our sampling frame.

Overall, the results in Tables 1–3 lend considerable support to our theoretical framework. Even down to the subject level, it appears our global-institutional argument is well equipped to account for worldwide changes in

Table 3 Constant-Case Versions of Tables 1 and 2

	1895–1944	1945–1994
Table 1		
Histories of the Colonial Powers (n = 15)	15.3	5.8
Histories of Particular Nation-States (n = 26)	33.6	32.6
Histories of Classical Greece and Rome (n = 34)	7.7	4.0
Histories of England (n = 34)	7.5	3.8
Histories of the United States (n = 34)	3.4	2.8
Ancient History (n = 35)	16.1	10.9
Table 2		
Supranational, International, and World Histories (n = 35)	15.5	16.6
Eastern Europe (n = 28)	0.6	2.5
Latin America and Caribbean (n = 28)	0.3	1.1
Africa and the Middle East (n = 31)	2.1	2.1
Far East (n = 29)	1.6	2.0
Contemporary History (n = 35)	24.6	31.1
Histories of Subnational Groups (n = 35)	2.0	4.2
Economic History (n = 35)	1.4	2.0

the academic core. Changing notions of action and structure reset the supply of assumptions available from world society and thus altered the subject priorities of history in universities throughout the world.

Conclusion

In this chapter we have extended the reach of our argument down another level of organizational analysis into the subject-matter emphases internal to the field of history. The teaching and research activities of universities worldwide map globally institutionalized realities, rather than the needs of society or interests of the powerful. During the period covered by our data, changes in the globally institutionalized cosmology and ontology together altered the taken-for-granted features of reality and thus fomented redistributions of academic emphases.

In substantive terms, we witness a shift over time from particular nation-states (especially dominant ones) to supranational, international, and global units of analyses in history. In the area domain, we see a diffusion of historical focus from Western Europe to the former peripheries of the world. Period-wise, ancient gives way to contemporary history. New social groupings also appear in the form of subnational groups. And more theorized and abstracted versions of history sprout up, such as economic history. All of these trends appear at the world level, and all follow, we argue, from changes in the global-institutional frame.

As in previous chapters, we can conclude that there are compelling reasons to analyze changes in the academic core as global phenomena. Universities in all kinds of countries derive from common sources and share common standards concerning what counts as history. Sometimes these standards come in quite concrete forms, as at UNESCO's Disarming History Conference in 1999, which recommended that history curricula throughout South Eastern Europe be reformed to represent what we call horizontal assemblies rather than vertical hierarchies. The goals in particular sought to rectify existing tendencies to emphasize "the national identity at the expense of the identity of others," "national aspects at the detriment of international, regional and local," and "the history of wars and violence to the detriment of giving due account of periods of peaceful coexistence, co-operation and cultural exchange, of mutual enrichment between different groups as well as between nations." UNESCO's standards for history – and for the university as a whole – are explicitly shaped for global application.[23]

Additionally as in previous chapters, we can reassert the benefits of considering university knowledge as an integrated body comprising the branches of learning, the basic and applied divisions, the disciplinary fields, and the subject matters within fields. We can now say with some assurance that every aspect of the broader whole is subject to encompassing forces of change.

Finally again we can demonstrate the usefulness of looking to the global-institutional frame for the causal roots of change. Revisions in the culture and organization of reality provide powerful guides to changes in university composition, as the analyses of historical subject matters that are contained in this chapter amply show.

Surely the subject composition of other university fields could be analyzed using the global-institutional framework we have employed here. It would be useful at least to compare the subject-matter trends in history with those exhibited by a natural and a social science field, say biology and sociology. Our assumption is that common trends would emerge. For present purposes, however, the exploration of history suffices in making our main point: that the effects of global-institutional reframing extend beyond the university's branches, divisions, and disciplinary fields into subject matters as well.

Notes

1. This chapter draws in part on David John Frank, Suk-Ying Wong, John W. Mayer, and Francisco O. Ramirez "What Counts as History: A Cross-National and Longitudinal Study of University Curricula." *Comparative Education Review* 44 (February): 29–53. Copyright © 2000 by the University of Chicago Press.

2. General worldwide and comparative data on disciplinary subject recomposition are more readily available for primary and secondary education than for tertiary education. See Meyer, Kamens, and Benavot (1992); Benavot (2004); McEneaney (2003); Mao (1995); and Wong (2004).

3. For example, see Higham (1970), Hobsbawm and Ranger (1983), and Teggart (1977).

4. From the 1909–10 Kansas State Agricultural Catalogue College Annual. The college later renamed itself Kansas State University.

5. Frank, Schofer, and Torres (1994) analyze changes in university history in the United States, 1910–90.

6. On history in Japan and the Germanys, see Dierkes (2001:36–7). On history in China, Taiwan, and Hong Kong, see Wong (2004).

7. See http://www.nd.edu/~history/department/mission.shtml.

8. Strikingly, Gabler (2002) finds that by the late twentieth century, biographies of Eleanor Roosevelt outnumbered those of Franklin Roosevelt among American children's books. Women, clearly, had been incorporated into U.S. history. Note that both types of functionalism have bases in the traditional sociology of knowledge, with the former view emanating from Merton (1973) and the latter from Mannheim (1936).

9. On the history of economics, see Solow (1997) and Barber (1997). For comparative views, see Babb (2001) and Fourcade-Gourinchas (2001).

10. See, for example, Abrams (1997) and Bryson (2005).

11. This capsule summary comes from Swidler and Arditi (1994). See also Foucault (1994).

12. Georg Iggers, quoted in Revel (2003:394). Of course we envision global-institutional reframing to drive not only the social-scientization of history but also the spectacular rise of the social sciences themselves. See Chapter 3.

13. See Mao (1995) and Wong (2004).

14. See Revel (2003:391).

15. For example on human rights, see Berkovitch (1999), Boyle (2002), Smith (1995), and Soysal (1994). On international nongovernmental organizations, see the papers in Boli and Thomas (1999).

16. See Frank and Meyer (2002).

17. See Hymans (2005).

18. See, for example, Gabler's (2002) analysis of children's nonfiction books 1960–2000 in the United States.

19. For additional details on the data, see Frank et al. (2000). The results presented here are culled from those included in that broader study.

20. Similarly, Wong (1991) shows a sharp decline in the proportion of secondary-school curricula devoted to the nation-state-oriented subjects of history, geography, and civics over the twentieth century at the same time as the more systems-oriented "social studies" grew enormously.

21. Benavot (2004) finds that the worldwide emphasis on official language instruction decreased as a percentage of total language instruction from the 1980s to the 2000s in grades 1–8 at the same time as the percentage of countries allocating instructional time to foreign language(s) sharply increased.

22. From Chatterjee (2003:490).

23. For more information on the conference, see http://www.marebalticum.se/disarminghistory.

CHAPTER 6

Conclusion: Universities and the Global-Institutional Frame

Despite the clear importance of the basic questions orienting our endeavors – concerning world-level transformations in the body of university knowledge – they have scarcely been raised, much less systematically addressed until now. The most closely related studies in the literature have been hamstrung empirically, usually focused on single countries and knowledge domains; thus, they have been theoretically constrained, typically emphasizing the roles of local actors in calling forth academic recomposition as a means of fulfilling and/or pursuing their interests, implicitly posing self-contained functionalist social systems.

In order to raise and subsequently address these basic questions, we made a tripartite innovation on the existing case-study standards. First we shifted the level of analysis. Although one generates only modest excitement by recalling that the university originated in medieval Europe and diffused throughout the world via missionaries and colonialists, just as one commands but passing notice by noting that universities throughout the periphery now aim as a matter of course to be "world class institution[s]," still most analysts conduct their work on academic priorities at local or domestic levels.[1] The facts of the university's global origins and global aspirations are treated as sideline curiosities, rather than determining features of the academic core. It is as if the propagandists had been convinced by the propaganda. Because the modern storyline renders universities as essential to the development of just and prosperous societies, the "natural" context for university studies – because it is the primary context in the modern storyline – is the nation-state. We treat the global origins and global aspirations of the university as matters of foremost importance to the analysis of academic priorities. Thus we pitch our research at the global level of analysis. Although the academic core of a particular university in Mexico, say, is surely subject to some unique forces of change, critical causal dynamics span across countries and continents (as a brief comparison of degree offerings, say, in Mexico, Korea, and Hungary in the years 1900 and 2000 would establish immediately).

Second, we shift the unit of analysis. Unto itself, the basic notion of common denominator, cross-sector forces of change – i.e., those that spur revisions in academic priorities across the university's organizational layers and sectors – is not controversial. Few, for example, would dispute that fundamental political changes, such as those that followed the dissolution of the Soviet empire, or deep-seated economic reconfigurations, such as those associated with the emergence of new knowledge economies, carry implications for study in many knowledge domains. Nevertheless, empirical work on academic-core revisions over time is almost always conducted within a single branch or field of learning. Again, a modern storyline seems to intervene in which, rather than representing a cultural and organizational package, the various knowledge domains are seen to represent essential aspects of reality, such that the "natural" analytical object is the stand-alone knowledge domain. But of course these demarcations are socially constructed. Thus our work treats the whole body of university knowledge as the unit of analysis. Although some causal factors are undoubtedly particular to the disciplinary standing of, say, astronomy, there are other more encompassing dynamics that pertain across fields simultaneously (as even a cursory study, say, of astronomy, literature, and history before and after the Copernican Revolution would readily show).

These two innovations, vis-à-vis level and unit of analysis, led us to seek and ultimately collect new measures of academic composition that would provide broad portraits of global changes in the body of university knowledge through time. Our faculty- and course-composition data, available for many countries throughout the twentieth century, open previously closed empirical vistas, allowing us to see beyond the narrow-gauge studies that have sparked so much consternation over the changing academic core. We present the first systematic evidence verifying that dramatic changes *are* afoot in university contents worldwide. While eliding local idiosyncrasies, our data articulate the wider contexts within which changes in particular countries and knowledge sectors occur, and thus they complement case-study evidence. In this broad-brushed view of university recomposition, we make our first main contribution to the literature, one that is primarily empirical.

From the new empirical perspectives offered by our data, existing theories of teaching-and-research priority shifts appear inadequate almost immediately.[2] What is striking at the world level is how similar university emphases appear and how standard are their compositions. Although the University of Zululand, for instance, claims to be a "unique comprehensive university," its academic programs suggest otherwise. Its four faculties – in Arts; Commerce, Administration, and Law; Science and Agriculture; and Education – bear no surprises, and its departments are by no means exotic. The *universalism* of the university is what stands out from the global purview – the notion that a single knowledge package is applicable to all. Thus we make our third innovation relating to existing case-study standards, shifting the explanatory framework so as to emphasize the centrality of the university's universalism. Drawing on global-institutional theory for guidance, we propose that university knowledge is an edifice resting on the framework of globally institutionalized "reality." Changes in the assumed nature of reality – in stories of origin and being, in definitions of action and structure – recast the substructure on which university knowledge arises and thus they provoke world-level reorderings of academic emphases.[3] Where change involves growing disarticulations between the premises of reality embedded in the global-institutional frame and the assumptions built into the definition of a particular knowledge sector, we anticipate relative demotions in university priority. Growing frame-sector articulations, of course, suggest the reverse – i.e., increased teaching and research emphasis for the salient branch of learning, disciplinary field, or subject focus over time.

The field of botany, to illustrate, carries outmoded blueprints of structure in its essential makeup. Botanists study *plants* as a fixed class of entities. The permanence of the category and the certain distinction of its boundaries (not dogs, not geodes) are defining features of the field. Assuming otherwise – i.e., to remove the timeless barriers that designate plants as particular kinds of thing that differ fundamentally from other kinds of things – is to locate oneself outside botany – in biology, ecology, chemistry, or physics, for example. Practitioners from these other fields may indeed study plants – so much so that overall plant studies in the university may well have increased over the century – but their assumptions about reality's structure mean plants fold in with other things. Botany, in short, assumes a structural model that is decreasingly tenable with global-institutional reframing. Given the growing disjoint between evolving models of reality and the definition of the field, our theory predicts botany's diminution in the university over the twentieth century, and indeed the discipline recedes. This is not to say that botany does not change internally: Chapter 5 on the subject matters of history strongly demonstrates that within-field adaptations can be substantial, changing in concert with evolving reality. But every knowledge sector is limited in some way by its disciplinary definitions and by interdisciplinary boundaries. To be a botanist is to study plants and plants only; to study the relationship between plants and people is to be a biologist. Even the seemingly flexible field of history has its limits – to be an historian is to study the past; to study the present is to be a sociologist. Thus shifts in the global-institutional frame condemned botany to increasing marginalization in the academic core. With this theoretical scheme, thus, we make our second main contribution to the literature.

The Whole is Greater than the Sum of Its Parts

Causal accounts along these lines – moving from global-institutional reframing to reorderings of academic priorities – are only partially persuasive on a case-wise basis because many proximate factors may offer compelling causal alternatives. Field x may be said to have grown by capitalizing on the success of a particular new technology, whereas field y may be said to have suffered from a particular theoretical dead end. Our argument for common denominators of change, across the levels and sectors of university knowledge, is much more persuasive when developments across the whole body are taken into account.

Thus, although it may be interesting, say, to note a correspondence between the upward swell of the university social sciences and the relocation of action capacities in the global-institutional frame, it is difficult on the basis of that observation alone to conclude that there is a causal relationship between the two. One's conviction increases, however, when a whole set of academic-core changes can be thus accounted for. In our analyses, for example, the constitution of the human actor over the twentieth century lent impetus *not only* to the social sciences (which require rational humans to captain vessels of progress) *but also* contributed to the enduring strength of art and music (which cultivate and validate the expressive capacities of human individuals) *and furthermore* had a negative impact on historical studies of the ancient period (which lose salience as meaning is sapped from moments of divine creation). The argument picks up persuasive steam as it is applied at greater scope across levels and domains of knowledge.

Likewise it is well and good to assert that stripping the gods of their sovereignty over knowledge and assigning it instead to humans foments decline in the humanities. But what is considerably more compelling is to tie this shift in the premises of reality *not only* to the humanities' slippage (which refuse to douse all sparks of inspiration with a complete demystification of knowledge) *but also* to the good showing of chemistry (in which experimentation leads to discovery and then, with repetition, to knowledge) *and also* to the rising within-discipline profile of economic history (which moves beyond narrating and into interpreting event sequences with abstractions, generalizations, and theorizations). As the accounts stack up on one other, the plausibility of the causal relationship increases exponentially.

Similarly in regard to structure, evidence suggesting a conduit between the vertical-hierarchy-to-horizontal-assembly transition in the templates of world society and the basic-to-applied transition in university emphases may warrant passing notice. What commands a whole lot more attention, however, is evidence suggesting a causal link between this facet of structural

redefinition and the rise of the applied disciplines (in which the everyday affairs of everyday people are elevated to everyday matters for university study)
and also the decline of the classics (which invoke a stratified reality even in
their title) and also the expansion of sociology (which is keenly focused on
documenting and eradicating inequalities). The whole is much greater than
the sum of its parts.

By the same token, to contend that the rearrangement of categorical orders
into dynamic networks in the culture and organization of world society un-
derlies the global expansion of geography may stimulate mild intrigue. What
is more arresting is to connect this same structural amendment *not only* to
the global prospects of geography (which bridges the human-nature divide
with webs of active interrelationship) *but also* to the heightened priority of
physics (which posits fundamental interconnections among all forms of matter) *and also* to the winning record of supranational, international, and world
subjects in history (which assume that human societies evolve conjointly and
interdependently with one another). In gathering the threads together, the
explanatory rope reveals its sturdiness.

Taken singly, in short, our accounts of change in the academic core
have but limited force. On a branch-by-branch, field-by-field, or subject-
by-subject basis, there are too many competing causal factors for the global-
institutional argument to stand out. Where our perspective distinguishes
itself is at the macro level, as a guide to the broad outlines of academic-core
change. With remarkable parsimony, our theory sheds light on the common bases of a great many world-level alterations in the body of university
knowledge throughout the twentieth century.

Unfinished Business: Remaining Questions for Future Research

We wish to at least mention several outstanding questions that are pertinent to and/or raised by our work. Many of them pose challenges for future
research.

Most strikingly, perhaps, we have left off questions concerning cross-
sectional levels of representation among the various knowledge domains: not
relative change from time 1 to time 2, but absolute representation at time
2. For instance, although it is good to understand why university economics

prospered more so than psychology over the twentieth century, it would also be good to know why at the end of the century economists were ten times more common on average in the world's universities than psychologists. Theoretically here, it is easy enough to say that we expect a general, if loose, correspondence between the importance of an entity or relationship in reality and the importance of that entity or relationship in the university. Practically, however, the task of determining the former is immensely challenging. *Changes* in the features of reality – our interest in the project at hand – are much easier to map than are static features of reality. The latter lie still on the social landscape, quietly escaping notice. Thus, although we find questions concerning the absolute composition of university knowledge to be highly interesting, we no more than dip our toes into that pool here.

Along these same lines, we have considered issues related to cross-national variation only in passing. Some comparative work on universities and university knowledge implies that different kinds of countries should have different kinds of academic priorities.[4] In Chapter 1, we showed convergence in university composition over the twentieth century, but interesting variations likely remain. Countries in the core may show dissimilar academic priorities from those in the periphery, long-time democratic countries may show different disciplinary dispositions from long-time socialist ones, countries with knowledge-based economies may have distinctive academic cores from those based in agriculture, and so on. One factor that almost certainly matters is colonial heritage, as evident in Table 1, which shows faculty numbers at the University College of Ibadan, Nigeria, in 1951–52. The stamp of British colonialism appears rather strikingly, so much so as to dampen expectations of cross-national variation. Although they lie beyond the scope of our immediate agenda, we see many questions along these lines that are well worth pursuing.

Along the same lines, we have said little about interdisciplinarity, one of the hot button topics in discussions of change in the academic core. Our data sources limited our capacity to address the issue, but our theoretical framework is unambiguous in its prediction: As dynamic networks replace categorical orders in the structural templates of world society, we expect to observe not only a breakdown of barriers and an elaboration of linkages between society and the university but also a breakdown of barriers and an elaboration of linkages among the various knowledge domains. In addition to increased

Table 1 Academic Composition by Number of Faculty at
University College of Ibadan, Nigeria, Calendar, 1951–52[1]

Faculty of Arts	
Classics	2
English	5
Geography	5
History	3
Mathematics	7
Religious Studies	2
Faculty of Science	
Botany	3
Chemistry	5
Physics	4
Biology	1
Parasitology	2
Zoology	3
Scientific French and German	1
Faculty of Medicine	
Anatomy	1
Physiology	2
Medicine	3
Surgery	2
Obstetrics and Gynecology	2
Preventive and Social Medicine	1
Pathology	2
Pharmacology	1
Forensic	1
Faculty of Agriculture & Veterinary Science	8
Department of Extra-Mural Studies	7
West African Institute of Social & Economic Research	2

[1] From the 1951–52 University College Ibadan *Calendar*.

intercourse with those nearby – for example, biochemistry, geophysics, social psychology – one should also see more extended reaches, as when the
humanities co-mingle with the sciences (for example in the ethics of science)
and when biology merges with art (for example in the evolutionary bases of
art).[5] The possibilities here seem rich: for example, "Linguistics is arguably
the most hotly contested property in the academic realm. It is soaked with
the blood of poets, theologians, philosophers, philologists, biologists, and
neurologists, along with whatever blood can be got out of grammarians."[6]

The applied/basic bridge should be crossed more frequently, too, in both directions. In fact, we did code the most popular interdisciplinary pursuits, and we did observe a sharp rise in such disciplines as astrophysics and biochemistry. But at the world level even during our final time interval, most joint endeavors were still negligible in size. Disciplinary inertia is substantial (which by extension suggests just how significant the changes we observed are). An anthropologist who wants to be granted tenure in an anthropology department has to publish in anthropology journals and thus take anthropological approaches to anthropological issues. Changes in the global-institutional frame may be starving anthropology of vital assumptions relative to sociology. But the anthropologist cannot simply switch allegiances. Disciplinary boundaries keep it so.

Near the beginning of our study, we noted that our data were relevant to the adaptation/selection debate in the organizational literature.[7] Does change in a population happen via selection (such that types x and y are present in the population to begin with, and type x dies out given environmental changes over time) or adaptation (such that only type x is present to begin with, evolving into type y given environmental changes over time)? Our data suggest a nested process, in which adaptation at level A occurs via selection at level B, and adaptation at level B occurs via selection at level C, and so on. Substantively speaking at the highest organizational level of analysis, we find powerful evidence of adaptation: The university survives and flourishes throughout the twentieth century, in part via academic-core transformations. These transformations, in turn, involve a dramatic process of selection among the three main branches of learning – against the humanities and, to a slightly less extent, the basic division. But of course the humanities do not disappear entirely, and to the extent they survive they do so by adapting, which involves selection among the disciplinary fields (philosophy, history, etc.). And so on. Neither adaptation nor selection can be said to be dominant in our findings: Rather they appear to be interdependent.

Finally there is the question of how our work can be situated in the wider sociology of science. From the seminal works of Mannheim, Merton, and Kuhn, sociologists have worked to identify the forces constituting and penetrating the knowledge system, producing and distorting what passes as truth.[8] The contributions to that work have been rich and varied, showing effects from an overlapping nest of contexts – laboratories, departments, disciplines, universities, nation-states, gender regimes, colonial networks, and so on. We envision our research here as taking one more step in this long sociological procession by exploring the relations between university knowledge and the global-institutional frame. Moreover, we imagine that over the twentieth century the lower-level nestings lose a degree of salience, given the increasing importance of universalizing forces, such as globalization and scientization. Our findings on convergence suggest as much. Additional research in this vein would be most useful.

Interpreting the Empirical Findings

Our empirical findings speak for themselves, confirming some previously advanced suppositions (for example, the decline of philosophy) and documenting trends that will surprise many (for example, the decline of law, our lone applied humanities field). We argue that shifts in the global-institutional frame neatly explain both the surprising and less surprising findings with respect to the academic core; however, we wish to emphasize here that declines *in university* knowledge do not necessarily mean declines in society at large.

Two examples help illustrate the point. Our data speak unequivocally on the trend in the humanities: The branch of learning dropped precipitously among university priorities during our period of study. At the same time, however, society at large took huge steps in the direction of incorporating and validating the expressive tastes and qualities of individual human beings, involving the Artist-to-artist transition discussed earlier. Fewer people read, more people write; fewer people studied painting, more people make paintings; fewer people contemplated great thinkers, more people have great thoughts.[9] The phenomenal expansion of blogging is but one expression of the spectacular rise in the numbers of people who act daily on the belief that their ideas, thoughts, opinions, and feelings have value and public standing. To some extent, thus, the assumptions at the root of the humanities – concerning the distinctive qualities of human thought and expression – were so thoroughly incorporated into and spread throughout society that the rationale for the humanities scholar or professor diminished. The point here is a simple one: Declining university activity need not mean declining activity.

The same case can be made for the basic natural sciences. Although the basic natural sciences lost ground in the academic core over the twentieth century, at the same time society underwent a process of massive scientization, with scientific assumptions coming to ground all kinds of activities in a highly routinized fashion.[10] Public policies and private choices of all sorts – from the fuel economy of cars to getting pregnant, from stealth technology in war to teenage rebellion – came to be understood in a day-to-day basis around basic natural scientific understandings. Once again, we witness a progression whereby the assumptions at the heart of a knowledge sector – concerning the laws of nature – were incorporated so deeply into society that formal university activities experienced a relative demise. The process at work here is the reverse of that which gave rise to the applied sciences over the century. In the latter case, society penetrated the university sciences. In the former case, the sciences penetrated society.

From this perspective, neither humanists nor basic natural scientists need despair at our findings. The university, in some measure, is a holding pen for forms of knowledge that have yet to be built into – presumably because they are new or blocked – the premises of society at large. More research on these matters is clearly needed.

Conclusion

Nowhere here do we mean to imply that the sole causal force behind shifts in university teaching and research emphases is global-institutional reframing. Although our primary efforts in the book clearly are devoted to developing and assessing this particular explanatory scheme, it does not follow that we see evolving models of reality as monopolizing the forces underlying academic recomposition. National and organizational factors indubitably operate in conjunction with global ones, just as economic and political factors most certainly operate in conjunction with institutional ones. Geology, for example, likely derived at least as much benefit from its association with petroleum engineering – in an era when countries waged war over oil – as it did from structural redefinition in the global-institutional frame.

This qualification notwithstanding, the study at hand demonstrates the richness of a global-institutional perspective on university change. Changes in the broad framework of reality seem to reconstitute the university's teaching and research agenda on a very broad basis, and the effect appears to strengthen with the intensification of world society over time.

We believe our framework can help enlighten many of the questions at the heart of the higher education literature. From the global-institutional perspective, for instance, the rise of corporate influence in the university appears more benign than malignant: In a horizontally networked society, it makes sense that the university commingles with other social institutions to establish priorities in the production of knowledge. By the same logic, the profusion of applied studies and professional schools makes sense: The forces eroding the historic barriers around the university are the same ones undermining formerly unambiguous barriers around civilizations, racial groupings, and virtuous women, for example. Structural blending is the modus operandi of the day, and its appearance in university-society relations cannot be separated from its appearance elsewhere. From the global-institutional perspective, what is more, "massification" and grade inflation in the university look less like declining standards than they do like opening opportunities. In a society where capacities to act and to know are attributed to humans inclusively, educational access is opened commensurately. The same elaboration of human actorhood stands behind extensions of the suffrage, behind the rights of individual to marry (and divorce) at will, and behind the respect won by individuals with formerly stigmatized identities, for example. The changing premises of reality in world society inform the whole range of higher educational developments at hand.

Returning to our primary phenomenon – evolving priorities in the academic core – our perspective sheds considerable light on the striking changes observed. Of course if one takes the argument on its terms, there is no reason to stop analysis at transformations in the academic core. The revision of all sorts of social institutions should follow in kind.

Notes

1. From the homepage of Nigeria's University of Ibadan, at http://www.ui.edu.ng/.

2. See Jepperson (2002).

3. Global-institutional studies in the sociology of education include Ramirez and Boli (1987) on the rise of mass schooling; Meyer, Kamens, and Benavot (1992) on

the changing content of school curricula; and Meyer, Ramirez, and Soysal (1992) on trends in enrollments.

4. See Clark (1995) and Dierkes (2001), for example.

5. For example, Dissanayake (1988) argues that art serves evolutionary functions.

6. From Rymer (1992).

7. See, for example, Young (1988).

8. See Kuhn (1962) and Berger and Luckmann (1966).

9. From Guthrie (2004).

10. See Drori et al. (2003).

Faculty Composition Data – Nation-States
Sampled by Time Period

Universities appearing in the *Commonwealth Yearbook* are highlighted.
Constant cases are highlighted in bold. (All nomenclature per 1995.)

1915–35 Mean Faculty Size: *159*	*1935–55* Mean Faculty Size: *226*	*1955–75* Mean Faculty Size: *270*	*1975–95* Mean Faculty Size: *711*
Algeria	Algeria		
	Afghanistan	Afghanistan	
		Albania	
		Angola	
Argentina	Argentina	Argentina	
Australia	**Australia**	**Australia**	**Australia**
Austria	Austria	Austria	
	Bangladesh	**Bangladesh**	**Bangladesh**

(*Continued*)

(*Continued*)

1915–35 Mean Faculty Size: *159*	*1935–55* Mean Faculty Size: *226*	*1955–75* Mean Faculty Size: *270*	*1975–95* Mean Faculty Size: *711*
Belgium	Belgium	Belgium	
		Bolivia	
		Botswana	Botswana
Brazil	Brazil	Brazil	
			Brunei Darussalam
Bulgaria	Bulgaria	Bulgaria	
	Burma	Burma	
		Burundi	
Canada	Canada	Canada	Canada
Chile	Chile	Chile	
China	China		
Colombia	Colombia	Colombia	
Colombo	Colombo	Colombo	
	Costa Rica		
Cuba	Cuba		
Czech Republic	Czech Republic		
Denmark	Denmark		
	Dominican Republic		
Ecuador	Ecuador		
Egypt	Egypt	Egypt	
England	England	England	England
Estonia	Estonia		
		Ethiopia	
Finland	Finland		
France	France	France	
Germany	Germany	Germany	
		Ghana	Ghana
	Gold Coast		
Greece	Greece	Greece	
Guatemala	Guatemala		
		Guyana	Guyana
Honduras	Honduras		
Hong Kong	Hong Kong	Hong Kong	Hong Kong
Hungary	Hungary	Hungary	
Iceland	Iceland	Iceland	

(*Continued*)

(Continued)

1915–35 Mean Faculty Size: 159	1935–55 Mean Faculty Size: 226	1955–75 Mean Faculty Size: 270	1975–95 Mean Faculty Size: 711
India	India	India	
		Indonesia	
	Iran	Iran	
		Iraq	
Ireland	Ireland	Ireland	
Israel	Israel	Israel	
Italy	Italy	Italy	
		Ivory Coast	
	Jamaica	Jamaica	
Japan	Japan	Japan	
		Jordan	
		Kenya	Kenya
		Korea	
		Kuwait	
Latvia	Latvia		
Lebanon	Lebanon	Lebanon	
		Lesotho	Lesotho
		Liberia	
Lithuania	Lithuania		
		Makerere	Makerere
		Malawi	Malawi
	Malaysia	Malaysia	Malaysia
Malta	Malta	Malta	Malta
		Mauritius	Mauritius
	Mexico	Mexico	
		Mozambique	
Netherlands	Netherlands	Netherlands	
New Zealand	New Zealand	New Zealand	New Zealand
		Nicaragua	
	Nigeria	Nigeria	Nigeria
Norway	Norway	Norway	
	Pakistan	Pakistan	
		Papua New Guinea	Papua New Guinea
		Panama	

(Continued)

(*Continued*)

1915–35 Mean Faculty Size: 159	1935–55 Mean Faculty Size: 226	1955–75 Mean Faculty Size: 270	1975–95 Mean Faculty Size: 711
Paraguay	Paraguay	Paraguay	
Peru	Peru	Peru	
Philippines	Philippines	Philippines	
Poland	Poland		
Portugal	Portugal	Portugal	
		Rhodesia	Rhodesia
Romania	Romania		
		Rwanda	
		Saudi Arabia	
	Senegal	Senegal	
Serbia	Serbia		
Sierra Leone		Sierra Leone	Sierra Leone
		Singapore	Singapore
South Africa	South Africa	South Africa	
		South Pacific	South Pacific
			Sri Lanka
	Sudan	Sudan	Sudan
			Swaziland
Sweden	Sweden	Sweden	
	Syria	Syria	
		Taiwan	
		Tanzania	Tanzania
		Thailand	
Turkey	Turkey	Turkey	
	Uganda	Uganda	Uganda
Uruguay	Uruguay		
USA	USA	USA	
Venezuela	Venezuela	Venezuela	
	Vietnam	Vietnam	
	West Indies	West Indies	West Indies
	Zaire	Zaire	
		Zambia	Zambia
		Zimbabwe	Zimbabwe

Course Composition Data – Nation-States Sampled by Time Period

	1895–1904	1905–1914	1915–1924	1925–1934	1935–1944	1945–1954	1955–1964	1965–1974	1975–1984	1985–1994
AFRICA										
Benin								x		x
Botswana								x	x	x
Burundi							x	x	x	
Cameroon									x	
Chad								x		x
Congo						x	x			
Egypt					x	x	x			
Ethiopia					x	x	x			
Gabon								x		x
Ghana						x			x	
Ivory Coast						x	x	x		

(*Continued*)

(*Continued*)

	1895–1904	1905–1914	1915–1924	1925–1934	1935–1944	1945–1954	1955–1964	1965–1974	1975–1984	1985–1994
Kenya							x	x	x	
Lesotho									x	
Liberia							x			
Libya							x			
Madagascar								x		x
Malawi								x	x	x
Mauritius										x
Niger								x		
Reunion								x		x
Rwanda								x	x	
Senegal						x	x	x		
S. Africa				x	x	x	x	x		x
Sudan								x		
Swaziland										x
Tanzania								x	x	
Uganda								x		
Zaire								x		
Zambia									x	
Zimbabwe								x	x	
AMERICAS										
Argentina				x	x	x		x	x	
Bolivia								x		
Brazil					x	x				
Canada		x	x	x	x	x	x	x	x	x
Chile				x				x		
Colombia						x	x	x		
Cuba	x	x	x	x	x			x		
Dom. Rep.						x	x			
Ecuador							x			
Guatemala							x			
Guyana									x	x
Mexico				x			x		x	
Neth. Antil.									x	x
Panama							x			
Peru							x			
Trinidad							x	x		
United States	x	x	x	x	x	x	x	x		x
Venezuela						x	x		x	

(*Continued*)

	1895–1904	1905–1914	1915–1924	1925–1934	1935–1944	1945–1954	1955–1964	1965–1974	1975–1984	1985–1994
MIDDLE AND FAR EAST										
Afghanistan							X			
Burma						X	X			
China		X	X	X	X				X	
Hong Kong		X	X	X	X		X	X		X
India		X	X	X	X	X	X			
Iraq							X			
Israel						X	X	X		
Japan	X	X	X	X	X	X	X	X	X	X
South Korea							X	X	X	
Lebanon		X	X	X	X	X	X	X		X
Malaysia							X	X		
Philippines		X	X	X	X	X	X	X		X
Singapore								X	X	
Syria		X	X	X						
Taiwan								X	X	X
Thailand							X		X	X
EUROPE										
Austria		X		X	X		X	X	X	
Belgium	X		X	X	X	X	X	X	X	X
Bulgaria		X	X	X	X		X	X	X	
Czechoslov.		X					X			
England		X	X	X	X	X	X	X	X	X
Estonia			X	X	X					
France	X	X	X	X	X	X	X			X
E. Germany	X	X	X	X		X	X	X	X	X
W.Germany.	X	X	X	X	X	X	X	X	X	X
Hungary			X	X	X		X	X		X
Ireland		X	X	X		X	X	X	X	
Italy	X	X	X	X	X		X	X	X	X
Lithuania			X							
Luxemb.									X	X
Netherlands				X	X	X	X	X	X	X
Poland		X	X	X		X	X	X		X
Portugal			X	X			X	X		
Spain				X	X	X	X		X	

(*Continued*)

(*Continued*)

	1895–1904	1905–1914	1915–1924	1925–1934	1935–1944	1945–1954	1955–1964	1965–1974	1975–1984	1985–1994
Switzerland	x	x	x	x	x	x	x	x	x	x
Russ./USSR	x								x	
Yugoslavia			x	x	x	x	x	x	x	x
OCEANIA										
Australia	x	x	x	x	x	x	x	x	x	
Fiji								x	x	x
Guam								x		
New Zeal.		x	x	x	x	x	x	x	x	x

Bibliography

Abbott, Andrew. 1999. *Department and discipline: Chicago sociology at one hundred.* Chicago: University of Chicago Press.

Abbott, Andrew. 2001. *Chaos of disciplines.* Chicago: University of Chicago Press.

Abrams, M. H. 1997. The transformation of English studies: 1930–1995. In *American academic culture in transformation: Fifty years, four disciplines,* ed. Thomas Bender and Carl E. Schorske, 123–49. Princeton, NJ: Princeton University Press.

Adelman, Clifford. 1995. *The new college course map and transcript files: Changes in course taking and achievement, 1972–1993.* Washington, DC: U. S. Department of Education.

Adjari, Sima. 2003. Professor criticizes social sciences. *New University: University of California, Irvine* 36:1, 4.

Altbach, Philip G. 1998. *Comparative higher education: Knowledge, the university and development.* Greenwich, CT: Ablex Publishing.

Amis, Martin. 2002. The voice of the lonely crowd. *Harper's,* August, 15–17.

Apple, Michael W. 1990. *Ideology and curriculum,* 2nd ed. New York: Routledge.

Ash, Mitchell G. 2003. Psychology. In *The modern social sciences*, Vol. 7 of *The Cambridge history of science*, ed. Theodore M. Porter and Dorothy Ross, 251–74. Cambridge: Cambridge University Press.

Association of Commonwealth Universities. 1914–95. *Commonwealth universities yearbook*. London: Association of Commonwealth Universities.

Babb, Sarah. 2001. *Managing Mexico: Economists from nationalism to neoliberalism*. Princeton, NJ: Princeton University Press.

Bain, Olga B. 2003. *University autonomy in Russian Federation since perestroika*. London: Falmer Press.

Balaram, P. 2001. The astrology fallout. *Current Science* 80:1085–86.

Banks, Arthur, ed. 1985. *Political handbook of the world*. New York: CSA Publications.

Barber, William J. 1997. Reconfigurations in American academic economics: A general practitioner's perspective. In *American academic culture in transformation: Fifty years, four disciplines*, ed. Thomas Bender and Carl E. Schorske, 105–21. Princeton, NJ: Princeton University Press.

Barrett, Deborah, and David John Frank. 1999. Population control for national development: From world discourse to national policies. In *Constructing world culture: International nongovernmental organizations since 1875*, ed. John Boli and George M. Thomas, 198–221. Stanford, CA: Stanford University Press.

Basu, Aparna, and B. S.Vinu Kumar. 2000. International collaboration in Indian scientific papers. *Scientometrics* 48:381–402.

Becher, Tony. 1989. *Academic tribes and territories: Intellectual enquiry and the cultures of disciplines*. Milton Keynes, England: Society for Research into Higher Education and Open University Press.

Beecher, Augustine. 2002. As college reopens principal vows to uphold educational standards. *Standard Times*, October 11, 2002. Freetown, Sierra Leone.

Benavot, Aaron, with the collaboration of Massimo Amadio. 2004. *A global study of intended instructional time and official school curricula, 1980–2000*. Background report commissioned by the International Bureau of Education for UNESCO's EFA Global Monitoring Report, The Quality Imperative (2005). Geneva, Switzerland: International Bureau of Education.

Bender, Thomas and Carl E. Schorske, eds. 1997. *American academic culture in transformation: Fifty years, four disciplines*. Princeton, NJ: Princeton University Press.

Bendix, Reinhard. 1978. *Kings or people: Power and the mandate to rule*. Berkeley, CA: University of California Press.

Bennett, J.A. 1987. *The divided circle: A history of instruments for astronomy, navigation, and surveying*. Oxford, England: Phaidon-Christie's.

Berger, Peter L., and Thomas Luckmann. 1966. *The social construction of reality: A treatise in the sociology of knowledge*. New York: Anchor.

Bergesen Albert J., and Omar Lizardo. 2004. International terrorism and the world-system. *Sociological Theory* 22:38–52.

Berkovitch, Nitza. 1999. *From motherhood to citizenship: International organizations and women's rights.* Baltimore: Johns Hopkins University Press.

Bertrams, Kenneth. 2004. Multiversity as an adapted response to entrepreneurial university? An historical perspective from the United States and Europe. Paper presented at a workshop organized by the Graduate Program "Entering the Knowledge Society" and the Institute for Science and Technology Studies, Bielefeld University, Bielefeld, Germany.

Biglan, Anthony. 1973. The characteristics of subject matter in different academic areas. *Journal of Applied Psychology* 57:195–203.

Binder, Amy J. 2000. Why do some curricular challenges work while others do not? The case of three Afrocentric challenges. *Sociology of Education* 73:69–91.

Binder, Amy J. 2002. *Contentious curricula: Afrocentrism and creationism in American public schools.* Princeton, NJ: Princeton University Press.

Bloom, Allan. 1987. *The closing of the American mind.* New York: Simon & Schuster.

Bloor, David. 1991. *Knowledge and social imagery*, 2nd ed. Chicago: University of Chicago Press.

Bocock, Jean, Lewis Baston, Peter Scott, and David Smith. 2003. American influence on British higher education: Science, technology and the problem of university expansion, 1945–1963. *Minerva* 41:327–46.

Bok, Derek. 2003. *Universities in the marketplace: The commercialization of higher education.* Princeton, NJ: Princeton University Press.

Boli, John, and Francisco O. Ramirez. 1987. The political construction of mass schooling – European origins and worldwide institutionalization. *Sociology of Education* 60:2–17.

Boli, John, and George M. Thomas. 1997. World culture in the world polity: A century of international non-governmental organization. *American Sociological Review* 62:171–190.

Boli, John, and George M. Thomas, eds. 1999. *Constructing world culture: International nongovernmental organizations since 1875.* Stanford, CA: Stanford University Press.

Botton, Alain de. 1999. What are the humanities for? *European Review* 7:19–25.

Bourdieu, Pierre. 1984. *Distinction: A social critique of the judgment of taste.* Cambridge, MA: Harvard University Press.

Bourdieu, Pierre. 1988. *Homo academicus.* Stanford, CA: Stanford University Press.

Boyle, Elizabeth Heger. 2002. *Female genital cutting: Cultural conflict in the global community.* Baltimore: Johns Hopkins University Press.

Boyle, Elizabeth H., and John W. Meyer. 1998. Modern law as a secularized and global model: Implications for sociology of law. *Soziale Welt-Zeitschrift Fur Sozialwissenschaftliche Forschung Und Praxis* 49:275–94.

Bradley, Karen,, and Francisco O. Ramirez. 1996. World polity and gender parity: Women's share of higher education, 1965–1985. In *Research in sociology of education and socialization*, ed. Aaron M. Pallas, 63–91. Greenwich, CT: JAI Press.

Braxton, John M., Jeffrey F. Milem, and Anna S. Sullivan. 2000. The influence of active learning on the college student departure process – Toward a revision of Tinto's theory. *Journal of Higher Education* 71:569–90.

Brint, Steven, ed. 2002a. *The future of the city of intellect.* Stanford, CA: Stanford University Press.

Brint, Steven. 2002b. The rise of the 'practical arts.' In *The future of the city of intellect*, 231–59. Stanford, CA: Stanford University Press.

Brint, Steven, Mark Riddle, Lori Turk-Bicakci, and Charles S. Levy. 2005. From the liberal to the practical arts in American colleges and universities: Organizational analysis and curricular change. *Journal of Higher Education* 76:151–80.

Brooks, Harvey. 1999. The symbiosis of pure and applied science – Who owns science? *UNESCO Courier*, May. Paris.

Brown, David K. 2001. The social sources of educational credentialism: Status cultures, labor markets, and organizations. *Sociology of Education* Extra Issue:19–34.

Bryson, Bethany. 2005. *Making multiculturalism: Boundaries and meaning in U.S. English departments.* Stanford, CA: Stanford University Press.

Bulterman-Bos, Jacquelien, Nico Verloop, Jan Terwel, and Wim Wardekker. 2003. Reconciling the pedagogical goal and the measurement goal of evaluation: The perspectives of teachers in the context of national standards. *Teachers College Record* 105:344–74.

Camic, Charles. 1995. Three departments in search of a discipline: Localism and interdisciplinary interaction in American sociology, 1890–1940. *Social Research* 62:1003–33.

Campbell, John L. 2002. Ideas, politics, and public policy. *Annual Review of Sociology* 28:21–38.

Cartwright, Nancy, Stathis Psillos, and Hasok Chang. 2003. Theories of scientific method: Models for the physico-mathematical sciences. In *The modern physical and mathematical sciences*, Vol. 5 of *The Cambridge History of Science*, ed. Mary Jo Nye, 21–35. Cambridge: Cambridge University Press.

Chabbott, Colette. 1999. Defining development: The making of the international development field, 1945–1990. In *Constructing world culture: International non-governmental organizations since 1875*, ed. John Boli and George M. Thomas, 222–48. Stanford, CA: Stanford University Press.

Chait, Richard. 2002. The 'academic revolution' revisited. In *The future of the city of intellect*, ed. Steven Brint, 293–321. Stanford, CA: Stanford University Press.

Chase-Dunn, Christopher. 1998. *Global formation: Structures of the world economy*, updated ed. Lanham, MD: Rowman & Littlefield.

Chatterjee, Partha. 2003. The social sciences in India. In *The modern physical and mathematical sciences*, Vol. 5 of *The Cambridge history of science*, ed. Mary Jo Nye, 482–97. Cambridge: Cambridge University Press.

Clark, Burton R. 1995. *Places of inquiry: Research and advanced education in modern universities.* Berkeley, CA: University of California Press, 1995.

Clark, Burton R. 2002. University transformation: Primary pathways to university autonomy and achievement. In *The future of the city of intellect,* ed. Steven Brint, 322–42. Stanford, CA: Stanford University Press.

Clark, Terry Nichols. 1973. *Prophets and patrons: The French university and the emergence of the social sciences.* Cambridge, MA: Harvard University Press.

Collins, Patricia Hill. 2000. *Black feminist thought: Knowledge, consciousness, and the politics of empowerment,* 2nd ed. New York: Routledge.

Collins, Randall. 1985. The mega-historians. *Sociological Theory* 3:114–22.

Collins, Randall. 1998. *The sociology of philosophies: A global theory of intellectual change.* Cambridge, MA: Belknap Press of Harvard University Press.

Colson, Elizabeth, and Max Gluckman, eds. 1959. *Seven tribes of British Central Africa.* Manchester, England: Manchester University Press.

Commoner, Barry. 2002. Unraveling the DNA myth: The spurious foundation of genetic engineering. *Harper's,* February, 39–47.

Davis, Deborah S., ed. 2000. *The consumer revolution in urban China.* Berkeley: University of California Press.

Dierkes, Julian. 2001. Absence, Déclin ou Essor de la Nation: Manuels d'Histoire D'Après-Guerre au Japon, et dans les deux Allemagnes. *Genèses – Sciences Sociales et Histoire* 44:30–49.

Dissanayake, Ellen. 1988. *What is art for?* Seattle, WA: University of Washington Press.

Douglas, Mary. 2002. *Purity and danger: An analysis of concepts of pollution and taboo.* London: Routledge.

Drori, Gili S., John W. Meyer, Francisco O. Ramirez, and Evan Schofer. 2003. *Science in the modern world polity: Institutionalization and globalization.* Stanford, CA: Stanford University Press.

Drori, Gili S., and Hyeyoung Moon. 2005. The changing nature of tertiary education: Cross-national trends in disciplinary enrollment, 1965–1995. In *The impact of comparative education research on institutional theory,* ed. David P. Baker and Alexander W. Wiseman. Oxford, England: Elsevier Science.

Dumont, Louis. 1986. *Essays on individualism.* Chicago: University of Chicago Press.

Dupré, John. 2003. *Darwin's legacy: What evolution means today.* Oxford, England: Oxford University Press.

Eakin, Emily. 1999. More ado (yawn) about Great Books. *New York Times,* April 8.

Evans-Pritchard, E. E. 1940. *The Nuer: A description of the modes of livelihood and political institutions of a Nilotic people.* Oxford, England: Clarendon Press.

Fisher, Nicholas. 1990. The classification of the sciences. In *Companion to the history of modern science,* ed. R.C Olby, G.N. Cantor, J.R.R. Christie, and M.J.S. Hodge, 853–67. London: Routledge.

Fish, Stanley. 2002. Postmodern warfare: The ignorance of our warrior intellectuals. *Harper's*, July, 33–40.

Foucault, Michel. 1994. *The order of things: An archaeology of the human sciences.* New York: Random House.

Fourcade-Gourinchas, Marion. 2001. Politics, institutional structures, and the rise of economics: A comparative study. *Theory and Society* 30:397–447.

Fourcade-Gourinchas, Marion, and Sarah Babb. 2002. The rebirth of the liberal creed: Paths to neoliberalism in four countries. *American Journal of Sociology* 108:533–79.

Frank, David John. 1997. Science, nature, and the globalization of the environment, 1870–1990. *Social Forces* 76:409–35.

Frank, David John, and John W. Meyer. 2002. The profusion of individual roles and identities in the post-war period. *Sociological Theory* 20:86–105.

Frank, David John, and John W. Meyer. Forthcoming. Interpreting worldwide expansion and change in universities. In *Towards a multiversity? Universities between national traditions and global trends in higher education*, ed. Georg Krücken. Bielefeld, Germany: Transcript-Verlag.

Frank, David John, John W. Meyer, and David Miyahara. 1995. The individualist polity and the centrality of professionalized psychology: A cross-national study. *American Sociological Review* 60:360–77.

Frank, David John, Evan Schofer, and John Charles Torres. 1994. Rethinking history: Change in the university curriculum, 1910–90. *Sociology of Education* 67:231–42.

Frank, David John, Suk-Ying Wong, John W. Meyer, and Francisco O. Ramirez. 2000. What counts as history: A cross-national and longitudinal study of university curricula. *Comparative Education Review* 44:29–53.

Frickel, Scott, and Neil Gross. 2005. A general theory of scientific/intellectual movements. *American Sociological Review* 70:204–232.

Gabler, Jay. 2002. The child, knowing: Trends in the subject matter of children's non-fiction books, 1960–2000. Unpublished paper, Department of Sociology, Harvard University.

Gabler, Jay. 2004. Victorian children in a postmodern world. Paper presented at the annual meeting of the American Sociological Association, San Francisco.

Gabler, Jay, and David John Frank. 2005. The natural sciences in the university: Change and variation over the 20th century. *Sociology of Education* 78:183–206.

Gastil, Raymond D. 1989. *Freedom in the world: Political rights and civil liberties.* New York: Freedom House.

Geiger, Roger L. 1986. *To advance knowledge: The growth of American research universities 1900–1940.* New York: Oxford University Press.

Geiger, Roger L. 2004. *Knowledge and money: Research universities and the paradox of the marketplace.* Stanford, CA: Stanford University Press.

Gibbons, Michael, Camille Limoges, Helga Nowotny, Simon Schwartzman, Peter Scott, and Martin Trow. 1994. *The new production of knowledge.* London: Sage.

Giddens, Anthony. 1979. *Central problems in social theory: Action, structure, and contradiction in social analysis.* Berkeley, CA: University of California Press.

Goldstein, Jan. 2003. Bringing the psyche into scientific focus. In *The modern social sciences*, Vol. 7 of *The Cambridge History of Science*, ed. Theodore M. Porter and Dorothy Ross, 131–53. Cambridge: Cambridge University Press.

Goodson, Ivor. 1995. *The making of curriculum: Collected essays*, 2nd ed. London: Falmer Press.

Gumport, Patricia J. 1999. Graduate education and research: Interdependence and strain. In *American higher education in the twenty-first century*, ed. Philip G. Altbach, Robert O. Berdahl, and Patty J. Gumport, 396–426. Baltimore: Johns Hopkins University Press.

Gumport, Patricia J., and Stuart K. Snydman. 2002. The formal organization of knowledge: An analysis of academic structure. *Journal of Higher Education* 73:375–408.

Guthrie, Julian. 2004. Venture capitalist rewrites the starving-author story. *San Francisco Chronicle*, September 26.

Haas, Peter. 1992. Epistemic communities and international policy coordination. *International Organization* 46:1–35.

Hannan, Michael T., and John Freeman. 1989. *Organizational ecology.* Cambridge, MA: Harvard University Press.

Haraway, Donna. 1989. *Primate visions: Gender, race, and nature in the world of modern science.* New York: Routledge.

Hawking, Stephen. 1988. *A brief history of time.* New York: Bantam.

Haynes, Roslynn D. 1994. *From Faust to Strangelove: Representations of the scientist in Western literature.* Baltimore: Johns Hopkins University Press.

Higham, John. 1970. *Writing American history.* Bloomington, IN: Indiana University Press.

Hironaka Ann. 2002. Changing meanings, changing institutions: An institutional analysis of patent legislation. *Sociological Inquiry* 72:108–30.

Hirsch, Eric Donald. 1987. *Cultural literacy: What every American needs to know.* Boston: Houghton Mifflin.

Hobsbawm, Eric, and Terence Ranger, eds. 1983. *The invention of tradition.* Cambridge: Cambridge University Press.

Huntington, Samuel P. 1968. *Political order in changing societies.* New Haven, CT: Yale University Press.

Hymans, Jacques E. C. 2005. What counts as history and how much does history count? The case of French secondary education. In *The nation, Europe, and the world: Textbooks and curricula in transition*, 61–81. New York: Berghahn.

International Monetary Fund. 1980. Government finance statistics [computer file]. Ann Arbor, MI: Inter-university Consortium for Political and Social Research.

Jang, Yong-Suk. 2000. The worldwide founding of Ministries of Science and Technology, 1950–1990. *Sociological Perspectives* 43:247–70.

Jencks, Christopher, and David Riesman. 1968. *The academic revolution.* Garden City, NY: Doubleday.

Jenniskens, Ineke. 2000. Governmental steering and innovations in university curricula. *Comparative Social Research* 19:139–64.

Jepperson, Ronald L. 2002. The development and application of sociological neoinstitutionalism. In *New directions in sociological theory: The growth of contemporary theories*, ed. Joseph Berger and Morris Zelditch, Jr., 229–66. Oxford, England: Rowman & Littlefield.

Kamens, David H., and Aaron Benavot. 1991. Elite knowledge for the masses – The origins and spread of mathematics and science education in national curricula. *American Journal of Education* 99(2):137–180.

Kamens, David H., Aaron Benavot, and John W. Meyer. 1996. Worldwide patterns in academic secondary education curricula, 1920–1990. *Comparative Education Review* 40:116–38.

Kay, Lily E. 1993. *The molecular vision of life: Caltech, the Rockefeller Foundation, and the rise of the new biology.* New York: Oxford University Press.

Kernan, Alvin. 1997. *What's happened to the humanities?* Princeton, NJ: Princeton University Press.

Kerr, Clark. 2001. *The uses of the university*, 5th ed. Cambridge, MA: Harvard University Press.

Kerr, Clark. 2002. Shock wave II: An introduction to the twenty-first century. In *The future of the city of intellect*, ed. Steven Brint, 1–19. Stanford, CA: Stanford University Press.

Kevles, Daniel J. 1979. *The physicists: The history of a scientific community in modern America.* New York: Vintage Books.

Kimball, Roger. 1990. *Tenured radicals: How politics has corrupted our higher education.* New York: Harper & Row.

Kirp, David. 2003. *Shakespeare, Einstein and the bottom line.* Cambridge, MA: Harvard University.

Knight, David M. 2003. Scientists and their publics: Popularization of science in the nineteenth century. In *The modern physical and mathematical sciences*, Vol. 5 of *The Cambridge history of science*, ed. Mary Jo Nye, 72–90. Cambridge: Cambridge University Press.

Knorr-Cetina, Karin. 1999. *Epistemic cultures: How the sciences make knowledge.* Cambridge, MA: Harvard University Press.

Krantz, Helen. 1985. The gentler time and the fast track. *New York Times*, October 27, Section 11, p. 27.

Krücken, Georg, ed. Forthcoming. *Towards a multiversity? Universities between national traditions and global trends in higher education*. Bielefeld, Germany: Transcript-Verlag.

Kuh, George D., C.R. Pace, N. Vesper. 1997. The development of process indicators to estimate graduate student gains associated with good practices in undergraduate education. *Research in Higher Education* 38:435–54.

Kuhn, Thomas. 1962. *The structure of scientific revolutions*. Chicago: University of Chicago Press.

Kuper, Adam. 2003. Anthropology. In *The modern social sciences*, Vol. 7 of *The Cambridge history of science*, ed. Theodore M. Porter and Dorothy Ross, 354–78. Cambridge: Cambridge University Press.

Lamont, Michèle. 1987. How to become a dominant French philosopher: The case of Jacques Derrida. *American Journal of Sociology* 93:584–622.

Lamont, Michèle. 2000. *The dignity of working men: Morality and the boundaries of race, class, and immigration*. Cambridge, MA: Harvard University Press.

Lara, Adair. 2004. The rants are lofty on new radio show. *San Francisco Chronicle*, March 27.

Latour, Bruno, and Steve Woolgar. 1979. *Laboratory life: The social construction of scientific facts*. Beverly Hills, CA: Sage.

Lenhardt, Gero. 2002. Europe and higher education between universalization and materialist particularism. *European Educational Research Journal* 1:274–89.

Lovejoy, Arthur O. 1936. *The great chain of being: A study of the history of an idea*. Cambridge, MA: Harvard University Press.

Loya, Thomas A., and John Boli 1999. Standardization in the world polity: Technical rationality over power. In *Constructing world culture: International nongovernmental organizations since 1875*, ed. John Boli and George M. Thomas, 169–97. Stanford, CA: Stanford University Press.

Mallard, Gregoire, Michèle Lamont, and Josh Guetzkow. 2004. What is originality in the social sciences and the humanities? *American Sociological Review* 69:190–212.

Mannheim, Karl. 1936. *Ideology and utopia: An introduction to the sociology of knowledge*. New York: Harcourt, Brace & World.

Mansfield, Harvey C. 2004. A more demanding curriculum. *Claremont Review of Books* V:75–78.

Mao, Weishun. 1995. World history in China mainland and Taiwan secondary school textbooks: A historical and comparative study. PhD diss., School of Education, Stanford University.

Massey, Douglas S., Camille Z. Charles, Garvey Lundy, and Mary J. Fischer. 2003. *The source of the river*. Princeton, NJ: Princeton University.

Mayr, Ernst, and William B. Provine, eds. 1998. *The evolutionary synthesis: Perspectives on the unification of biology*. Cambridge, MA: Harvard University Press.

Mazlish, Bruce. 2000. Rethinking the social sciences. Paper presented at The Future of the City of Intellect Conference, UC-Riverside.

McEneaney, Elizabeth H. 1998. The transformation of primary school science and mathematics: A cross-national analysis, 1900–1995. PhD diss., Department of Sociology, Stanford University.

McEneaney, Elizabeth. 2000. Models of science in primary school textbooks. Paper presented at the annual meeting of the Society for the Comparative Study of Education, San Antonio.

McEneaney, Elizabeth H. 2003. Elements of a contemporary primary school science. In *Science in the modern world polity: Institutionalization and globalization*, ed. G. S. Drori, J.W. Meyer, F. O. Ramirez, and E. Schofer, 136–54. Stanford, CA: Stanford University Press.

McEneaney, Elizabeth H., and John W. Meyer. 2000. Theories and research on the content of the curriculum. In *Handbook of sociology of education*, ed. Maureen T. Hallinan, 189–211. New York: Plenum.

Mead, George Herbert. 1934. *Mind, self, and society.* Chicago: University of Chicago Press.

Meek, V. Lynn, L. Goedegebuure, Osmo Kivinen, and Risto Rinne, eds. 1996. *The mockers and mocked: Comparative perspectives on differentiation, convergence and diversity in higher education.* Oxford, England: Pergamon-Elsevier.

Merton, Robert K. 1973. *The sociology of science: Theoretical and empirical investigations.* Chicago: University of Chicago Press.

Meyer, John W. 1994. Rationalized environments. In *Institutional environments and organizations: Structural complexity and individualism*, ed. W. Richard Scott and John W. Meyer, 28–54. Thousand Oaks, CA: Sage.

Meyer, John W., John Boli, and George M. Thomas. 1987. Ontology and rationalization in the Western cultural account. In *Institutional structure: Constituting state, society, and the individual*, ed. George M. Thomas, John W. Meyer, Francisco O. Ramirez, and John Boli, 12–37. Newbury Park, CA: Sage.

Meyer, John W., John Boli, George M. Thomas, and Francisco O. Ramirez. 1997. World society and the nation-state. *American Journal of Sociology* 103:144–81.

Meyer, John W., and Ronald L. Jepperson. 2000. The 'actors' of modern society: The cultural construction of social agency. *Sociological Theory* 18:100–20.

Meyer, John W., David H. Kamens, and Aaron Benavot. 1992. *School knowledge for the masses.* London: Falmer Press.

Meyer, John W., Francisco O. Ramirez, and Yasemin N. Soysal. 1992. World expansion of mass education, 1870–1980. *Sociology of Education* 65:128–49.

Miller, Arthur. 2001. American Playhouse: On politics and the art of acting. *Harper's*, June, 33–43.

Montessus de Ballore, Robert de. 1919–55. *Index generalis.* Paris: Gauthier-Villars et cie.

Morgan, Mary S. 2003. Economics. In *The modern social sciences*, Vol. 7 of *The Cambridge history of science*, ed. Theodore M. Porter and Dorothy Ross, 276–305. Cambridge: Cambridge University Press.

Morton, John. 1999. Anthropology at home in Australia. *Australian Journal of Anthropology* 10:243–58.

Musgrave, P. W. 1994. Curriculum: Sociological perspectives. In *The international encyclopedia of education*, Vol. 3, ed. Torsten Husen and T. Neville Postlethwaite. Oxford, England: Pergamon.

Narváez-Berthelemot N., J. M. Russell, R. Arvanitis, R. Waast, and J. Gaillard. 2002. Science in Africa: An overview of mainstream scientific output. *Scientometrics* 54:229–241.

Oreskes, Naomi, and Ronald E. Doel. 2003. The physics and chemistry of the earth. In *The modern physical and mathematical sciences*, Vol. 5 of *The Cambridge history of sciences*, ed. Mary Jo Nye, 538–57. Cambridge: Cambridge University Press.

Pinch, Trevor. 1990. The sociology of the scientific community. In *Companion to the history of modern science*, ed. R.C. Olby, G.N. Cantor, J.R.R. Christie, and M.J.S. Hodge, 87–99. London: Routledge.

Popkewitz, Thomas S., ed. 1987. *The formation of school subjects: The struggle for creating an American institution*. New York: Falmer Press.

Porter, Theodore. 2002. Statistical utopianism in an age of aristocratic efficiency. *Osiris* 17:210–27.

Porter, Theodore M. 2003. Genres and objects of social inquiry, from the Enlightenment to 1890. In *The modern social sciences*, Vol. 7 of *The Cambridge history of science*, ed. Theodore M. Porter and Dorothy Ross, 13–39. Cambridge: Cambridge University Press.

Porter, Theodore M., and Dorothy Ross. 2003. Introduction: Writing the history of social science. In *The modern social sciences*, Vol. 7 of *The Cambridge history of science*, ed. Theodore M. Porter and Dorothy Ross, 1–10. Cambridge: Cambridge University Press.

Powell, Walter W., and Jason Owen-Smith. 2002. The new world of knowledge production in the life sciences. In *The future of the city of intellect*, ed. Steven Brint, 107–30. Stanford, CA: Stanford University Press.

Powell, Walter W., and Kaisa Snellman. 2004. The knowledge economy. *Annual Review of Sociology* 30:199–220.

Ramirez, Francisco O. 2002. Eyes wide shut: University, state, and society. *European Educational Research Journal* 1:256–73.

Ramirez, Francisco O. 2003. The global model and national legacies. In *Local meanings, global schooling: Anthropology and world culture theory*, ed. Kathryn M. Anderson-Levitt. New York: Palgrave Macmillan.

Ramirez, Francisco O., and John Boli. 1987. The political construction of mass schooling: European origins and worldwide institutionalization. *Sociology of Education* 60:2–17.

Ramirez, Francisco O., and Elizabeth H. McEneaney. 1997. From women's suffrage to reproduction rights? Cross-national considerations. *International Journal of Comparative Sociology* 38:6–24.

Ramirez, Francisco O., Yasemin Soysal, and Suzanne Shanahan. 1997. The changing logic of political citizenship: Cross-national acquisition of women's suffrage rights, 1890–1990. *American Sociological Review* 62:735–45.

Ramirez, Francisco O., and Marc J. Ventresca. 1992. Building the institution of mass schooling. In *The political construction of education*, ed. B. Fuller and R. Rubinson, 47–59. New York: Praeger.

Ramirez, Francisco O., and Christine Min Wotipka. 2001. Slowly but surely? The global expansion of women's participation in science and engineering fields of study, 1972–92. *Sociology of Education* 74:231–51.

Readings, Bill. 1996. *The university in ruins*. Cambridge, MA: Harvard University Press.

Reuben, Julie. 1996. *Making of the modern university: Intellectual transformation and the marginalization of morality*. Chicago: University of Chicago Press.

Revel, Jacques. 2003. History and the social sciences. In *The modern social sciences*, Vol. 5 of *The Cambridge history of science*, ed. Theodore M. Porter and Dorothy Ross, 391–406. Cambridge: Cambridge University Press.

Riddle, Phyllis. 1993. Political authority and university formation in Europe, 1200–1800. *Sociological Perspectives* 36:45–62.

Robertson, Roland. 1992. *Globalization: Social theory and global culture*. London: Sage.

Robic, Marie-Claire. 2003. Geography. In *The modern social sciences*, Vol. 7 of *The Cambridge history of science*, ed. Theodore M. Porter and Dorothy Ross, 379–90. Cambridge: Cambridge University Press.

Robinson, Karen. 2005. The rise of individualism and the elective system in higher education. Unpublished paper, Department of Sociology, University of California-Irvine.

Rose, Nikolas. 1996. *Inventing our selves: Psychology, power and personhood*. Cambridge: Cambridge University Press.

Rosenau, James N., and Ernst-Otto Czempiel, eds. 1992. *Governance without government: Order and change in world politics*. Cambridge: Cambridge University Press.

Rosner, Lisa, ed. 2002. *Chronology of science*. Santa Barbara, CA: ABC-CLIO.

Ross, Dorothy. 2003. Changing contours of the social science disciplines. In *The modern social sciences*, Vol. 7 of *The Cambridge history of science*, ed. Theodore M. Porter and Dorothy Ross, 205–37. Cambridge: Cambridge University Press.

Rowe, David E. 2003. Mathematical schools, communities, and networks. In *The modern physical and mathematical sciences*, Vol. 5 of *The Cambridge history of science*, ed. Mary Jo Nye, 113–32. Cambridge, England: Cambridge University Press.

Rymer, Russ. 1992. Annals of science. *The New Yorker*, April 13.

Schissler, Hanna, and Yasemin Nuhoglu Soysal, eds. 2004. *The nation, Europe, and the world: Textbooks and curricula in transition.* Oxford, England: Berghahn Books.

Schlesinger, Arthur M. 1998. *The disuniting of America: Reflections on a multicultural society*, rev. ed. New York: W. W. Norton.

Schofer, Evan. 1999. The rationalization of science and the scientization of society: International science organizations, 1870–1995. In *Constructing world culture: International nongovernmental organizations since 1875*, 249–66. Stanford, CA: Stanford University Press.

Schofer, Evan. 2003. The global institutionalization of geological science associations, 1800–1990. *American Sociological Review* 68:730–59.

Schofer, Evan, and John W. Meyer. 2005. The worldwide expansion of higher education in the twentieth century. Paper presented at the Towards a Multiversity? Workshop. Bielefeld University, Bielefeld, Germany.

Schweber, Libby. 2004. *Disciplining statistics: Demography and vital statistics in France and England, 1835–1885.* Unpublished book manuscript, University of Reading, England.

Scott, W. Richard. 1992. *Organizations: Rational, natural and open systems*, 3rd ed. Englewood Cliffs, NJ: Prentice Hall.

Shils, Edward. 1997. *The calling of education.* Chicago: University of Chicago Press.

Shinn, Terry. 2003. The industry, research, and education nexus. In *The modern physical and mathematical sciences*, Vol. 5 of *The Cambridge history of science*, ed. Mary Jo Nye, 133–53. Cambridge: Cambridge University Press.

Sichone, Owen. 2003. The social sciences in Africa. In *The modern social sciences*, Vol. 7 of *The Cambridge history of science*, ed. Theodore M. Porter and Dorothy Ross, 466–81. Cambridge, England: Cambridge University Press.

Simpson, George Gaylord, and William S. Beck. 1965. *Life: An introduction to biology*, 2nd ed. New York: Harcourt, Brace, and World.

Slaughter, Sheila. 2002. The political economy of curriculum-making in American universities. In *The future of the city of intellect*, ed. Steven Brint, 260–89. Stanford, CA: Stanford University Press.

Slaughter, Sheila, and Larry L. Leslie. 1997. *Academic capitalism: Politics, policies, and the entrepreneurial university.* Baltimore: Johns Hopkins University Press.

Slaughter, Sheila, and Gary Rhoades. 2004. *Academic capitalism in the new economy.* Baltimore: Johns Hopkins University Press.

Small, Mario L. 1999. Departmental conditions and the emergence of new disciplines: Two cases in the legitimation of African-American studies. *Theory and Society* 28:659–707.

Smith, C. 2000. New humanities dean settles in. *University of Chicago Magazine*, December: 18.

Smith, Jackie. 1995. Transnational political processes and the human rights movement. In *Research in social movements, conflict and change*, ed. Louis Kriesberg, Michael Dobkowski, and Isidor Walliman, 185–220. Greenwood, CT: JAP Press.

Smith, Robert W. 2003. Remaking astronomy: Instruments and practice in the nineteenth and twentieth centuries. In *The modern physical and mathematical sciences*, Vol. 5 of *The Cambridge history of science*, ed. Mary Jo Nye, 154–73. Cambridge: Cambridge University Press.

Smocovitis, Vassiliki Betty. 1996. *Unifying biology: The evolutionary synthesis and evolutionary biology*. Princeton, NJ: Princeton University Press.

Soares, Joseph A. 1999. *The decline of privilege*. Stanford, CA: Stanford University Press.

Solow, Robert W. 1997. How did economics get that way and what way did it get? In *American academic culture in transformation: Fifty years, four disciplines*, ed. Thomas Bender and Carl E. Schorske, 57–76. Princeton, NJ: Princeton University Press.

Soysal, Yasemin Nuhoglu. 1994. *Limits of citizenship: Migrants and postnational membership in Europe*. Chicago: University of Chicago Press.

Stinchcombe, Arthur. 1965. Social structure and organization. In *Handbook of organizations*, ed. James G. March, 142–93. Chicago: Rand McNally.

Strang, David. 1990. From dependency to sovereignty: An event history analysis of decolonization 1870–1987. *American Sociological Review* 55:846–60.

Swidler, Ann, and Jorge Arditi. 1994. The new sociology of knowledge. *Annual Review of Sociology* 20:305–29.

Szeman, Imre. 2003. Culture and globalization, or, the humanities in ruins. *CR: The New Centennial Review* 3:91–115.

Teggart, Frederick J. 1977. *Theory and processes of history*, 2nd ed. Berkeley, CA: University of California Press.

Thaman, K. H. 2003. Decolonizing Pacific studies: Indigenous perspectives, knowledge, and wisdom in higher education. *Contemporary Pacific* 15:1–17.

Thomas, George M. 2001. Religions in global civil society. *Sociology of Religion* 62:515–33.

Thomas, George M., John W. Meyer, Francisco O. Ramirez, and John Boli. 1987. *Institutional structure: Constituting state, society, and the individual*. Newbury Park, CA: Sage.

Tsutsui, Kiyoteru, and Christine Min Wotipka. 2004. Global civil society and the international human rights movement: Citizen participation in human rights international nongovernmental organizations. *Social Forces* 83:587–620.

Turner, Victor. 1967. *The forest of symbols: Aspects of Ndembu ritual*. Ithaca, NY: Cornell University Press.

United Nations Population Fund. 1997. *The state of world population 1997. The right to choose: reproductive rights and reproductive health*. New York: United Nations.

van Vught, Frans A., ed. 1989. *Government strategies and innovation in higher education*. London: Jessica Kingsley Publishers.

Wagner, Peter. 2003. The uses of the social sciences. In *The modern social sciences*, Vol. 7 *of The Cambridge history of science*, ed. Theodore M. Porter and Dorothy Ross, 537–52. Cambridge: Cambridge University Press.

Wallerstein, Immanuel. 1984. *The politics of the world economy.* Cambridge: Cambridge University Press.

Wallerstein, Immanuel. 1991. *Unthinking social science: The limits of nineteenth century paradigms.* Cambridge: Polity Press.

Wallerstein, Immanuel. 1999. *The end of the world as we know it.* Minneapolis, MN: University of Minnesota Press.

Watanabe, Teresa. 2000. Academia rediscovers religion as a subject for study. *Los Angeles Times,* November 25.

Weber, Max. 1946 (1919). Science as a vocation. In *From Max Weber: Essays in sociology,* ed. H.H. Gerth and C. Wright Mills, 129–56. New York: Oxford University Press.

Weber, Max. 1946. Bureaucracy. In *From Max Weber: Essays in sociology,* ed. H.H. Gerth and C. Wright Mills, 196–244. New York: Oxford University Press.

Weber, Max. 1978. *Economy and society.* Berkeley, CA: University of California Press.

White, Lynn. 1967. Historical roots of our ecological crisis. *Science* 155:1203–7.

Wong, Suk-Ying. 1991. The evolution of social science instruction, 1900–1986. *Sociology of Education* 64:33–47.

Wong, Suk-Ying. 2004. The standardization and globalization of world history teaching in three Chinese societies. Paper presented at the annual meeting of the American Sociological Association, San Francisco, California.

Workman, Bill. 1994. Stanford classicists mourn decline of humanities. *San Francisco Chronicle,* April 8, A19.

World Bank. 2000. *Higher education in developing countries: Peril and promise.* Washington, DC: World Bank.

World Resources Institute (WRI). 1998. *World resources 1998–99 database.* Washington, DC: World Resources Institute.

Yearley, Steven. 1996. *Sociology, environmentalism, globalization.* London: Sage.

Young, Ruth C. 1988. Is population ecology a useful paradigm for the study of organizations? *American Journal of Sociology* 94:1–24.

Zils, Michael. 1971, 1976. *World guide to universities.* New York: R. R. Bowker.

Index

Abbott, Andrew, 41n16
academic core: adaptation and selection in
 changes in, 205; boundaries
 surrounding, 14; branches of learning
 reconfigured, 47–88; changing
 conceptions of reality affecting, 17–32,
 197–209; convergence toward
 isomorphism of, 78–81, *80*;
 cross-national variation in, 12, 203;
 data and methods of this study, 34–39;
 existing literature on changes in, 5–15,
 197; indicator comparisons for changes
 in, 81–82; as mapping reality, xiii,
 14–17; mechanisms of change in,
 32–34; national and organizational
 factors affecting, 207; ongoing
 reconstruction of, 1–46; questions for
 future research on, 202–6; some forms
 of understanding excluded from, 16.
 See also humanities; natural sciences;
 social sciences
academic integrity, 13, 17
accreditation, 13, 42n33
action: branches of learning affected by
 redefinition of, 56–59, 62, *63*, 201;
 educational access due to elaboration of
 human actorhood, 208; humanities
 affected by redefinition of, 56–57, 58,
 62, *63*, 65, 93–98, *103*; natural sciences
 affected by redefinition of, 58–59, 62,
 63, 148, 150, 153, 155; in ontology, 17,
 20; prioritized subject matters of
 history affected by redefinition of,
 178–80, *185*; redefined in twentieth
 century, 24–28, 47; social sciences

affected by redefinition of, 57, 58–59,
 62, *63*, 121–26, *131*
active learning techniques, 97–98
adaptation/selection debate, 205
Adelaide, University of, 61–62
advertising, *49*
aesthetics, *9*, 11
Africa, history courses on, *190*, 191, *193*
agriculture: as applied natural science, *49*,
 146; at Ibadan, *204*; at Jordan, 12; at
 land-grant universities, 7; at Tokyo, 7, *9*
agronomy, *51*
alchemy, 45n70
American Museum of Natural History,
 171n46
American Revolution, 28, 29
ancien régime, 30
ancient history, 178–79, *185*, *187*, 189,
 193, 194
anthropology: action's redefinition
 affecting, 123–24; at American
 Museum of Natural History, 171n46; as
 basic social science, *49*; coalescence as a
 field, 119; convergence toward
 isomorphism in, *80*; cross-national
 variation in, 143n34; disciplinary
 boundaries affecting, 205; dualities in
 basic intellectual apparatus of, 129,
 136; faculty composition over time,
 133, 136, 138–39; fields gaining less
 than double their original shares, *133*,
 138, 138–39; functionalism and, 140;
 global-institutional reframing affecting,
 131, 132; hierarchy as ideological
 substructure of, 127, 136; at